THE SENTIMENTAL COURT

Modern law seems to be designed to keep emotions at bay. *The Sentimental Court* argues the exact opposite: that the law is not designed to cast out affective dynamics but to create them. Drawing on extensive ethnographic fieldwork – both during the trial of former Lord's Resistance Army commander Dominic Ongwen at the International Criminal Court's headquarters in the Netherlands and in rural northern Uganda at the scenes of violence – this book is an in-depth investigation of the affective life of legalized transitional justice interventions in Africa. Jonas Bens argues that the law purposefully creates, mobilizes, shapes, and transforms atmospheres and sentiments and further discusses how we should think about the future of law and justice in our colonial present by focusing on the politics of atmosphere and sentiment in which they are entangled.

JONAS BENS is a postdoctoral researcher at the Institute of Social and Cultural Anthropology and the Collaborative Research Center "Affective Societies" at Freie Universität Berlin. His work focuses on law, statehood, and colonialism in capitalist modernity. His books include *The Indigenous Paradox: Rights, Sovereignty and Culture in the Americas* (2020).

CAMBRIDGE STUDIES IN LAW AND SOCIETY

Founded in 1997, Cambridge Studies in Law and Society is a hub for leading scholarship in socio-legal studies. Located at the intersection of law, the humanities, and the social sciences, it publishes empirically innovative and theoretically sophisticated work on law's manifestations in everyday life: from discourses to practices, and from institutions to cultures. The series editors have longstanding expertise in the interdisciplinary study of law, and welcome contributions that place legal phenomena in national, comparative, or international perspective. Series authors come from a range of disciplines, including anthropology, history, law, literature, political science, and sociology.

Series Editors

Mark Fathi Massoud, *University of California, Santa Cruz*
Jens Meierhenrich, *London School of Economics and Political Science*
Rachel E. Stern, *University of California, Berkeley*

A list of books in the series can be found at the back of this book.

THE SENTIMENTAL COURT

The Affective Life of International Criminal Justice

Jonas Bens

Freie Universität Berlin

CAMBRIDGE
UNIVERSITY PRESS

CAMBRIDGE
UNIVERSITY PRESS

Shaftesbury Road, Cambridge CB2 8EA, United Kingdom

One Liberty Plaza, 20th Floor, New York, NY 10006, USA

477 Williamstown Road, Port Melbourne, VIC 3207, Australia

314–321, 3rd Floor, Plot 3, Splendor Forum, Jasola District Centre, New Delhi – 110025, India

103 Penang Road, #05–06/07, Visioncrest Commercial, Singapore 238467

Cambridge University Press is part of Cambridge University Press & Assessment, a department of the University of Cambridge.

We share the University's mission to contribute to society through the pursuit of education, learning and research at the highest international levels of excellence.

www.cambridge.org
Information on this title: www.cambridge.org/9781009069359

DOI: 10.1017/9781009072342

First published 2022
First paperback edition 2026

A catalogue record for this publication is available from the British Library

Library of Congress Cataloging-in-Publication data
Names: Bens, Jonas, author.
Title: The sentimental court : the affective life of international criminal justice / Jonas Bens, Freie Universität Berlin.
Description: Cambridge, United Kingdom ; New York, NY : Cambridge University Press, 2022. | Series: Cambridge studies in law and society | Includes bibliographical references and index.
Identifiers: LCCN 2021055059 (print) | LCCN 2021055060 (ebook) | ISBN 9781316512876 (hardback) | ISBN 9781009072342 (ebook)
Subjects: LCSH: International criminal courts – Psychological aspects.
Classification: LCC KZ7230 .B46 2022 (print) | LCC KZ7230 (ebook) | DDC 345/.01–dc23/eng/20220128
LC record available at https://lccn.loc.gov/2021055059
LC ebook record available at https://lccn.loc.gov/2021055060

ISBN 978-1-316-51287-6 Hardback
ISBN 978-1-009-06935-9 Paperback

CONTENTS

FIGURES

MAPS

ACKNOWLEDGMENTS

This book and the ethnographic fieldwork on which it is based were made possible through a grant by the German Research Foundation for the research project "Sentiments of Justice and Transitional Justice" (DFG-SFB1171-B04) within the Collaborative Research Center "Affective Societies" at Freie Universität Berlin. My thanks go to Olaf Zenker, the project's principal investigator, and Birgitt Röttger-Rössler, the director of the research center. Without the support of these two extraordinary anthropologists, this book would most likely never have come to fruition. Olaf's passion, inspiration, and unyielding curiosity have been an invaluable resource and driving force for this work. It is a rare privilege to be able to work in a collaborative environment of scholars from different disciplines in which the participants not only aspire to create something that is more than the sum of its parts but actually realize such an aspiration in collegiality and friendship. It is first and foremost the result of Birgitt's openness, wisdom, and well-practiced craft of tenacious diplomacy that this became a reality with the CRC "Affective Societies" in Berlin. I had the privilege to serve on the board of this exceptional research center and to work closely with Anne Fleig, Ulrike Geiger, Henrike Kohpeiss, Doris Kolesch, Katharina Metz, Christian von Scheve, and Jan Slaby, whose dedication and leadership helped make this experiment in interdisciplinary affect and emotion research a success.

The book is based on ethnographic fieldwork in northern Uganda. To Lioba Lenhart from the Institute of Peace and Security Studies at Gulu University, I owe more than I can say. I am deeply grateful for the rare opportunity to collaborate with such an exceptionally intelligent and knowledgeable colleague who is also a delight to spend time with. Without the skillful navigation of Arthur Owor, I would never have found my way in Gulu. His insights and social networks benefited this project enormously. I thank two bright MA students from Gulu University with whom I had the pleasure to collaborate on a semiquantitative survey headed by Lioba Lenhart: Loum Janani, and Julius Omony. My thanks also go to my collaborators in Gulu – Kenneth Oyet Odong, Elivs Kilama, and Lucy Auma – and, of course, to the many people who were willing to spend time with me to talk about their sentiments about the Dominic Ongwen case.

During my time in The Hague, I was fortunate to be affiliated with the Van Vollenhoven Institute for Law, Governance and Society at the University of Leiden. My thanks go to Jan-Michiel Otto and Adriaan Bedner for their support. In my time in The Hague, I developed a wonderful intellectual friendship with Keebet von Benda-Beckmann. I owe much to her perspectives, comments, and writings. I also thank the professionals at the International Criminal Court with whom I had the pleasure of discussing my work, particularly Jimmy Otim, Maria Mabinty Kamara, and Caroline Maurel.

The work on the manuscript was further supported through the research project "Negotiating International Criminal Law" at the University of Jyväskylä, funded by the Academy of Finland. Along with Baudouin Dupret, I had the privilege of teaming up with the project's principal investigator Sigurd D'hondt. This collaboration has developed into a wonderful intellectual friendship with these two exceptional scholars. I owe much to the exchange with the research team in Jyväskylä, particularly Juan Pablo Perez-Léon-Acevedo, Elena Barrett, and Fabio Ferraz de Almeida. A further grant from the German Research Foundation and the German Federal Ministry of Education and Research for the "Affect and Colonialism Web Lab" enabled my friends and colleagues Fabian Bernhard, Rosa Cordillera A. Castillo, Débora Moura Medeiros, Verena Straub, and myself to delve deeply into the affective lives of colonialism and to connect with wonderful scholars, artists, and activists from all over the world – an indispensable treasure trove from which to draw ideas for this book.

After the first four years, I was fortunate enough to continue my work in Berlin in the framework of the research project "Contested Property" (DFG-SFB1171-A06), with Paola Ivanov as principal investigator. It has been a wonderful opportunity to collaborate with such a bright and generous colleague. With great patience and generosity, she cheerfully tolerated the distractedness and inefficiency that can so often (for me at least) surface in the home stretch of finishing a manuscript.

There are numerous colleagues and friends who have been indispensable both as generous intellectual allies and supportive intellectual critics. The work of Kamari Clarke has been a great inspiration for this book, and my discussions and meetings with her have been invaluable. She is one of the keenest analysts of the pressing issues of our time and an inspirational and strong critical voice. Two wonderful colleagues, Adam Branch and Thomas Scheffer, took up our invitation to discuss the material on which this book is based in workshops in Berlin. I benefited greatly from their insights. My thinking on affect and emotion has been shaped over hours of discussions with Gabriel Scheidecker and Antje Kahl. Jan Slaby's intellectual drive and his ability to get genuinely enthusiastic about new ideas in spite of the often backbreaking demands of the neoliberal university are remarkable. I consider my discussions with him on questions of affect and politics a great privilege.

This book also owes much to the discussions of the working group "Affect, Emotion and the Political." There, I would additionally like to thank Aletta Diefenbach, Thomas John, Hauke Lehmann, Matthias Lüthjohann, Dominik Mattes, Friederike Oberkrome, Hans Roth, Gerhard Thonhauser, Nur Yasemin Ural, Dina Wahba, Robert Walter-Jochum, and Mehmet Ragıp Zık for their knowledge, ideas, and openness. For much of the time I was writing this book, I had a "writing partner" – my Affective Societies colleague Kerstin Schankweiler – who, in my biased opinion, is one of the smartest, funniest, and most insightful and original image theorists of our time. We met daily to write our books, sitting next to each other in the library and discussing our respective progress during coffee breaks. This constellation was a great gift that undoubtedly served this book very well.

During the course of writing this book, I was fortunate to have been given the opportunity to present parts of this book and have them subjected to insightful scrutiny and illuminating comments at the Discourse Hub at the University of Jyväskylä, the Center for Advanced Studies at Ludwig Maximilians University in Munich, the Institute of Social Anthropology at Georg August University in Göttingen, the Law & Anthropology Department at the Max Planck Institute for Social Anthropology in Halle/Saale, the Max Planck Institute for Human Development in Berlin, the Law and Society Institute at Humboldt University in Berlin, and the Institute of Anthropology and African Studies at Gutenberg University in Mainz.

I would also like to thank the panel organizers, discussants, and participants of the various international conferences where I presented my work related to this book, including at meetings of the German African Studies Society (VAD), the European Association of Social Anthropologists (EASA), the European Conference on African Studies (ECAS), the German Anthropological Association (DGSKA), the American Anthropological Association (AAA), the Association of Social Anthropology (ASA), the International Union of Anthropological and Ethnological Sciences (IUAES), the European Philosophical Society for the Study of Emotion (EPSSE), and the Capacious Conference.

Some material in this book has already been published elsewhere. A shortened version of Chapter 1 has appeared as "The Courtroom as an Affective Arrangement: Analysing Atmospheres in Courtroom Ethnography" (*Journal of Legal Pluralism and Unofficial Law* 50 (3): 336–355, 2018). A previous version of Chapter 2 has been published as "Transitional Justice Atmospheres: The Role of Space and Affect in the International Criminal Court's Outreach Efforts in Northern Uganda" in *Normative Spaces and Legal Dynamics in Africa* (Routledge, 2020, edited by Katrin Seidel and Hatem Ellisie). An abridged version of Chapter 4 is published as "Affective Witnessing in the Courtroom" (*Parallax* 26 (3): 271-285, 2020).

Over the years I have had the opportunity to discuss my ideas with many other colleagues, among them are Jan Beek, Tamar Blickstein, Thomas Bierschenk, Giorgio Brocco, Heath Cabot, Hansjörg Dilger, Heike Drotbohm, Marcos Freire de Andrade Neves, Mark Goodale, Antje Gunsenheimer, Valerie Hänsch, Cilija Harders, Elfriede Herrmann, Markus Höhne, Brandaan Huigen, Omar Kasmani, Sirin Knecht, Michael Kraus, Matthias Krings, Andrea Lauser, Christian Mader, Laibor Kalanga Moko, Jean-Pierre Olivier de Sardan, Žiga Podgornik-Jakil, Katerina Ragkou, Martin Ramstedt, Michael Richardson, Theresa Schütz, Katrin Seidel, Larissa Vetters, Jana Weiß, and Deniz Yonucu. My thanks go out to all of them as well.

It was a great privilege to have been able to collaborate with two extraordinarily bright student assistants over the course of writing this book, first with Leonie Benker and later with Lisa Maier. They saved the day more than once and provided me with more than just a bit of critical insight. Brian Donahoe has worked tirelessly to edit this manuscript; it has been a great intellectual endeavor to go through the process of bringing into shape a book with such a hugely insightful and exceptionally smart fellow anthropologist. Finally, profound thanks go to the editors of the Cambridge Studies in Law and Society, Jens Meierhenrich, Mark Massoud, and Rachel Stern, as well as the publishing team at Cambridge University Press, particularly Finola O'Sullivan, Marianne Nield, and Robert Judkins who believed in this book and brought it to publication.

ABBREVIATIONS

CAR	Central African Republic
DRC	Democratic Republic of Congo
ICC	International Criminal Court
ICTR	International Criminal Tribunal for Rwanda
ICTY	International Criminal Tribunal for the Former Yugoslavia
IDP	internally displaced person
ISO	Internal Security Organization (a Ugandan secret intelligence agency)
LRA	Lord's Resistance Army
NRM	National Resistance Movement (the government party in Uganda)
OTP	Office of the Prosecutor (of the International Criminal Court)
SPLA	Sudan People's Liberation Army
UPDF	Uganda People's Defence Force (the Ugandan army)

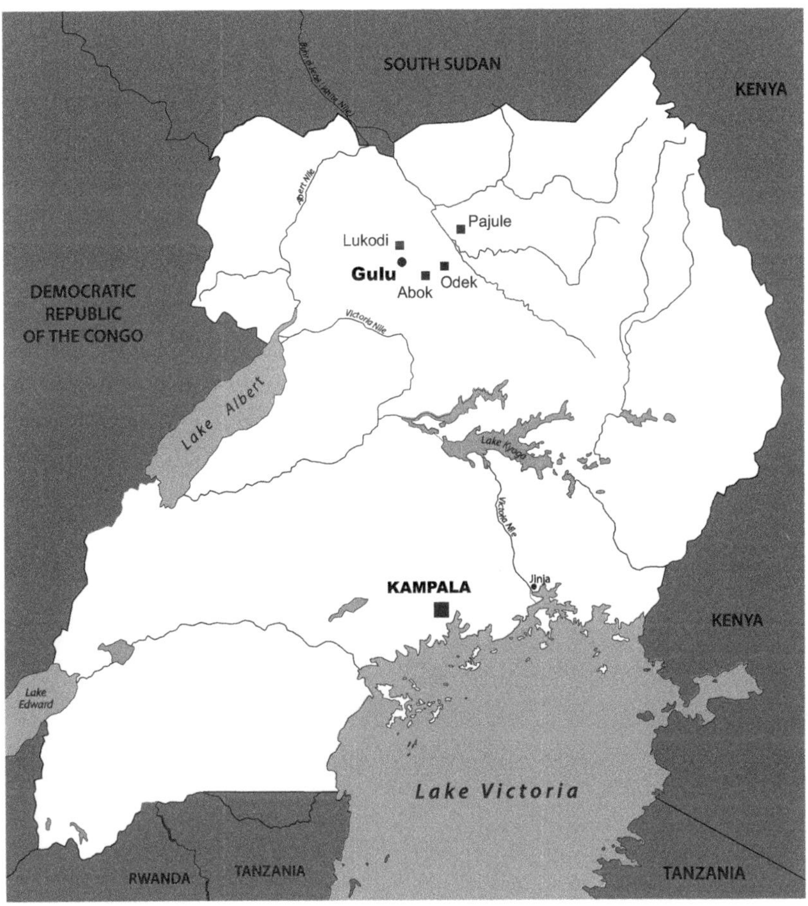

i.1 The four massacre sites formally included in the ICC case *The Prosecutor* v. *Dominic Ongwen*

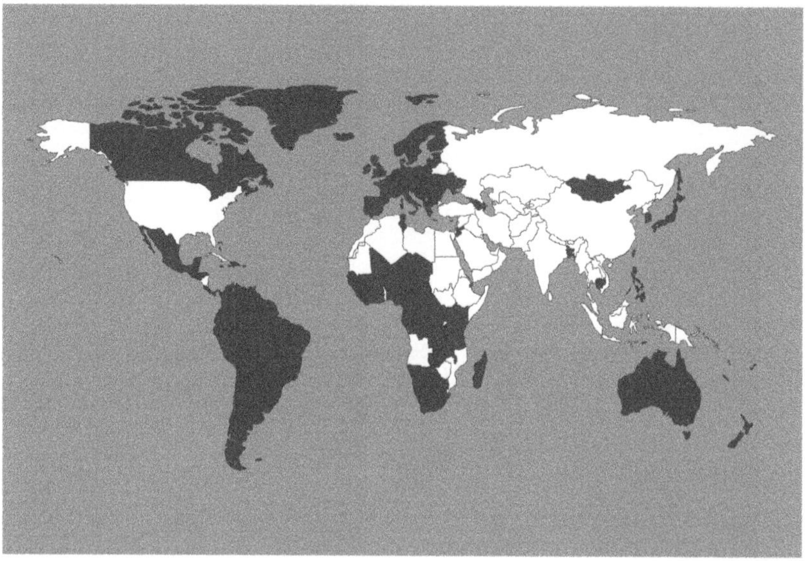

i.2 The member states of the Rome Statute accepting jurisdiction of the International Criminal Court as of April 2021 (in gray)

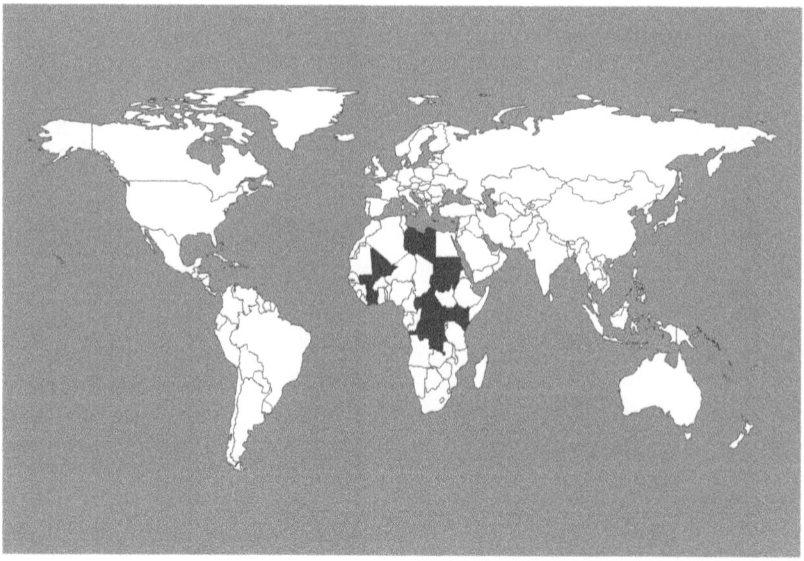

i.3 Countries and regions that are the location of crimes tried in ongoing and completed cases before the International Criminal Court as of April 2021 (in gray)

INTRODUCTION

Affect, Emotion, and the Law

> *Die formalen Qualitäten des Rechts entwickeln sich dabei aus seiner Kombination von magisch bedingtem Formalismus und offenbarungsmäßig bedingter Irrationalität im primitiven Rechtsgang … zu zunehmend fachmäßig juristischer, also logischer Rationalität und Systematik und damit – zunächst rein äußerlich betrachtet – zu einer zunehmend logischen Sublimierung und deduktiven Strenge des Rechts und einer zunehmend rationalen Technik des Rechtsgangs.*[1]
>
> Max Weber, *Wirtschaft und Gesellschaft* (1921)

In May 2017, two and a half years after starting the research project of which this book is the outcome, I approached the headquarters of the International Criminal Court (ICC) in Scheveningen, on the outskirts of The Hague, the capital of the Netherlands. As I had done many times before, I walked along the footpath leading from the bus station to the Court's main entrance. On that particular day, however, for some reason I stopped and looked more closely at the huge sculpture in front of the building (Figure i.1).

Although it is prominently positioned in front of the ICC, I had not paid it any attention before. The artwork, a metal and concrete structure, is several meters wide and at least five or six meters high. At first sight it appears to be an abstract cubist form, made up predominantly of straight lines and sharp angles. Suddenly finding myself curious about this sculpture, I read the small plaque in front of it. It told the visitor that this work of art, called *The Gift* by artist Navid Nuur, was presented by the Netherlands to the ICC to mark the official opening of the new permanent premises of the ICC in 2016. The "powerful and energetic sculpture," the plaque read, "is based on salt crystals found in tears and in the water of the nearby sea. These elements," the explanation

Figure i.1 *The Gift*, a sculpture by Navid Nuur in front of the permanent premises of the ICC in The Hague. (A black and white version of this figure will appear in some formats. For the color version, please refer to the plate section.)
Source: Jonas Bens

continued, "symbolise the universal expression of the emotions of joy and sorrow and the sea that connects all continents." I was astonished. This sculpture claimed to represent precisely those things that I was researching, that is, how international criminal justice as a transnational phenomenon is embedded in affective and emotional dynamics.

From the beginning of my research in 2015, I knew that the workings of international criminal justice could not be observed in one place only. The legalized and politicized processes of coming to terms with a past of large-scale violence, often called *transitional justice* (Teitel 2000; Hinton 2010b; Buckley-Zistel et al. 2013), become manifest in all kinds of different locales. To observe this globalized process I was prepared to go to multiple field sites for my ethnographic work (on multisited fieldwork, see Marcus 1995) and to engage in "deterritoriaialized ethnography" (Merry 2006b, 28). I decided to start my fieldwork at the most obvious site, the courtroom of the ICC, and to take it from there. I soon became most interested in the case *The Prosecutor v. Dominic Ongwen*, in which a former high-ranking commander of the Lord's Resistance Army (LRA), a rebel militia from northern Uganda, was being tried for war crimes and crimes against humanity. I decided to follow the case back to northern Uganda and to visit the places where the alleged violence had been perpetrated. I wanted to find out how transitional justice would find its way from the courtroom to Uganda and back again. This book recounts my exercise in deterritorialized ethnography in order to come to terms with this transnationally globally legalized process. With its reference to "the sea that connects all continents," Navid Nuur's sculpture was already pointing to that transnational dimension of justice.

The second remarkable aspect of this work of art was that the plaque's text connects this global, even universal, aspiration for international criminal justice to the salty tears of joy and sorrow. I found all this paradigmatic of my entire research project. When I started to investigate the role of affect and emotions in international criminal justice, I had expected it to be an interesting but somewhat difficult thing to do. Affect and emotions are generally seen as antithetical to legal forms and processes. The law demands reason and tries to exclude emotions. Affective dynamics trouble the law. From what I had read in the literature on law-and-emotion research, the law is always keen to obscure its affective and emotional undercurrents (Bandes 2001; Bornstein and Wiener 2010). I had already been to the Court dozens of times to attend proceedings. Spending hours and hours in the public gallery, I was always on the lookout for emotions and where I might find them, wondering how I would be able to recognize the affective elements and dimensions that I assumed must be present. And during all this time there was this unmistakable attempt to represent the universality of emotions directly in front of me, in metal and concrete, meters high and tons in weight, staring me in the face every day as I walked by. I had failed to see it because I was not schooled in where to look for it. Like this sculpture in front of the ICC, affect and emotions in international criminal law are hidden in plain sight. They are everywhere, clearly visible, obtrusive even, but one has to learn how to see them.

I suppose I had not made the connection between the large sculpture and the emotions it was intended to symbolize mainly because of its outward appearance. The straight lines, the sharp angles, the cubic form, the steel and concrete, the crystalline structure – these features did not express emotionality and affectivity to me. Rather, to my mind this sculpture symbolized the "iron cage" of rationalized modernity, to borrow Max Weber's famous phrase (1905, 108).[2]

In his monumental work *Economy and Society* (1921), Weber provides a grand theory of European modernity and the role of law in it. Modernity, according to Weber, means rationalization. In European modernity, reason increasingly governs all aspects of human life in society: economy, science, politics, bureaucracy, family, personal relationships. The main instrument for realizing this proliferation of reason is the law. To rationalize, and therefore modernize, society means, for Weber, to legalize it. Weber's analysis is certainly intuitive. In the more than one hundred years since Weber published his most celebrated works, modern law has indeed conquered the world. The system of international criminal law, with the ICC at its center, is certainly one important example. But for all the ingenuity and insight with which Weber analyzed and described modernity, he was certainly also afraid of it. His theory of reason is a theory of disenchantment. For Weber, "reasoning" means pure thinking, a thinking purged of magic, of religion, and, most importantly, of passion. Legal reasoning, first and foremost, means thinking *without* feeling. Weber's modernity is steel and concrete – not unlike the sculpture in front of the ICC. He even famously described the future of the modern world as "the polar night of icy darkness and hardship" (1919, 66).[3]

Such a conception of rational modernity can easily amount to a cliché. It has rationality at its core but cannot define it other than by what it is not, namely feeling. In this book, I will deviate from this stereotypical idea of legal reasoning. In the following chapters I will show that rationality – legal reasoning in particular – is not the opposite of affect and emotion, but a culturally and historically specific mode of meaning making that includes thinking *and* feeling. I want to take Weber at his word and explore the emotional and affective undertones implicit in his astute observations of rational law. If the modern world actually amounts to "a polar night of icy darkness" (in itself quite an emotion-evoking metaphor), then this is quite a visceral affair. Modern law is as much felt as it is thought.

This is not only a question of high theory. Thinking of modern law as deeply saturated with affect opens up exciting perspectives on many highly relevant, practical questions in the scholarship on law and society: How can we come to terms with the fact that courtroom performance, rhetoric, and spatial arrangement can so powerfully influence the outcome of a court proceeding? By what means do courtroom spectacles affect audiences, grab their attention, and connect to their senses of justice? How do we come to terms with the fact that legal reasoning is based on assertions regarding which audiences need to develop a subjective feeling of plausibility? Can we fully comprehend legal objectivity if we limit our conception of it to the lack of passion, or might there be other conceptual options, including the possibility of its affective production? Can we better understand complex legal-political debates such as the crisis of legitimacy of the ICC in Africa if we describe them as a competition of sentiments? All of these questions will be addressed in the following chapters as I shed light on the affective life of international criminal justice by developing and deploying two main analytical concepts: atmosphere and sentiment.

ATMOSPHERE

With my thoughts still on Navid Nuur's evocative sculpture, I continued my way to the entrance building of the ICC. When you want to enter the ICC, you must go through one of three revolving doors, line up at one of two counters, and present your identification papers to one of the ICC's security guards. The feeling is similar to waiting in the passport control line at an airport. You have to declare the purpose of your visit – whether you have an appointment or you simply want to observe one of the hearings that are being held that day – and you are handed a visitor's pass that you wear on a lanyard around your neck. When leaving the building later, you have to use the pass as a kind of key to exit through an automated door that is really quite futuristic. I realized that even after I had done this dozens of times, I still felt a little tense when I waited in line. In my head I would begin to practice what to say to the security guard, how I would go through the metal detector, even in what order I would put my personal effects on the conveyor belt at the security check.

I remembered reading an article by the anthropologist Nigel Eltringham, who has done ethnographic fieldwork at the International Criminal Tribunal in Rwanda (ICTR). In this article Eltringham describes what it feels like to enter the courtroom building of the ICTR, how the architecture of the building is intended to have a certain effect on the visitor, to imprint on him or her the power of the legal institutions, and to show what it means to be a spectator of justice (Eltringham 2012). In terms of social theory, this refers to the Foucauldian notion of *dispositif*, the idea of investigating the workings of power by looking at the apparatuses of governance, that is, ensembles composed of a large number of discursive and nondiscursive elements.[4] Institutions, organizations, and structures of all kinds produce their subjects by subjecting them to the *dispostif.* The state and its bureaucracy become inscribed in the subjective experiences of the people who are subjected to it – a process anthropologists call *affective governance* (Stoler 2002; Navaro-Yashin 2012; Laszczkowski and Reeves 2017; Freire de Andrade Neves 2018).[5]

People who find themselves in offices, courtrooms, museums, or universities, filled with all kinds of people and things that embody and symbolize the mystical trappings of the "state," feel something. They often experience these feelings not as coming from their deep inner selves, but – at least to a large degree – as the result of the wider arrangement in which they find themselves. Although people are generally aware of these experiences, the feelings are inchoate and difficult to put into words. It is this phenomenon that I am referring to when I use the noun "affect" or the adjective "affective." It is an important contention of this book that the workings of international criminal justice are, in important ways, affective.

After passing through the metal detectors, I would leave the small entrance building of the Court through an automatic door. To get to the main building where the courtrooms are located, one must cross a bridge over a waterway that surrounds the main building. To my mind, the arrangement evoked the image of a medieval castle with a moat around it, a traditional symbol of power and security with specific reference to the European past. To enter the main building, one must go through yet another revolving door. I became aware of how many doors one must pass through to get to the courtrooms. With each boundary that I crossed I became more and more immersed in the affective workings of the ICC. It seems that the power of affect is, to an important degree, "immersive power," as Rainer Mühlhoff (2018) has put it. All the different arrangements composed in the context of international criminal justice, of which the courtroom is but the most obvious example, have the effect of immersing those who venture within. The "overall feel" that these affective arrangements create and that affect people I call *atmospheres*. I contend that it is important to investigate this atmosphere making in order to understand how international criminal justice works, which is why the first part of this book is devoted to examining how the system of international criminal justice and its actors create atmospheres.

Chapter 1 will take us into the ICC courtroom in The Hague to observe the Dominic Ongwen trial. Law and society scholars have generally analyzed courtroom performances as speech events, focusing on how orators verbally discuss the law and mobilize the art of rhetoric to influence their audiences. I broaden the perspective by including audio, visual, spatial, and discursive material and components in my analysis of atmosphere to assess the workings of courtroom performance. Actors carefully arrange and rearrange these courtroom elements into an "affect-ctive arrangement." Challenging the widely held assumption that a courtroom is designed to cast out affect and emotion, I argue that courtrooms are actually designed to create affect and emotion and to regulate them in specific ways. Legal proceedings depend to a large degree on lawyers' ability to create courtroom atmospheres and manage affective arrangements. How they curate these atmospheres is often decisive for the outcome of a court case.

Chapter 2 takes us to a rural village in northern Uganda where the Dominic Ongwen proceedings are shown in a public screening – one of the outreach activities the ICC regularly conducts. Although not a legal setting in the narrow sense, these outreach events are carefully curated in order to create a specific transitional justice atmosphere. Sometimes these attempts succeed, other times they do not. I argue here that the production of atmosphere is a vital aspect of the success or failure of transitional justice projects. Transitional justice research has often focused on matters of translation between global norms and local politics. In these analyses, the translation of international criminal law either succeeds because it allows the participants "on the ground" to follow its reasoning or it fails because the cultural mismatch between the global and the local is too great. In the latter case, the explanations tend to create analytical dissonance leading to oversimplifications that often take the form of dichotomies – Western justice/African justice, law/politics – which sometimes cloud an analysis instead of providing clarity. I argue that focusing on the creation of atmospheres in transitional justice allows for fine-grained, ethnographically grounded analyses of why transitional justice succeeds or fails – and for whom. From this perspective, one cannot assume that transitional justice is only, or even mainly, about translating concepts from one legal context into another; rather, it is about creating a relational arrangement in which certain ways to bring about justice feel more just than others.

SENTIMENT

After I had entered the ICC's main building on this day in May 2017, waited in line before the large front desk, and presented my credentials,

I turned to the right and walked down the corridor to a small cafeteria where one can have a cup of coffee and a piece of cake, something I did regularly during my fieldwork. This is the one place where everyone who works at the Court – judges, prosecutors, administrators – and all those who visit the court – students, tourists, anthropologists – can encounter one another. As I looked out of the large windows – the whole building is of steel and glass – I was reminded of the first interview I conducted for this research project, right in this very cafeteria.

The conversation took place in January 2016. It was with a member of the ICC's outreach unit, which is responsible for connecting the Court's activities to the outside world. They do this by talking to the press, disseminating information leaflets and videos, and conducting outreach events of various types. The public screenings in northern Uganda that I describe in Chapter 2 are one example of this outreach work. We were not long into our conversation when we began to discuss the political context that largely structures the whole project the ICC is conducting – what some rather brusquely call "the ICC's Africa problem" (Dersso 2016) and what one could also call, conversely, "Africa's ICC problem." When the ICC began its work in 2002, it was the first institution of its kind: an international court set up to prosecute "the most serious crimes of concern to the international community as a whole," as it says in the Rome Statute, the international treaty that established the legal foundation for the ICC's work.[6] Before the ICC was established, there were only ad hoc international criminal tribunals for specific situations of large-scale violence. The military tribunals of Nuremberg and Tokyo following the Second World War in the 1940s and the two large international criminal tribunals on the genocidal violence in Yugoslavia and Rwanda in the 1990s are prominent examples. The ICC is intended to be a permanent institution for bringing individuals, mostly military and political leaders, ideally from all over the world, to trial. They should be prosecuted for war crimes and crimes against humanity in situations so extreme that a single state is not able or not willing to handle the criminal process.[7]

But the reality looks quite different. At the time of writing this book, the Court had only managed to prosecute Africans for international crimes perpetrated in Africa.[8] For some time now, many African politicians and public intellectuals have painted the Court as a neocolonial institution. Although most African nation-states had initially been in favor of the establishment of the ICC, the winds started shifting when the ICC put out an arrest warrant for Omar Hassan Ahmad al-Bashir, the then-sitting president of Sudan (Jalloh, Akande, and Plessis 2011; Cole 2013). Since then, the African Union has been critical of the indictment practices of the ICC. Its member states have argued in several decisions and resolutions that the ICC was specifically targeting African leaders and purposefully ignoring the international law principle of sovereign immunity, that is, the principle that state officials such as heads of state and government cannot be brought before the courts (see Chapter 6 for a critical discussion of this principle).[9] This discussion on the legitimacy of the ICC's transitional justice interventions in Africa forms a larger discursive frame for much of the work that the ICC does on an everyday basis.

When I asked my conversation partner from the ICC's outreach unit about the "Africa problem," she readily admitted that there was indeed a problem and that it stemmed from the fact that the ICC had thus far only tried perpetrators from Africa. A few days earlier, the chief prosecutor, Gambian lawyer Fatou Bensouda, had announced that her office would start a preliminary investigation into possible war crimes and crimes against humanity committed during the conflict between Russia and Georgia in and around South Ossetia in 2008. The ICC outreach officer said that this announcement came as a bit of a relief because it would be the first formal investigation in Europe and could alleviate some of the criticism that the ICC was targeting Africans. She complained that African politicians were mobilizing enormous resources to campaign against the ICC, while her unit only had very limited capacity to rebut the criticism and influence these debates.

I asked her quite directly what role she thought emotion played in her work in the context of these debates on the ICC's legitimacy in Africa. Her immediate reaction was to insist that, of course, it was her job and that of her colleagues to objectively inform the public, especially the victims in the African "situation countries," and to "put the emotions aside." She went on to say that, naturally, all actors would be highly emotionally involved in these kinds of cases, but the ICC's outreach work must try to inform people without getting into emotional discussions; it was important to stick to the facts: how the process before the ICC works, what happens when, who has what rights, and so on.

Our conversation went on for a little while longer, and I asked the outreach officer what she personally thought about the criticism that the ICC was a neocolonial institution. She acknowledged the problem and noted that the structure of the global legal order did not allow for complete equality before international criminal law.

There are three ways of bringing a case before the ICC. The standard way is used when crimes are committed in a member state of the Rome Statute. In this case, the chief prosecutor can first open an investigation and then apply for an arrest warrant. The problem is that there are a number of countries that are not members of the Rome Statute. The United States, China, Russia, and India have not ratified the treaty, nor have most of the countries in Asia and the Pacific region, with the notable exceptions of Australia, Bangladesh, New Zealand, and Japan. That means that the standard way of bringing a case before the ICC is mainly limited to countries in Europe, the Americas, and Africa.

A second way of bringing a case before the ICC is for one of the member states of the Rome Statute to refer a case to the ICC, but there is only a limited number of situations in which this is a realistic option. In the case of the LRA, the Ugandan government referred the situation in northern Uganda to the ICC at a time when the government under President Yoweri Museveni thought that doing so would be an effective way to solicit international help in his government's fight against the LRA.

A third option is for the United Nations Security Council (UNSC), the most powerful body of the UN, to refer a situation to the ICC for investigation, which can be done even for crimes that were committed in countries that are not parties to the Rome Statute. This has, for example, been done in the case of Sudan. But three of the five veto members of the UNSC are themselves not signatories to the Rome Statute, and they tend to block investigations against themselves and their allies.

These structures have resulted, as the ICC outreach officer conceded, in severe limitations on the ICC's efficacy in prosecuting international crimes. Nevertheless, she still found the campaign of African politicians against the ICC to be unjustified. Her main argument was that most of the cases that were now being tried before the ICC had been initiated by precisely those governments that were now criticizing the ICC's trials as illegal interventions into their internal affairs, Uganda among them.

While my conversation partner was explaining these things, she said something that did not strike me as remarkable at the time but jumped out at me later when I reread the notes I had taken. Summing up her assertion that the African politicians' criticisms were unjustified, she concluded that the anti-ICC campaign only proved that many of these politicians were, in fact, afraid of the ICC. When Fatou Bensouda's predecessor as chief prosecutor, Luis Moreno Ocampo, issued an arrest warrant against then-sitting Sudanese President Al-Bashir, every African head of state and government realized that they themselves could be brought before the ICC if they engaged in similar crimes. "They are afraid," she said, "and the fact that they are afraid shows that we are doing a good job."

When I looked back on this conversation, it became clear to me that international criminal law seems to be about emotions after all, even in the descriptions and explanations given by the actors most responsible for enforcing it. It is true, as Elizabeth Mertz has shown in her impressive ethnography of a law school in the United States, that "legal training demands a bracketing of emotion and morality (as it is commonly understood) in dealing with human conflict and the people who appear in legal conflict stories" (2007a, 121; for the Swedish legal system, see Flower 2014). At the same time, in the theories of criminal punishment that all law students have to learn early on in their legal educations, one important function of criminal punishment is deterrence. The idea is that potential criminals are afraid of going to jail, and that is why they tend to adhere to the law. In fact, in many aspects, emotions are an explicit component of any legal order and the work of its practitioners. And these explicit emotions exist side by side with a self-understanding that requires people to "put their emotions aside." In their seminal work *Professional Emotions in Court* (2018), Stina Bergman Blix and Åsa Wettergren introduce the idea that lawyers constantly experience "background emotions" that influence their decision-making – even in those proceedings that are expressly supposed to be unemotional. They, therefore, do not see the presence of emotions in lawyering as an aberration from proper judicial work, and in fact conceive of law at work as, first and foremost, the production of an "emotive-cognitive judicial frame" (Blix and Wettergren 2018, 7). From this perspective, all kinds of organizations and institutions, including those of the law, appear inherently emotional – a point that has been well-established by sociologists of emotion (Sieben and Wettergren 2010; Celermajer et al. 2019).

Apart from the affective workings of the law and these subtle atmospheres that are difficult to describe, there is another emotion-related component of feeling at work in international criminal law that is much closer to our everyday understanding of "feeling." What I have in mind here are those phenomena that people experience and for which they have concrete words, with more or less clear concepts behind them: fear, love, hate, and anger, to name but a few. This is what I am referring to when I use the noun *emotion* or the adjective *emotional*. While people usually have to provide detailed explanations to describe their affective experiences, emotion words are culturalized condensations of such felt experiences. People use these emotion concepts with the expectation that their counterpart will get the message. While there are emotion words in every language, emotion concepts and emotional experiences differ, sometimes drastically, according to the cultural context in which they appear, something anthropologists have investigated in great depth (Benedict 1946; Briggs 1970; Levy 1973; Rosaldo 1980; Lutz 1988; Röttger-Rössler 2004). The sculpture in front of the ICC spoke of the tears that connect all people. But while it might be true that all humans have the biological capacity to cry, not all people are experiencing the same feelings when they do, nor do they use the same emotion concepts to verbalize those feelings. Also, they do not necessarily understand each other any more clearly in those moments when they do experience emotion.[10]

In the course of this book, we will encounter many instances in which emotional dynamics govern the workings of international criminal law. The ICC outreach officer mentioned the fear of prosecution. We will also find anger toward those who have killed a relative or a friend, the forgiving empathy of a pious churchgoer toward a perpetrator, righteous indignation over a breach of the law by a believer in the liberal justice system, the honest pride of having mastered a crisis by a victim of violence, the quiet satisfaction felt by an uninvolved bystander when a criminal is punished. These emotions, although they are experienced by individuals, do not originate in individual experience. They are, as anthropologists (being, after all, social scientists) have insisted, the product of cultural socialization (Röttger-Rössler, Scheidecker, and Funk 2015; Scheidecker 2017). Claiming that emotions play a role in human behavior is not the same as contending that people react like biologically preprogrammed robots vis-à-vis the complexity of the world. It means, rather, that culture and society not only surround people, but are also inscribed in how they experience themselves, others, and the world. It also means insisting that the way people experience themselves, others, and the world shapes their actions.[11]

The realm of feeling is not, as such, antithetical to other registers of engaging with the world. Indeed, anthropologists have argued that a strict separation of emotion and reason, thinking and feeling, affect and cognition is a particularly Western idea that does find not many followers across cultures (Lutz 1988; Surrallés 2003). Anthropologist Michelle Rosaldo put it very nicely when she described emotions as "embodied thoughts" (1984), implying that thinking and feeling are not mutually exclusive realms but inextricably entangled. The opinions people form and the decisions they make are at some level intermingled with their subjective experiences of the world, with their feeling lives. One's opinion for or against the policies of the ICC can be formed out of fear of prosecution, thirst for revenge, hope for retribution, love of justice, or some other kind of emotional dynamics, but also against the background of an atmosphere of mistrust, the gut feeling that something is not right about all this, or the vague sensation that this might be the time to make things right. It is this role of affect and emotion in the formation of political opinions, normative assessments, and assertions of justice or injustice that I am referring to when, in the course of this book, I use the term *sentiment*.

What I like about the English word "sentiment" is that it can mean both "opinion" and "emotion." "I agree with your sentiment," means that I agree with somebody's opinion, but at the same time that I also sympathize with that person's emotional experience. I use the term "sentiment" in the course of this book to focus on the foundational role that affective and emotional experiences have on the way people make sense of the world. In this sense, I follow the famous anthropologist Bronislaw Malinowski, who, in his insights into the workings of culture, used sentiment widely as an analytical term. He explained that "the love or hate or devotion we feel for a parent, a country or a life-pursuit, . . . the ties which bind us to the various members of our family, patriotism, ideals of truth, righteousness, devotion to science – all these are sentiments" (1927, 139). With this in mind, I therefore define sentiments as evaluative regimes of meaning that are embedded in and colored by affective and emotional dynamics.[12] Put differently, emotions and affects can also be sentiments if they concern processes of normative meaning-making, such as differentiating between right and wrong, just and unjust, good and bad. In the second part of this book, I will try to explain my contention that the project of international criminal justice can be described as a project to evoke, produce, shape, and maintain sentiments. Chapters 3 to 7 deal with the role of sentiment in international criminal law; they approach central concepts of legal theory and practice – plausibility, objectivity, and justice – in their emotional dimension.

In Chapter 3 I investigate legal truth by analyzing the production of legal plausibility. In a legal proceeding it is not important if things *are* true; it is of practical importance only that things *appear* to be true to specific relevant actors – judges, for example. Courtroom actors spend a great deal of time and effort trying to make things appear true to their audiences. A central strategy in this respect is what I call *affective framing*: the practice of evoking affective arrangements in such a way that an action or an event is *felt* to be more or less plausible. All of the principal actors involved in the Dominic Ongwen case were engaging in affective framing. His defense lawyers described his life in an army camp to make plausible the duress he was under in his time in the LRA. His prosecutors talked about ambition and prowess to make his guilt more plausible. His victims built memorials to create an affective frame that would make their demands for justice and reparations more plausible. Although their projects were different, all these actors understood that certain actions and events appear plausible or implausible in light of the affective arrangement in which they are presented, and that legal reasoning is based on these plausible facts.

In Chapter 4, I explain my take on objectivity in terms of sentiment. Objectivity is not the opposite of affectivity; to the contrary, my argument is that objectivity is a kind of affect. In a somewhat unconventional way, I argue that legal objectivity has to be seen as an affective mode in which objects are assembled in an affective arrangement. In the Dominic Ongwen case, the lawyers brought people, books, videos, and even spirits from northern Uganda into the courtroom. They were constantly trying to arrange the relevant objects and subjects in such a way that their own arguments would appear to be supported by *objects* (and would therefore be more *objective*), and their counterparts' arguments would appear mainly to be supported by *subjects* (and thus be more *subjective*). Analyses of courtroom argumentation often implicitly assume that convincing a courtroom audience of one's arguments is a competition for "credibility points"; in other words, that lawyers try to load their own pieces of evidence with credibility and try to siphon credibility off from their counterparts' pieces of evidence. Awareness of the sentiment involved shifts this perspective. Courtroom actors go far beyond playing a game of crediting and discrediting. They aim to manipulate the whole arrangement under which certain bodies in the courtroom can be credited or discredited. As such, they are simultaneously playing the game and changing the rules as they go along.

In Chapter 5, I focus on the debate in northern Uganda regarding the legitimacy of the ICC. To the people there, the legitimacy of the ICC is neither abstract nor absolute; it is a very concrete matter of whether the ICC is the best conflict resolution mechanism for the given circumstances. Other normative systems are also available to address the violence of the past: Ugandan state law, traditional law, and religious ethics. Sentiment sheds light on how people navigate this normative pluralism. Not only do different legal systems compete with one another, but different sentiments of justice do as well. The judgments on justice that people make cannot be understood simply by referring to differences in their culturally socialized values. People make their assessments regarding the justice or injustice of a specific case, such as the trial against Dominic Ongwen, always in relation to the normative orders that present them with the criteria to assess it. People navigate this normative pluralism by evoking, producing, shaping, and maintaining sentiments. Recent approaches to justice in Africa have proposed that law and justice must be analyzed separately, insisting that justice always goes beyond legality. Studies on the role of emotions in transitional justice seem to agree that emotions are something the law cannot accommodate and argue that transitional justice must go beyond legal measures to create forums in which emotions can come to the fore – truth and reconciliation commissions, for instance. In my view, there is a twofold misconception at work in these lines of argumentation: when one looks for the emotions only outside of the law, namely in the realm of justice, one tends to underestimate both how the law is imbued with affect and how justice is imbued with law. A focus on sentiment circumvents such misleading separations between law and justice and has the potential to provide a fresh perspective on some of the dead ends in transitional justice research.

THE POLITICS OF ATMOSPHERE AND SENTIMENT

When I had finished my coffee on that day in 2017, I made my way to one of the courtrooms. To reach it, I had to pass through yet another security check and a metal detector. At the security check, I was handed a leaflet listing the rules I had to adhere to when visiting a court proceeding (Figure i.2). You are not allowed to bring electronic devices such as mobile phones into the public gallery, nor books or other papers; only a notebook and a pencil.

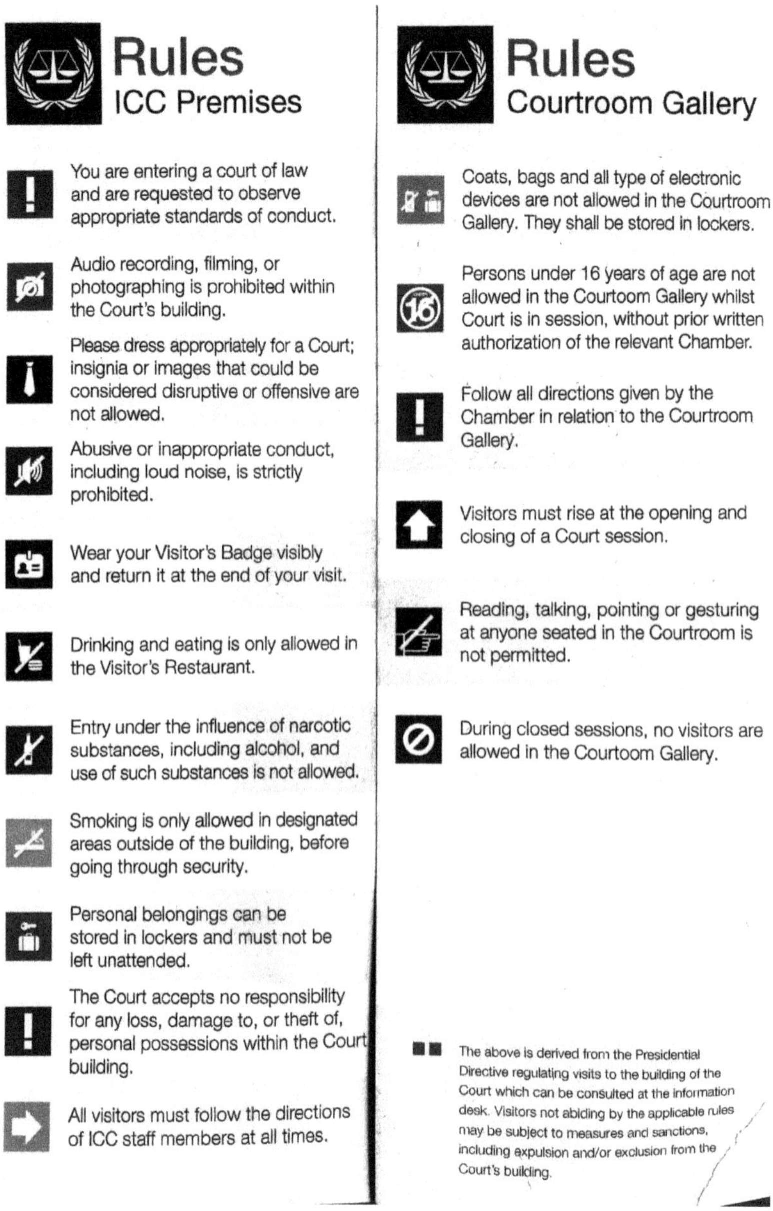

Rules
ICC Premises

You are entering a court of law and are requested to observe appropriate standards of conduct.

Audio recording, filming, or photographing is prohibited within the Court's building.

Please dress appropriately for a Court; insignia or images that could be considered disruptive or offensive are not allowed.

Abusive or inappropriate conduct, including loud noise, is strictly prohibited.

Wear your Visitor's Badge visibly and return it at the end of your visit.

Drinking and eating is only allowed in the Visitor's Restaurant.

Entry under the influence of narcotic substances, including alcohol, and use of such substances is not allowed.

Smoking is only allowed in designated areas outside of the building, before going through security.

Personal belongings can be stored in lockers and must not be left unattended.

The Court accepts no responsibility for any loss, damage to, or theft of, personal possessions within the Court building.

All visitors must follow the directions of ICC staff members at all times.

Rules
Courtroom Gallery

Coats, bags and all type of electronic devices are not allowed in the Courtroom Gallery. They shall be stored in lockers.

Persons under 16 years of age are not allowed in the Courtoom Gallery whilst Court is in session, without prior written authorization of the relevant Chamber.

Follow all directions given by the Chamber in relation to the Courtroom Gallery.

Visitors must rise at the opening and closing of a Court session.

Reading, talking, pointing or gesturing at anyone seated in the Courtroom is not permitted.

During closed sessions, no visitors are allowed in the Courtoom Gallery.

The above is derived from the Presidential Directive regulating visits to the building of the Court which can be consulted at the information desk. Visitors not abiding by the applicable rules may be subject to measures and sanctions, including expulsion and/or exclusion from the Court's building.

Figure i.2 Rule sheet for visitors to the ICC. (A black and white version of this figure will appear in some formats. For the color version, please refer to the plate section.) Source: Jonas Bens

In the public gallery, there are two large screens, one on the left side and one on the right, that transmit live video of the proceeding. This same video feed is also streamed online via the ICC's website. Visitors tend to look at these screens rather than through the glass wall into the courtroom itself. Then, after a while they begin to realize this and shift their view back and forth between the screens on the side and the glass wall into the courtroom. It is through this peculiar spatial arrangement that I became aware of the multiplicity of audiences that are connected to these court proceedings simultaneously. Seeing the courtroom through the glass wall but simultaneously seeing on the screens what another, wider audience sees outside the public gallery points to the central role publics (in the plural) play in these kinds of trials. Transitional justice is largely dependent on connecting legal proceedings with mass audiences. In the course of this book, I contend that it is through affect and emotion that these audiences are being connected to the project of transitional justice.

Numerous studies have highlighted the role of affect and emotion in mass politics, particularly when it comes to social movements, political mobilization, or democratic elections (Goodwin, Jasper, and Polletta 2001; Marcus 2002; Gould 2009; Coleman 2013). Scholars seem to become interested in affect and emotions when they want to explain excitement, outbursts, movement, volatility, and trouble – all of which they associate with politics. They are much less inclined to write about affect and emotions when they want to explain calm deliberation, moderation, composure, and order – all of which are associated with law. If scholars write about the power of courts to influence the emotions of mass audiences, it is usually in the context of "political trials" (for classic accounts, see Kirchheimer 1961; Arendt 1963; Shklar 1964). But the fact that these courtroom spectacles grab the emotional attention of the audience is attributed not to law, but to politics, a politics that contaminates the workings of the law in these trials (but cf. Ertür 2015 for a notable exception). From the perspective I advocate in this book – that atmosphere and sentiment pervade the law – this crude law–politics divide becomes suspect. As studies of political trials show, courts, including international courts, are crucial players in influencing atmospheres and sentiments in the political sphere and engage in its economy of attention. My argument is that this is not in spite of the fact that they are legal processes but largely because of that fact.

Understanding that international criminal justice derives its power from its ability to create, maintain, transform, and reject atmospheres and sentiments is of crucial importance to law and society research first and foremost because it opens up a fresh perspective on the legitimacy of bodies such as the ICC. Mainstream approaches to legitimacy inspired by procedural justice insist on connecting the perceived legitimacy of legal institutions to whether or not these institutions operate according to their self-proclaimed rationality. Most of the time, such an approach neglects the affective and emotional dimensions of people's meaning making in relation to the law.

In Chapter 6, I describe the workings of atmosphere and sentiment in the political controversies swirling around the legitimacy of the ICC's legal interventions in Africa. I argue that to forcefully make an argument regarding legitimacy, actors will try to create a certain political atmosphere with the right political sentiments to further their goals. A successful strategy of doing so is to create predictable discursive devices to navigate atmosphere and sentiment. There are many such discursive devices; here I shall focus on what I call *indignation regimes*. I see indignation as a central political emotion in the mass-media polity, as it serves as a marker of relevance for political issues. Political actors try to regulate how their audiences will feel indignation about the issues they bring to the fore. Being able to create or use relatively stable discursive regimes to create indignation is hence a powerful tool that is used by virtually all political actors in a political public, not only by so-called *populist* politicians, as many in political theory and practice seem to believe.

If one theorizes affect and emotion, atmosphere and sentiment, as constitutive elements of international criminal law and the politics in which it is embedded, I believe the consequences are far reaching. The debate on the ICC in Africa cannot be properly understood without coming to terms with the European modernity's inextricable entanglement with European colonialism. The contestations over the ICC are also struggles over whose emotions are allowed to come to the fore and what form these emotional utterances are allowed to take. Think back to the large metal sculpture in front of the ICC in The Hague that I introduced at the beginning of this chapter: its design represents an ideal type of modernity – massive, made of metal, simple, crystalline, technical. It has become part of conventional wisdom to think of emotion as antithetical to the modern world. As a consequence, affect and emotion tend to be attributed either to a premodern past or, as many postcolonial thinkers such as Frantz Fanon and Edward Said have shown, to a non-European, premodern other.

But such a division of the globe into the reasonable and the emotional parts of the world is based on the attempt to make invisible the fact that European modernity and international criminal law as one of its components are themselves based on specific sentiments. Assessing the role of emotion in (post)modern life has become integral to assessing present and future in relation to the past and the Global North in relation to the Global South. Thinking about emotion as constitutive of modernity is hence targeting the very core of the conception of Western modernity. Bruno Latour famously coined the phrase "We have never been modern." I believe he was right. In Chapter 7, I build on this assertion and add: We have also never been rational.

As I sat in the public gallery in the ICC (Figure i.3) waiting for proceeding to begin, a class of university students in their early twenties occupied the seats near me. They were most likely from one of the international master's programs at one of the nearby Dutch universities that specialize in "genocide studies" or "human rights and development." They started to engage in whispered conversations with each other, pointing to actors in the courtroom and trying to figure out which of them was the prosecutor and which the defense lawyer. One group even started to giggle. All of these activities are listed as strictly

Figure i.3 A public gallery in the ICC. (A black and white version of this figure will appear in some formats. For the color version, please refer to the plate section.)
Source: ICC-INT

forbidden on the sheet of rules that they were handed at the security check. Consequently, one of the security guards approached the group and reprimanded them.

I was reminded of Arlie Hochschild's famous book *The Managed Heart* (1983), in which she explains the concept of "feeling rules." All social arrangements are governed by such rules, which regulate who is allowed to have what kinds of feelings at what time. They go beyond mere display rules, for example, that you should not giggle in a courtroom where war crimes are being tried. They govern the feeling itself: you should not even *feel* like giggling in a courtroom where war crimes are being tried. Of course, the ICC is no exception. It is also structured by feeling rules, and there are security guards to enforce them.

This is a moment when all the concepts I have described so far – affect, emotion, atmosphere, and sentiment – can be observed coming together and intertwining. The public gallery is designed to produce a specific atmosphere, and this atmosphere seems to be a vital part of the attempt to produce specific sentiments. The production of affect plays a role in curating these atmospheres, and the presence and absence of certain emotions, such as joy, seem to be necessary as well. In the scholarship there are many who make a great deal of the distinction between affect and emotion (Massumi 2002), usually with the aim of asserting that affect is the more basic, more important, and more relevant thing to study. While I agree that there is a point in distinguishing affect from emotion to a certain degree, I see them more as two perspectives on the question of how people experience the world and what matters to them (Lutz 2017). This is basically what this book is about: to show the mechanisms through which international criminal justice matters to, concerns, and affects people. My main analytical lenses are atmosphere and sentiment, and the processes I observe are their production, deployment, and management in a transnational space. Through this kind of analysis, I am trying to explain in the following chapters what I mean when I assert that the ICC is a *sentimental court*.

PART I

ATMOSPHERES

1

COURTROOM ATMOSPHERES

The Courtroom of the ICC as an Affective Arrangement

> *The proceedings happen on a stage before an audience, with the usher's marvelous shout at the beginning of each session producing the effect of the rising curtain. Whoever planned this auditorium in the newly built Beth Ha'am, the House of the People (now surrounded by high fences, guarded from roof to cellar by heavily armed police, and with a row of wooden barracks in the front courtyard in which all comers are expertly frisked), had a theater in mind, complete with orchestra and gallery, with proscenium and stage, and with side doors for the actors' entrance.*
>
> Hannah Arendt, *Eichmann in Jerusalem: A Report on the Banality of Evil* (1963)

Why is there such a thing as a courtroom? From a practical standpoint, there might also be other convenient places to hold a legal proceeding. One could settle a family dispute in the home of the concerned parties, discuss the merits of a claim for damages at the defendant's place of business, or hold a criminal proceeding at the scene of the crime. At these places, the relevant evidence would usuallay be present, questions that arise in the course of the proceeding could be investigated quickly by asking witnesses who typically live or work nearby. But this is not how it is usually done. Instead, the law seems to require a special place at which the proceedings can be performed. The people involved in a legal proceeding are forced to interrupt their daily business, leave their homes and workplaces, and enter a place where many other trials and proceedings have taken place in the past and will take place in the future.

In ancient Athens, a murder case would be tried at the *Areopagos*, a rock at the northeastern end of the city's Acropolis (Lanni 2006). In medieval Germany, important legal decisions would be made at the *Thing* (assembly), a central place in the community often featuring a linden tree under which the proceedings would be held (Schild 1980). In nineteenth-century northern Uganda, people met in the hut of the *rwot*, the village chief, for disputes to be settled (Girling 1960). In twenty-first-century Netherlands, people meet to hold war crimes trials at the headquarters of the International Criminal Court (ICC) in The Hague. While the law-spaces that humans have used in the past and still use might differ considerably from each other in terms of aesthetic composition and spatial arrangement, they have one thing in common: once set up, the basic design does not change much over time, and it serves as a ritual forum where all kinds of cases are heard.[1] It seems that the law's aspirations to truth, objectivity, justice – all of which are thoroughly discussed in this book – are best furthered by a specific space that is used over and over again. There appears to be a connection between how the law can be performed and how persons and things are arranged in space while it is being performed.

The law enters the social world as a performance. People come together at a certain time and a certain place to play it out. Those who approach the law ethnographically have developed a good sense for the fact that one cannot understand the social life of law without understanding exactly how the various performances through which it enters people's lives take place.[2] The court proceeding is, of course, the most important of these performances – although, as we will see, by far not the only one.

Traditionally, courtroom ethnographers have therefore paid particular attention to the most prominent aspect of this performance: talk. This stands to reason, as talking is the main thing people do in courtrooms. The insights that have been derived from linguistic-oriented courtroom ethnography are invaluable.

I argue, however, that for a complete analysis of the workings of the courtroom, one must go beyond talk and strive to understand the role of *atmosphere* in the law. Talking is indeed one important practice aimed at shaping the atmosphere of a courtroom. Actors do their best to influence the atmosphere in the courtroom through their talk because they believe that doing so has an impact on the outcome of the court proceeding. To shape an atmosphere, one must try to arrange the persons and things assembled and to relate them to one another in specific ways so that the overall arrangement conveys a certain *feeling*. This art of creating, recreating, and shaping the courtroom atmosphere is a key technique that one must master to be an effective lawyer. In this line of thinking, I conceptualize the courtroom not as a bland container filled with the language of the law but as a much more complex thing: an *affective arrangement*.

This approach differs considerably from the commonly held notion that modern courtrooms are somehow designed to cast out emotions in order to create a neutral space where the rational law is allowed to unfold.[3] I am arguing quite the opposite. The courtroom is not designed to cast out affect and emotion but to create and arouse them. Anybody who has set foot in a courtroom will recall that it gives rise to a specific feeling. That this feeling is different from the feeling they experience when going about their everyday business is no accident. The courtroom is intentionally designed to produce a certain atmosphere, and actors spend a great deal of time and effort in shaping it to their advantage.

A COURTROOM ATMOSPHERE

In January 2016, I attended the confirmation of charges hearing in the case *The Prosecutor* v. *Dominic Ongwen* in The Hague. Dominic Ongwen, a Ugandan national, was accused of committing war crimes and crimes against humanity when he was a commander of the Lord's Resistance Army (LRA). The LRA is an armed rebel group that was formed after the current president of Uganda, Yoweri Kaguta Museveni, took over the government in 1986. It fought a twenty-year war in northern Uganda against the Ugandan army, the Uganda People's Defence Force (UPDF), with the explicit aim of overthrowing the Museveni government. The conflict between the LRA and the Ugandan government has a complex history involving many outside actors (Behrend 1993; Allen 2006; Lenhart 2006; Finnström 2008, 63–98; Dolan 2009, 39–71; Allen and Vlassenroot 2010b). It is only since 2006 that the LRA, which still exists albeit only as quite a small group, has been prevented from conducting military operations on Ugandan soil.[4] In the course of this book, I will discuss a number of aspects of this difficult history.

One high point of the conflict in northern Uganda was the early 2000s. At that time, the military conflict had become so fierce that nearly 90 percent of the population of northern Uganda, about 1.5 million people, was forced to live in camps for internally displaced persons (IDPs) (Allen 2006, 53). The humanitarian conditions in these camps were catastrophic. Hundreds of people died every day from malnutrition and disease (Dolan 2009, 107–158). At about the same time, the ICC first started its operations. The Ugandan government under Yoweri Museveni decided to refer the situation in northern Uganda to the ICC and asked the then chief prosecutor, Luis Moreno Ocampo, to open an investigation into possible war crimes and crimes against humanity. This referral of the LRA conflict to the ICC was a key moment in the history of the conflict. Chief Prosecutor Ocampo conducted an investigation into actions of both the LRA and the UPDF. In 2005, however, Ocampo decided to apply for only five arrest warrants, all for top LRA commanders, including the leader of the LRA, Joseph Kony. Among those high-ranking commanders was also Dominic Ongwen. The warrants were issued by the ICC in July 2005.

Ongwen was charged for crimes he committed while commanding LRA soldiers in the early 2000s. His charges included the conscription and use of child soldiers, rape, forced marriage, and sexual slavery. At the heart of the charges were four massacres in IDP camps in the villages of Lukodi, Odek, Abok, and Pajule in the years 2003 and 2004 that Ongwen allegedly ordered and commanded.[5] For nearly ten years, Ongwen and the other LRA commanders wanted by the ICC remained at large. Ongwen avoided arrest until the end of 2014, when he was captured under somewhat murky circumstances by Séléka rebels[6] in the Central African Republic.[7] On January 16, 2015, Ongwen was delivered to the ICC in The Hague.

It took a little more than a year for the Office of the Prosecutor to put together its case. Before Ongwen could be put on trial, the prosecution had to convince the Court in a confirmation of charges hearing that it had enough evidence for a trial proceeding.[8] It was this confirmation of charges hearing that I attended as a visitor in the public gallery in early 2016. The prosecution convincingly presented a summary of the evidence that it had assembled against the accused, and Dominic Ongwen was committed to trial, beginning on December 6 of the same year.

At the heart of the prosecution's thoroughly choreographed presentation were several audio files. During the war in northern Uganda, the Ugandan security forces had intercepted radio communications between LRA commanders. Members of both the Ugandan army (UPDF) and the Internal Security Organization (ISO), a Ugandan secret intelligence agency, wrote down in shorthand what they had heard over the radio. At a later time, they transcribed their handwritten shorthand jottings in longhand into a logbook. As their superiors in the army and the secret intelligence service were mostly from the south of Uganda, these logbook transcriptions were mainly made in English rather than in the original Acholi. From 2003 onward, many of these intercepted radio transmissions were also recorded with a tape recorder. Some of these recordings, especially those in which Dominic Ongwen himself can be heard talking over the radio, were highly incriminating evidence. The Office of the Prosecutor collected these tape recordings, had them transcribed in their original Acholi, and had them translated into English. As these recordings and their several transcriptions were at the heart of the prosecution's evidence, the prosecution lawyers decided to introduce them on the first day of the proceedings.

Jeremy Elderfield, one of the junior trial lawyers on the prosecution team, took responsibility for that task. He began by explaining to the participants in the courtroom why the intercepted radio transmissions had been recorded in the first place. He said that the "tape recordings were used primarily as a backup in case radio operators missed the meaning or the content of the communication during the live broadcast."[9] Having these tapes available, along with their shorthand jottings, meant that the members of the UPDF and the ISO were able "to go back to check what had been said to complete their logbook entry." The moment Elderfield had finished that sentence, a photograph of one of the tapes appeared on every computer screen in the courtroom.

The courtroom of the ICC is a high-tech environment (Figure 1.1). Every participant inside the courtroom is seated in front of a personal computer with a large screen. The participants use these personal computers to display the relevant court documents; it is more convenient and efficient than carrying large quantities of paper around with them and having to pass exhibits around the courtroom. While a few participants still prefer to bring folders into the courtroom, most rely on the computer and have only a small notebook with them to scribble down some notes. The parties also use the computer system to accompany their oral arguments with audiovisual presentations. These presentations are viewed by all participants, and those parts that do not contain confidential information are also shown to the public. Elderfield had prepared such an audiovisual presentation.

When the photograph of the tape appeared on all screens, Elderfield went on to explain: "The tape on this slide was produced by the ISO. It is numbered 693, which means that it was the 693rd tape that the ISO recorded of LRA radio communications. This tape records communications from 8 to 10 October 2003, the date of the Pajule attack." Right after finishing this sentence, Elderfield lifted up a compact cassette to the height of his breast, held it in front of his body, and said: "I have the

Figure 1.1 The ICC courtroom with IT workspaces including monitors and the audio system for simultaneous translation (foreground). The elevated booths where interpreters sit are visible in the back of the room. Cameras are positioned on the walls. (A black and white version of this figure will appear in some formats. For the color version, please refer to the plate section.)
Source: ICC-INT

original of this tape also with me in the courtroom." He then paused for a few seconds, still holding the tape in front of him. Elderfield went on with his presentation by announcing that he intended to play to the audience "a short segment of the tape."

The ICC courtroom has a sophisticated audio system that facilitates simultaneous translation into English and French. In the Dominic Ongwen case, which was primarily conducted in English, there was a third simultaneous translation into and from Acholi – the native language of Dominic Ongwen. All seats in the courtroom as well as in the public gallery are equipped with headphones and a device with which the user can select an audio channel. One channel transmits the audio as it is spoken on the courtroom floor, the so-called floor language. Other channels transmit the voice of an English, French, or Acholi interpreter. The interpreters are seated in raised, glass-enclosed booths on the right and left sides of the courtroom – on the same level as the public gallery (see Figure i.3). They interpret during those moments when the trial participants are not speaking the language that they are responsible for translating into. These different feeds also serve as the audio for the video stream that is transmitted online and into the public gallery.

Elderfield referred to the use of the sound and translation system by explaining that although the people on this tape were speaking "in Acholi, you will get a sense of its quality and of how LRA commanders talked to each other on the radio." He went on to explain that "there is no transcript because the substance isn't crucial." Then, he looked up and addressed the interpreters sitting on the upper level: "And just before I start this audio, I'd like to confirm with the Acholi interpretation booth that there is no need to interpret."

Elderfield stopped talking. After a few seconds, the audio file of not more than one minute began to play. At first, one could only hear static. After a few seconds, two men began speaking to each other in Acholi. The speakers were talking fast, ending their sentences with "over" in the style of a military radio call. A translation was not transmitted. For those participants who did not speak Acholi sufficiently well, the content of the conversation was not revealed. Nevertheless, all present in the courtroom seemed to listen attentively. At one point during the exchange, the two men burst into a long, loud laugh. After they stopped laughing, they seemed to go on with their conversation. Shortly after, the audio file stopped playing.

When the prosecution lawyer resumed his oral presentation, he did not comment on what people had heard. Instead, another photograph of a compact cassette appeared on the trial participants' screens. Elderfield stated: "This tape was made by the UPDF. You can see from the writing on the tape's shell that it covers from 6:30 in the evening of 30 April to 9 a.m. on 10 May 2004." Directly after these words, Elderfield went on to another piece of evidence.

Witnessing this scene from the public gallery, I immediately sensed that this short sequence of the proceeding was a highly intense moment. If I were asked to describe the situation in colloquial terms, I would use phrases such as "it pushed a button" or "it really got to me." The way the prosecutor introduced the audio file and played it for the courtroom audience created an intense atmosphere that was almost certainly important and perhaps even decisive in the outcome of the court proceeding. How this is done and how it can be analyzed from an ethnographic standpoint is the focus of this chapter.

AFFECTIVE LANGUAGE AND BEYOND

Anthropologists have long been fascinated by the intricate workings of the courtroom (see, e.g., Conley and O'Barr 1990; Merry 1990; Hirsch 1998; Matoesian 2001; Richland 2008; D'hondt 2009; Scheffer 2010). These studies are based on the simple but compelling proposition that the law cannot adequately be described as a mere set of rules governing the lives of people, but that it has to be understood as a practice and that it takes a whole set of actors to bring it into existence on a daily basis. Court proceedings are not well understood by simply focusing on the grammar of the law; one has to come to terms with the pragmatics of the law. The question becomes: How do actors construct the reality of legal proceedings through linguistic utterances, in other words, through discourse (see Conley and O'Barr 2019)?

This approach has traditionally put the linguistic utterances of humans at the center of analysis. This analytic logocentrism exists for good reasons, as a court's main function is the transformation of real-life events into discourse (Vismann 2011). To understand courtroom proceedings of any kind, it is important to be mindful of their complicated spatiality and temporality. While a criminal trial is an event at a certain place and a specific time, the purpose of a trial is to attach legal significance to past events that have transpired elsewhere. The law is hence always faced with a difficult gap in time and space – a gap that separates the trial from the events it has to assess. Dominic Ongwen commanded a group of soldiers armed with weapons and purportedly ordered them to attack a camp and not to spare civilian lives – ten years ago and thousands of kilometers away. How can this be made legible in a courtroom in The Hague in the present? The courtroom must serve as an apparatus that allows participants to transcend time and space. In this perspective, the courtroom is a time machine (Bens 2019b).[10] A performance is staged in order to reenact and re-localize the past crime in the present proceeding (Diehl et al. 2006; Reinelt 2006; Cole 2009).

The idea that court proceedings are to be seen as performances is already deeply inscribed in law-and-language approaches. Language in the courtroom is performed. Performing language means first and foremost engaging in a bodily practice in the real world; it is, as Chomsky (1965, 10–15) put it, *doing language*. It means furthermore to act with language in such a way as to transform the outside world, hence *doing something with language* (Austin 1962).[11] Finally, and in its broadest meaning, performing language means *doing something with language in a social-relational setting* that is structured by the audience's expectations and established aesthetic canons (Goffman 1956; Bauman 1977; Turner 1987; Bauman and Briggs 1990). The way this performance unfolds shapes the processes of distinguishing fact from fiction, truth from lies, guilt from innocence, legality from illegality.

To recreate the past crime in the present courtroom by way of performance is, as every lawyer knows, a craft of narration. People tell stories, some more convincing than others, which necessarily mention some things while omitting others, highlight some aspects while obscuring others. What is recreated in the courtroom does not necessarily reflect how the people who personally witnessed the crime experienced it or even remember it. Courtroom ethnographers have shown time and again how these discursive registers in which courts necessarily operate entail processes of decontextualizing and dehistoricizing, sometimes with harmful consequences for those in marginalized positions (Eades 2008; Ehrlich 2012).

The scene represented above is part of this discursive performance of the law. But it also presents us with a conundrum: the most intense moment of this whole day in court, at least if I judge it from my own emotional reaction and my observations of the reactions of others in the courtroom, was the one when the act of people talking was highlighted, but practically nobody understood what they were talking about. Is this indicative of the discursive power of the law, or does it point to something else? The answer to both questions, I believe, is yes. The scene illustrates the performative power of language, but we can only understand it fully when we see it as embedded in an atmosphere. Only in this entirety can we approach the law's affective theater of power.

We have learned from linguistic anthropology that people can be moved by language in many different ways. Referring to feeling in the propositional content of speech, for example, by using emotion words, is only one of these ways. Anthropologists have insisted that signs convey meaning on many levels (Mertz 2007b). Silverstein (1976) has called this the *plurifunctionality of language*. When a speaker utters words, these words communicate, of course, specific information. Words can do that because they function as symbols and refer to states or objects in the world – "referents" in linguistic terms. This most straightforward dimension of meaning that can be conferred through language is called *referential meaning*. Most members of the audience were not able to understand the referential meaning of the LRA fighters' utterances. Unaccustomed to the symbolic system of the Acholi language, they do not know which symbols refer to which referents.

But communication through language goes beyond referential meaning. When a speaker makes an utterance, he or she also communicates by pointing to states or objects that co-occur in the context of the utterance. To put it in linguistic terms, the utterance functions as an "index" and conveys *indexical meaning*. Laughter, as in our case, is an example of this. When a speaker laughs, for instance, while he or she is uttering certain words, the laugh points to, or indexes, the speaker's emotional state. Laughing when discussing a military conflict, maybe a massacre even, can communicate to listeners that the speaker feels joy or pleasure in the face of war.

Courtroom actors often purposefully use the tensions that emerge between referential and indexical meanings. A prosecution lawyer might ask a witness, "Where were you on the night of the murder?" The witness (in a low voice, avoiding eye contact with the lawyer): "Uhh . . . me? I, ehm, was at home . . . alone." The prosecution lawyer will then often try to deliberately direct attention away from the propositional content of the witness's account ("I was at home alone"), its referential meaning. He or she might highlight instead the possible indexical meaning that is conveyed by the witness's hesitation, low tone of voice, avoidance of eye contact, and similar paralinguistic components of the utterance. The indexical meaning here could communicate to the judge the emotional state of the witness. Perhaps the witness is nervous. Why might the witness be nervous? Maybe the witness is afraid of being found out as a liar. The linguistic strategy that courtroom participants employ to highlight indexical meaning over referential meaning has been described as "metapragmatic regimentation" (Matoesian 1998; Maryns 2014; D'hondt 2019). Metapragmatic discourse makes the practice of speaking itself the semantic topic of an utterance (Silverstein 1993).[12] The prosecution lawyer might use a phrasing that comments on the way the witness has given his or her answer: "Why are you hesitating?" "Can you speak louder please?" "You sound as if you were not so sure about this. Were you really at home alone?"

What Elderfield did on that day in the courtroom can be read as an example of metapragmatic regimentation. He attempted to purposefully suspend the referential meaning of the LRA fighters' speech. He advised the listeners to disregard the content of the radio conversation and only to listen to the sound of the voices; he also instructed the interpreters not to provide a translation of the recorded interaction. And the result was powerful. The vast majority of the listeners did not understand the content of the performed speech. This made it possible to focus even more on the laughter that served as an index pointing to the emotional state of the speakers.

At this point, we are in an analytic space, initially opened up by the idea of the indexical function of language, in which we can poach in the field of language and affect (Besnier 1990, 438). When analyzing the affective workings of the courtroom, it is crucial to go beyond the explicit semantic evocation of emotion through emotion words. The affective workings of language include the full array of linguistic practices, including paralinguistic means such as intonation, gesture, and other poetic devices (Ochs and Schieffelin 1989; Rosenberg 1990). Linguistic anthropologists have criticized their colleagues in psychological anthropology for focusing too much on the referential meaning of emotion words rather than taking full stock of the indexical dimension of language (Ochs 2012). It then becomes clear that speakers constantly index their own feelings and the feelings of others. The resulting strictly social-relational perspective shows how speakers influence the emotions of their listeners, purposefully or not. They *affect* their audiences through their speech. In a way, this is a reminder of old insights. It is no coincidence Aristotle used the term "affect" in the second book of *The Art of Rhetoric* (2018) – that part of his theory of public speech that is devoted to the concept of persuasion. An effective speaker knows the emotional state of his or her audience, predicts its emotional responses, and evokes the right emotions at the right moment.

Affective language is thus always also bodily experienced both by the speaker and the audience (Ochs 2012). Lawyers try to affect their audiences to persuade them all the time. They try to create "vivid images" and "a realistic picture" of the issues relevant to the case. Such oratory affects audiences viscerally. A great orator commands the courtroom in such a way that the participants "can 'relive' the actions, emotions, and events of the reported situation" (Matoesian 1999, 74). They often do so by repeating those words that were spoken at the time of the crime, if such reported speech is available – a particularly powerful and affectively charged device to influence listeners' emotions (Besnier 1994, 286; Matoesian 1999, 75). The indexical power of the laughter on a tape recording, highlighted by a lawyer's metapragmatic regimentation, is a great candidate for having an emotional impact on a courtroom audience.

Still, there comes the moment in any such analysis when it becomes clear that the investigation of speech acts itself reveals only half of the story. Even when it is possible to show that speakers aim to evoke emotions in their listeners and to identify the rhetorical and linguistic devices, especially indexical devices, by which they fulfill this aim, it is still unclear whether the speakers succeed in their attempts (Bens 2019c). When people in the courtroom heard the laughter on the tape recording, what did they feel? How did it affect them? It is the investigation of people's experience, for example, the emotional experience of a member of an audience as he or she listens to a speaker, that promises some insights into this black box.

Anthropologists have long been interested in how people in different social and cultural contexts experience the world differently. Such a phenomenological approach is inherent in any ethnographic endeavor, but some have clearly prioritized the investigation of how people experience reality and make sense of it subjectively (Desjarlais and Throop 2011; Jackson 2012). Regarding the conflict between the LRA and the Ugandan government, Sverker Finnström (2008) has written an ethnography of how people in northern Uganda, especially young people, experienced the war and made sense of their sometimes highly precarious lives in the course of it. Coming to terms with affect, emotion, and feeling is central to this approach. Indeed, in the field of the anthropology of emotions, one can differentiate those works that are more linguistically oriented and take culture-dependent emotion words and concepts as the starting point of their investigations (Rosaldo 1980; Abu-Lughod 1986; Lutz 1988) from those that are more phenomenological in outlook and are focused on the subjective experience of emotion (Levy 1973; Throop 2010; Stodulka 2016). The latter approach also includes a thorough self-investigation of the researcher's subjective experiences, including the ethnographer's own emotions and how affective dynamics include him or her (Stodulka 2015). Such phenomenological ethnographic studies usually circumvent the difficulty of describing affect and emotion from observational data by focusing on narrative interviewing as a central technique to capture people's subjective experiences. In ethnographic writing, phenomenologists often describe people's experiences in their own words – complemented by and triangulated with self-reflections on how the ethnographer him- or herself has felt.[13]

In a way, it was this self-observation that prompted me to become interested in the scene with the laughter on tape in the first place. There was talk performed in the courtroom, and I felt something happening to me in the course of it. This feeling led me to suspect that what had made such an impression on me may well have affected others similarly. This dialectic of self-observation and the observation of others is a key aspect in any ethnographic endeavor. The ethnographer's own emotions are an epistemic resource to better understand the field he or she is emerged in (Stodulka, Selim, and Mattes 2018). To confirm or deny these initial suspicions, the ethnographer has to try and find out how others might have experienced the moment.

During the lunch break following the presentation of the prosecution, I engaged in a conversation with two other visitors who were having lunch in the ICC's cafeteria. I asked them, in the type of open questioning that is typical of narrative ethnographic interviewing, what they felt about all this. Unsurprisingly, perhaps, they highlighted the prosecution's presentation of the audio files as having affected them particularly powerfully. They were sure that the prosecution was making a very convincing and gripping presentation by bringing to the fore the cruelty and violence with which Dominic Ongwen had operated during the conflict.

However, despite having recognized the prosecution's rhetoric for the performance that it was and having gauged how the audience experienced this performance, I was still left somewhat dissatisfied. People talking in a courtroom and audiences being affected by it is a mysterious thing. The playing of the audio file with the LRA fighters' laughter on it – highlighted by the prosecutor's metapragmatic regimentation – is the main thing that happened there, but does an analytic description of this suffice to convey "the feel" of the whole arrangement of the courtroom that shapes how people are able to experience it? While language and feeling interconnect and co-constitute each other (Abu-Lughod and Lutz 1990; Wilce 2009), it would be misleading to reduce affect and emotion to discourse (Desjarlais 1992; Lyon 1995; Leavitt 1996; Röttger-Rössler 2002).

How can we come to terms with feeling in the courtroom if we want to go beyond the linguistic utterances made in the room? It is my argument in this chapter, and indeed throughout this book, that the affective and emotional dynamics that occur in the courtroom of the sentimental court go far beyond a few words well put and a few images skillfully displayed. Although the myriad of single linguistic and paralinguistic utterances made in the courtroom are crucial to creating and shaping the atmosphere that emerges in a courtroom, the participants also feel an atmosphere as an integrated whole, not only as the sum of individual components. I argue that thorough ethnographic observation is key to analyzing atmosphere, an observation not only of individual bodies and their utterances but of a whole of relationally entangled human and nonhuman bodies co-present in space.

AFFECT, AFFECTIVE ARRANGEMENT, AND ATMOSPHERE

To analyze atmosphere in the courtroom I propose to mobilize ideas from affect theory (Clough and Halley 2007; Gregg and Seigworth 2010). Affect theory is a particular strand of scholarship in the research of feeling that has gained prominence since the 1990s in philosophy (Massumi 1995), as well as in cultural studies and queer studies (Sedgwick and Frank 1995). While affect theory is a broad intellectual movement, a number of approaches directly connect to the philosophical work of Baruch de Spinoza, most notably his *Ethica* (1677) and particularly in the way Gilles Deleuze has interpreted him (Deleuze 1968, 1970).[14] At the center of such approaches in affect theory is Spinoza's concept of the *body*. Bodies are defined as all entities that have the "power (or potential) to affect or be affected" (Massumi 2002, 15). As such, bodies in a Spinozan sense are not only biological bodies, but all kinds of entities, including nonhumans, inanimate objects, and even immaterial phenomena (Papoulias and Callard 2010; Blackman 2012; Seyfert 2012).[15] "These bodies do not conform to our expectations of clearly defined boundaries between the psychological, social, biological, ideological, economic, and technical" (Blackman 2012, x).

Affect, then, is understood most broadly as all that which relationally transpires between bodies (Slaby and Mühlhoff 2019). Affect theory can hence be taken, similar to social science emotion research (Röttger-Rössler and Markowitsch 2009; Burkitt 2014), as a critique of individualistic accounts of feeling (Scheve 2018). A perspective on affect challenges us to engage in a thoroughly *relational* account of culture and society.

It is easy to see that such an affect theory approach significantly broadens the field of inquiry when it comes to feeling. When basically all that relationally transpires between bodies is analyzed in terms of affect, then affect is not a particular subject to study in culture and society, as is often assumed in the research of emotion, but something that permeates culture and society at the most fundamental level; in other words, affect is everywhere. The intellectual appeal of such an approach is compelling, and many anthropologists in recent years have not been able to resist incorporating the concept of affect into their ethnographic analyses of micropractices (see, e.g., Skoggard and Waterston 2015; Rutherford 2016).[16]

Those anthropologists who refer to affect theory usually do not mobilize established approaches from the anthropology of emotion but refer instead to more recent scholarship in affect studies – much to the regret of some anthropologists of emotion.[17] I believe that bypassing the anthropology of emotion is a mistake because it has contributed much to our understanding of the social and cultural life of feeling. But affect theory has brought with it an overweening universalist ambition that may well prove to be fruitful for anthropology, challenging anthropologists to think affective dynamics into everything they research and to use their ethnographic methods to do so. This ambition perhaps feeds into a delusion of grandeur on the part of some anthropologists, but it does make a powerful plea against the highly relativistic tendencies and idiosyncratic "butterfly collecting" that anthropology is always in danger of falling into. In an important respect, this book is inspired by this delusion of grandeur in that it tries to argue that the law is likewise always grounded in affect, even in the most unexpected places.

For the purposes of courtroom ethnography, affect theory highlights the fact that affect manifests itself not only in people's perceptions, but also in the concrete arrangements in which events take place. Affect theory imagines the social as an assemblage of bodies that constantly affect – and are being affected by – each other. From an ethnographic perspective, then, it would seem to be apt to engage in a description of how these bodies are arranged, how they relate to one another, and what dynamics take place in these relational interactions. The courtroom as well as other ensembles in which events unfold can, therefore, be seen as *affective arrangements*:

> Affective arrangements are heterogeneous ensembles of diverse materials forming a local layout that operates as a dynamic formation, comprising persons, things, artifacts, spaces, discourses, behaviors, and

> expressions in a characteristic mode of composition and dynamic relatedness. Our approach facilitates microanalyses of affective relationality as it furthers both an understanding of the entities that coalesce locally to engender relational affect, and also the overall "feel," affective tonality or atmosphere that prevails in such a locale.
>
> (Slaby, Mühlhoff, and Wüschner 2019, 4)

In one important respect, affective arrangements are spaces. As I have been arguing since the beginning of this chapter, the law must not only be performed to be brought to life but it must also always be performed somewhere, at a specific place (Müller-Mall 2013, 79). These places, such as a courtroom, are filled with material objects that play a key role in providing stability and guidance for the speech acts (Scheffer 2004). Affect research in anthropology, sociology, and human geography has shown that every place filled with objects is always entangled in affective dynamics (Löw 2008; Thrift 2008; Navaro-Yashin 2009) that create atmospheres (Philippopoulos-Mihalopoulos 2015).

But the idea of affective arrangement goes beyond the affective quality of a place. The analysis of an affective arrangement approaches feeling as a relational flow during events. Such an account must always begin with a description of the multiplicity of bodies in the arrangement and from that try to explore their affective relationality.[18] In a way, such an approach takes up the linguistic anthropology credo of the courtroom as a performance and, consequently, applies it by including additional dimensions such as "scenery and stage props" (Goffman 1956, 13), voice, gesture, spatial arrangements, and visual regimes. It takes seriously the fact that "bodies of evidence" are brought into the affective arrangement to reenact the past in a quasi-theatrical sense. All bodies in a courtroom perform as a "team" (Goffman 1956) that includes human as well as nonhuman performers. The result of this team performance is an atmosphere.[19]

In the most general terms, atmosphere describes the affective tonality, the overall "feel" or mood that unfolds at a specific time and place.[20] From the perspective of humans inside an affective arrangement, an atmosphere is an affective experience that comes not (only) from one's inner self but also from the surroundings within which one is embedded (Griffero 2014; Riedel 2019). An atmosphere is the result of an affective arrangement and is itself a kind of affect (Anderson 2009). While the idea of affective arrangement has a spatial connotation, denoting the "local layout" for affective relationality, an atmosphere is not a locale itself, but it does extend into a specific place and becomes concrete within that specific place.

Any affective arrangement constantly produces some kind of atmosphere. But, as theorists of atmosphere have highlighted, atmosphere is a liminal phenomenon that is experienced as different from other atmospheres that one has experienced earlier (Riedel 2019). Actors feel atmospheres mostly in those moments when they change. It is precisely those moments when the constellation of bodies changes in such a significant way that another "overall feel" is being established that can serve as entry points for an ethnography of atmospheres.

THE COURTROOM'S AFFECTIVE THEATER OF ATMOSPHERE

Let us return to the courtroom scene described at the beginning of this chapter and first try to take stock of the different bodies assembled in the affective arrangement. There is, of course, the main speaker, Jeremy Elderfield. Then there are the other human participants at the hearing: the judges, the defense team, the interpreters in the interpretation booths, and the visitors in the public gallery, including myself. But one can also think of nonhuman bodies. There is, for instance, the compact cassette containing a recording of intercepted LRA radio communication that Elderfield lifted up in the air at one point. The technical infrastructure comes to mind, especially the large computer screen displaying images of other tapes and the headphones transmitting the audio of the radio call between two LRA fighters and the voices of the interpreters. But the presence of bodies in the courtroom goes beyond persons and things. Let us think of the voice of the LRA fighters as a sound that was a crucial part of the affective dynamics during the sequence described earlier. The fighters' contribution to the affective arrangement was no less important than those human bodies physically present. From the perspective of feeling, their presence was even more strongly felt than that of one of the many clerks sitting in one of the back rows. One can also think of images as relevant bodies, for example, those of the tape that was played and the label on the tape with information about the date and time of the recording.

But these bodies were not only "there" in the courtroom. They functioned as components of an arrangement that was both put to work and had its own workings. The way these human and nonhuman bodies interrelated in the affective arrangement of the courtroom arguably created the atmosphere that prevailed at the moment of the proceeding. The affective arrangement of a courtroom is a contentious place in which actors are constantly engaged in rearranging bodies in ways that further their agenda of presenting the "right" performance.

The prosecution lawyer did this by introducing bodies into the arrangement and relating them to each other and to the other bodies already present in the courtroom. There is the compact cassette he brought with him and held up in the air during his speech. But that was not the only body he introduced. He in effect brought in several other tapes by displaying images of them on the computer screens and, of course, the two LRA fighters by playing the audio recording of their voices. The light and the sound filled the whole room. All these bodies together formed an affective arrangement and, by performing together, created an atmosphere.

This perspective has, of course, methodological implications. The mood and overall feel of a room that is produced by performing bodies can only partially be reconstructed from written transcripts or even audio and video files, as the performance depends to a large degree on the co-presence of bodies in space. Ethnography means to affectively immerse oneself in the field with all of one's senses (Stoller 1989). More recently, courtroom ethnographers have begun to pay closer attention to the necessity – and not least the *affective* necessity – of "being there" in the courtroom, which is the only way to gain a full understanding of its workings (Dahlberg 2009; Eltringham 2012; D'hondt 2021). This seems relevant not only because the ethnographer can use his or her own feelings of the event as an epistemic resource, as phenomenological approaches rightly argue (Stodulka, Selim, and Mattes 2018), but also because feelings serve as heuristic devices reminding the ethnographer to approach the event itself and the atmosphere that prevails there as more than just the sum of its parts.

I contend that trial lawyers have a very good understanding of the relevance of atmosphere in court. During the presentation of the evidence, the prosecution lawyer, as a human body, was at the center of the scene and tried to affect his listeners not only through his speech but beyond his speech as well. To a large degree, he did the work of mobilizing other nonhuman bodies to help him in his presentation by purposefully placing them in the affective arrangement of the courtroom. When he brought the compact cassette with him into the room, it seemed not to be enough to verbally announce that he had the tape with him. He also took it in his hand and held it up in the air for everybody to see. He obviously thought this would have a stronger impact on his audience than, for instance, just saying that the tape was sitting in the other room in a box and that those interested could look at it later. The presence of the body changed the affective arrangement and hence also the atmosphere in the room.

Thinking of the court as an affective arrangement producing an atmosphere makes it necessary to pay close attention to the material and infrastructural outlets of law-spaces. During the presentation of the evidence, Jeremy Elderfield used both the computer screens and the audio equipment as infrastructures to introduce bodies into the affective arrangement. The infrastructure as material bodies is then mostly there to bring bodies into the courtroom, by way of images and sounds. If one thinks of the fact that a computer screen sends beams of light into the room and that an audio speaker causes the air to vibrate and produce sound, it is easy to see how these infrastructures create atmosphere. Light and sound count among the main conduits by which one feels the presence of bodies.

As such, the courtroom atmosphere largely depends on visual regimes.[21] When the prosecution lawyer made his presentation, he showed images of tapes. By doing so, he wanted to show that the Ugandan military forces had collected large amounts of incriminating evidence in a meticulously organized manner. To that end, he not only orally described the procedures of recording and labeling tapes but also showed the tapes and the labels on the computer screen. Like the actual cassette he brought with him, these images of tapes were brought into the courtroom to help him with his argument.

Similarly important are the auditory regimes of the courtroom.[22] Playing the audio file brought the voices of the LRA fighters as nonhuman bodies into the courtroom. Their voices filled the whole room and became part of the atmosphere beyond the referential meaning they communicated. Although most of the audience could not understand the semantic content, everybody listened attentively. All listeners could identify the speakers laughing, and it was possible for me to observe how the human bodies and the behavior of the listeners changed. They were sitting still, not engaging in whispered conversations as is often done during court proceedings. One can argue that at this moment the nonhuman bodies of the fighters' voices dominated the affective arrangement, as most of the human bodies in the courtroom focused exclusively on them.

The perspective I am advocating reveals how much of a courtroom performance is made up of the work of introducing and relating bodies in an affective arrangement. But it would be misleading to think that the atmosphere in a courtroom only depends on the affective arrangement as it emerges on the micro-level of a courtroom proceeding. As I have argued, an affect theory perspective pushes ethnography to take the event itself seriously and places great emphasis on "being there" in the moment of the proceeding. One must, however, not lose sight of the workings of historically embedded macro-level processes of power. As I will show in the course of this book, affective arrangements form the basis for the production, maintenance, and transformation of sentiments that far surpass in their impact the concrete events which bring them about or in which they inscribe themselves. But even if we remain focused exclusively on the atmosphere, we must still acknowledge that it results not only from the arrangement work done there and then, but that it also depends on larger structural forces.

This points to a more basic problem of legal ethnography, even ethnography in general. Courtroom ethnography takes seriously the event of the court proceeding itself and assumes that what people say and do during these proceedings matters for the outcome of the legal process of which the proceeding is a part. As such, courtroom ethnography as a methodology has to face a certain tension with more processual and structural approaches to legal anthropology that see the outcome of individual legal processes as largely determined by structural and historical forces that lie far beyond an individual court proceeding (Moore 1978; Starr and Collier 1989). At the same time, only events of relatively short duration are conducive to ethnographic investigation. What ethnography can do is observe and record events. What ethnography often wants to achieve is to understand the processes that bring events about. Ethnographic events do have pasts and futures. One could call this the *event-and-process dilemma* in the ethnographic study of law. For courtroom ethnography it has been rightly argued that this dilemma should be approached by taking seriously both the individual court proceeding and the larger structural processes shaping it (Scheffer 2007).[23]

This means first and foremost providing "context" for court proceedings by bringing past developments and actors' sometimes hidden agendas into the ethnographic description by way of triangulation.[24] It is important to show at what points these larger forces structure the atmosphere of the event. As such, the courtroom serves as a time machine (Bens 2019b). The affective performances of the courtroom can have the form of reenactments of the past and pre-enactments of the future. Larger processes and the event's historical position in them do influence how an event can take place per se, but only as past and present materialize, in one form or another, at the time of the event.[25]

In this context, it is important to remember where the prosecution got its evidence from, namely the Ugandan government. When I was in northern Uganda and asked people about the time when the ICC began its investigation, I was told that most people saw the ICC as a tool of the Ugandan government, used to pressure the LRA, rather than as an independent actor. A few people mentioned a press conference that the chief prosecutor at the time, Luis Moreno Ocampo, held with the Ugandan President Yowero Kaguta Museveni. This signaled to many that the ICC was in the camp of the government. In a way, these suspicions have been proven true. Although many people in northern Uganda claim that the Ugandan army was also guilty of war crimes (Dolan 2009), no indictments have been brought against its commanders. The trial against Dominic Ongwen was at the time of writing the only one related to the conflict in northern Uganda. This is largely due to the fact that the prosecution relied heavily on materials provided by the army as evidence against Dominic Ongwen and the other LRA commanders. The ICC was under great pressure to produce results and hence urgently needed the support of the Ugandan government. Adam Branch has argued that the Dominic Ongwen case shows how much the ICC is dependent on the cooperation of national governments to be able to prosecute its cases, yet it is precisely those governments that are often under investigation (Branch 2017). The ICC faces heavy criticism from several sides. Some argue that it is not efficient enough in enforcing international criminal law in Uganda, as local politics regularly trump the ICC's attempts to prosecute (Peskin 2009). Others argue that the Court is widely perceived as being biased against Africans, as all trials up to now have been against African perpetrators (Clarke 2009). These legitimacy issues are serious and are inscribed to a large degree into the atmosphere that is created, right down to the level of individual courtrooms.

The prosecutor tried very hard to assemble bodies to reenact these past events and to affectively charge the room with the credibility and authenticity of these tapes. He brought in several images of tapes to reenact the way the Ugandan military forces produced the data that he was now using to incriminate Dominic Ongwen. An image reenacted the process of intercepting, recording, and transcribing LRA radio communications by the Ugandan military. Additionally, a physical tape was displayed before the Court and made to "perform." Then, finally, the LRA fighters themselves had to perform, mediated by their voices on tape. And, finally, again an image was shown.

This multiplicity of "bodies of evidence" in the affective arrangement is striking, especially as their provenance was highly precarious. Despite general concerns about the fact that most of the evidence against the LRA did in fact derive from their former enemy in a military conflict, it became evident during the trial proceedings that the methods used by Ugandan military personnel to intercept LRA radio communications were at times chaotic. Tapes were overwritten because there was an insufficient supply; radio calls in Acholi were transcribed in English shorthand, then rewritten in longhand (to be understandable for the Ugandan army leadership), and then retranslated from English into Acholi by the ICC for the court proceedings. Every one of these steps represented an opportunity to falsify the evidence. This structured the way the tapes could perform in court and the special effort the prosecution had to exert to bring them into the affective arrangement of the courtroom.

***

Why is there a need for courtrooms? The law needs a specific space to be performed because of the atmosphere it creates, and atmosphere is created by the way bodies are related to each other in an affective arrangement. The law has not only to be spoken and heard, it also has to be felt. A regular, fixed place for the law makes the highly volatile politics of atmosphere, at least in some aspects, predictable. This understanding of atmosphere shows that the law is not at all about the suppression of affect, but about the creation of affect.

There is a tradition of scholarship on the role of emotion in the law that has long been dominated by psychologists, lawyers, philosophers, and neuroscientists (Abrams and Keren 2009; Bandes and Blumenthal 2012). They have made a forceful plea for treating emotions as an integral part of the law, a plea that is based on the following premise: There is an overarching legal ideology to be debunked, namely that "the sphere of law admits only to reason; and vigilant policing is required to keep emotion from creeping in where it does not belong" (Maroney 2006, 120). In countering this claim, law-and-emotion scholarship takes account of emotions in legal proceedings in order to come to a better understanding of the law (Abrams and Keren 2009, 2000; Bandes and Blumenthal 2012, 162).

This book is, in a way, a contribution to that project. However, I believe my starting point – the perceived anti-emotional legal ideology – is only part of the story. Sure, many lawyers would readily agree that legal decisions should not be based on emotion. But in many practical respects they are deeply convinced of the role of affect in their work. The "vigilant policing" to keep emotions at bay can itself be read as a strategy to create a specific atmosphere, a courtroom mood in which a legal proceeding can take place the way it is intended to by legal actors. In the following chapters I will argue that key concepts in legal theory that are presumed to be grounded in rationality are in fact sentiments, the results of the production of specific affects.

In contradistinction to the baseline of law-and-emotion research, I argue that the law is not about favoring rationality over emotion. Rather, it favors, in specific situations, certain affective modes over others. In this context, the rational itself is one of these affective modes. The production of atmosphere is one way of approaching this complicated field of law and affect.

Such an approach has, in my opinion, methodological implications as well. Instead of looking for the emotions at specific moments in the trial, which makes it necessary to make many theoretical decisions beforehand, the researcher should not predecide which constellations between which bodies will become decisive for the affective workings of law. One does not look so much for emotional expressions in legal proceedings – the shouting, the crying, the righteous indignation – nor for explicit references to emotions through the use of emotion words. One tries, rather, to sketch out in a more exploratory way the relational dynamics between bodies that might affect what happens in court. This includes, of course, emotional displays and the use of emotion words in courtroom speech (Bens 2018b), but it goes far beyond that. It means conceptualizing the courtroom in a very broad sense as a machine designed to create affect.

2

TRANSITIONAL JUSTICE ATMOSPHERES

The ICC's Outreach Work in Northern Uganda

> *I have experienced numerous social occasions where I assumed other people were feeling what I was feeling, and that the feeling was, as it were, "in the room," only to find out that others had felt quite differently. I would describe such spaces as "intense." Shared feelings are at stake, and seem to surround us, like a thickness in the air, or an atmosphere. But these feelings not only heighten tension, they are also in tension. Emotions in their very intensity involve miscommunication, such that even when we feel we have the same feeling, we don't necessarily have the same relationship to the feeling.*
>
> Sara Ahmed, *The Cultural Politics of Emotion* (2004b)

What can the law contribute to coming to terms with the crimes of the past? On a very general level, criminal law exists to respond to violent breaches of the social and cultural order, to sanction the breaking of rules, to punish perpetrators, to convey some kind of satisfaction to victims, to recognize the wrong for the public, to deter future violence. All of these are, in a way, attempts to settle an account that was left open by something that occurred in the past.

International criminal law extends these aspirations by scaling them up to the highest possible level of society. International criminal proceedings are performed in a court, but they are only part of a much larger project of bringing justice to entire societies that have been torn apart by violence. Regarding the ICC's legal basis, the Rome Statute says that the Court is there to prosecute and punish "the most serious crimes of concern to the international community as a whole" (Art. 5). This entails the idea that certain crimes are so severe that they violate all of humanity – a concept that is inscribed in the term "crimes against humanity."[1] In the end, international criminal justice exists to bring justice to the whole of mankind, to settle an account left open for every human being on the planet.

Clearly, then, the aspirations of international criminal justice extend far beyond the courtrooms at the headquarters of the ICC in The Hague. International criminal trials are seen as a strategy to facilitate transitional justice, the project of bringing about justice in the aftermath of regime change; to give an answer to past rights violations and to further a non-violent future. There are many ways to facilitate transitional justice for a society. The international criminal justice approach sees it as crucial that the international community step in and put on trial those individuals who bear the most responsibility for the mass-scale violence that has plagued the society. Only on the basis of their punishment, so the idea goes, can a society heal.

To be able to heal, the society must see justice at work. That is why international criminal trials are highly mediatized events. In fact, the ICC spends a great deal of time and effort to inform the wider public about its work. The Court has its own outreach unit to facilitate this communication process. In addition to communicating to the mass media, the ICC also tries to get in direct contact with people by organizing events in those places where the violence took place. In the introduction to this book, I wrote that the people working for the ICC outreach unit see their work as the dispassionate dissemination of information. I argue in this chapter, however, that they are at least as consciously engaged in the production of atmospheres to further their outreach work as their colleagues in The Hague are engaged in the production of courtroom atmospheres.

Sanction, punishment, satisfaction, recognition, deterrence, justice – all these terms have their place in the logic of international criminal law. But it is easy to see how they transcend the boundaries of the law. They are socially and culturally grounded ideas and values that are inscribed into the lives of people not least through feeling. If it is the goal of international criminal justice proceedings to deliver these values, it cannot be done without taking stock of the feelings of people and without attempting to impact people's feeling lives. The most basic way to do that in the context of transitional justice is to produce transitional justice atmospheres.

AN OUTREACH EVENT IN NORTHERN UGANDA

On December 6, 2016, I traveled from Gulu, one of the small urban centers in northern Uganda where I was staying, to Abok, a village about ninety minutes away. From the late 1990s until a little over ten years ago, Abok had been the location of a camp for internally displaced persons (IDPs). At the height of the war in northern Uganda, in the early 2000s, the majority of northern Ugandans were living in these camps. Like many others, the camp in Abok was poorly defended by the Ugandan army. On June 8, 2004, the LRA raided the IDP camp in Abok and massacred dozens of civilians. On that day it was Dominic Ongwen, then a brigade commander for the LRA, who commanded the fighters.

The ICC had held a confirmation of charges hearing against Ongwen in January of the same year, which I had attended as a visitor (see Chapter 1). It was afterward that I went to northern Uganda to conduct ethnographic fieldwork, specifically at those massacre sites relevant to the case. My goal was to come to terms with how people there understood these proceedings and how they assessed their legitimacy (see Chapter 5). In the meantime, the judges had decided that there was sufficient evidence against Ongwen to put him on trial and scheduled the trial opening for December 6, the very day that I went to Abok. The ICC's outreach unit had planned a large two-day event to screen the trial opening for the villagers. I had also heard that the registrar, the administrative director of the ICC headquarters in The Hague, was traveling to Uganda and planning to attend the Abok screening. Media representatives were also expected.

I had arrived there in the morning with two colleagues from northern Uganda. We could see that two large tents had been set up next to the administration building, a small structure in the middle of an open field. Trucks had brought in enough plastic chairs to seat about 2,500 to 3,000 visitors. People started to arrive in large numbers and, after a while, it became clear that the number of visitors was going to far exceed the seating capacity. Only two small televisions had been put up, and it was obvious that it would be difficult for everyone to see what was going to be displayed on these TV screens (Figure 2.1).

As people were gathering, the mood of the place gradually changed. It seemed to us that something was "hanging in the air" – there was a sense of excitement and expectation of what was to come. These initial impressions, gleaned within a few minutes of our arrival, led our conversation around to the topic of this chapter. Conducting an outreach event means, first and foremost, creating an affective arrangement. In order to do that, a number of bodies have to be assembled in one place: villagers, ICC employees, television sets, and plastic chairs, for instance. The way in which this affective arrangement is engineered

Figure 2.1 Public screening of the first day of the Dominic Ongwen trial before the ICC, December 6, 2016, Abok, northern Uganda. (A black and white version of this figure will appear in some formats. For the color version, please refer to the plate section.)
Source: Jonas Bens

has consequences for the mood that unfolds during the event; in other words, the outreach event has an *atmosphere*. In this chapter, I explore the role of atmosphere in conducting transitional justice events. I claim that the ICC's outreach efforts strive to create transitional justice atmospheres that are aimed at influencing people's sense of justice in relation to the past violence and their demands for a just future.

THE INTERNATIONAL CRIMINAL COURT AND TRANSITIONAL JUSTICE IN NORTHERN UGANDA: THE AFFECTIVE MICROWORKINGS OF LEGAL TRANSLATION

As I have already noted at the beginning of the chapter, the ICC tries individuals for committing mass-scale atrocities in military conflicts, seeing this as an important contribution to a larger project of transitional justice (Okafor and Ngwaba 2014). Transitional justice describes the processes and practices that facilitate coming to terms with past mass-scale violence in a society, usually after a regime change. Transitional justice is, however, a broader concept than that of international criminal justice, as it often includes not only criminal prosecution of those individual actors most responsible for the mass violence but also truth and reconciliation commissions, institutional reforms – whether relating to the security sector or the administrative and political branches of government – and other nonjudicial measures (Teitel 2000).[2] In the literature on transitional justice, a major focus is on the kinds of measures that are more or less effective in facilitating a democratic transition and in bringing about justice after mass violence. One important point of contention in these debates is on the question of whether criminal justice measures should be at the heart of transitional justice (Teitel 2000) or, conversely, if an overly strong insistence on legal measures and punishment hinders the possibility of coming to terms with a violent past (Kieran 2007).

In recent years, the ICC's legal interventions in Africa have caused significant controversy. After the ICC started its operation in the early 2000s, the Office of the Prosecutor (OTP) made the decision to prosecute sitting heads of state and government in Africa: first by putting out an arrest warrant against the Sudanese President Omar Al-Bashir in 2009, then by indicting Kenyan Deputy Prime Minister Uhuru Kenyatta in 2010, who later became the president of Kenya. Since then, many African governments have turned against the ICC and insisted that sitting heads of state and government must be exempt from prosecution. Beyond this *Realpolitik* inside the African Union, many politicians and academics inside and outside Africa have begun to criticize the Court as a neocolonial institution that tends to impose homogenizing Western notions of justice on the complex political and economic realities in Africa (see Clarke 2009, 2019; Clarke, Knotterus, and de Volder 2016).

The ICC's engagement in northern Uganda has proven similarly controversial, although not always along the lines of the macro discourse on neocolonialism. In the early 2000s, the Ugandan government referred the situation in northern Uganda to the ICC (Akhavan 2005). Some celebrated the Court's intervention as an important transitional justice measure (Allen 2006), while others criticized the ICC's criminal justice approach as counterproductive (Branch 2011, 179–215). Especially in the beginning, the ICC was seen by many observers in northern Uganda and elsewhere as a possible impediment to a workable peace process (Branch 2007). Along the lines of the broader "peace versus justice" debate, some feared that the ICC's intervention would provide a disincentive for the LRA leaders to enter into a peace agreement, as they might have to face criminal prosecution in The Hague afterward (Armstrong 2014). Others argued that instead of pitting peace and justice in mutually incompatible opposition to each other, peace negotiations had to be complemented by and work together with criminal prosecutions (Clark 2010).[3]

Many thought then (and still do) that an African solution tailored to the specific challenges in northern Uganda would better address the violence than the internationalized, one-size-fits-all approach of international criminal justice (Clarke 2009, 117–150). Even now, ten years after the conflict, at a time when most people in northern Uganda no longer fear that LRA violence will be reignited immediately, people remain largely skeptical of the ICC. The ongoing case against Dominic Ongwen is no exception (Branch 2017).

Not least to strengthen its perceived legitimacy in light of these controversies, the Court conducts outreach activities in the so-called situation countries, including Uganda. These efforts include organized public screenings of the trial proceedings in the regions where the violence has taken place. The ICC sees such outreach activities as part of its transitional justice mandate, which includes letting the victims participate in the trial (Carayon and O'Donohue 2017). The idea is that doing so contributes to the larger goal of coming to terms with past violence and facilitates a transition from the violent past into a future of democracy, accountability, and justice (Anders and Zenker 2014b). The specific temporality of international criminal law is crucial here. International criminal proceedings are slow, and the time when the proceedings take place is typically far removed from the time of the atrocities (Benda-Beckmann 2014, 7). In this context, one function of the international trials at the ICC is to provide a historical record of past abuses (Wilson 2011), and outreach events play an important role in that.

By its own description, international criminal justice is not subject to spatial demarcations (Benda-Beckmann, Benda-Beckmann, and Griffiths 2009, 5). As international crimes can take place all over the world, international criminal law provides a universally applicable set of rules to prosecute and punish them equally around the globe. Anthropologists have, however, insisted that the universal aspirations of international criminal law must always be analyzed in the context of the specific localities in which they become manifest (Merry 2006a).

Such places include, for example, courtrooms in The Hague, UN conference rooms in New York City, activist meetings all over the world, and, in our case, trial screenings in rural northern Uganda. These localities matter for how international law, although global in its outlook, comes into being and is maintained, challenged, and transformed.

Gerhard Anders has elaborated on this global–local dialectic in his ethnographic work on the Special Court for Sierra Leone (Anders 2009). He has shown that although international criminal law strives to be independent of local concerns, it cannot but be shaped by them to a large degree. The particular history and power relations in Sierra Leone had a significant impact on how the Special Court could deliver justice. In-depth ethnography can make an important contribution to understanding the complex interplay of the inner workings of international criminal law and the (political) influences of the diverse localities in which it becomes manifest (Anders 2009, 154).[4]

The degree to which the local sneaks into international criminal law can also be observed in the ICC's intervention in northern Uganda. In the Dominic Ongwen case, local political matters in Uganda had a significant influence on the international legal proceedings (Branch 2017). It was Uganda's President Yoweri Museveni, essentially a party to the conflict, who invited the ICC to investigate the LRA's crimes in December 2003 (Freeland 2015). Since then, the Court has been perceived by many in northern Uganda as an instrument of the government in its conflict with the rebel forces (Allen 2006, 84; Branch 2011, 191). As I explained in Chapter 1, the OTP is still largely dependent on the Ugandan government's cooperation to make its case and to get access to crucial evidence and witnesses.

The remoteness of the trial in The Hague provoked some controversy in northern Uganda regarding the appropriate location of the proceedings. Thus, one example of a broader discussion in transitional justice circles concerns the question of whether transitional justice should be conducted in a much more localized fashion (Shaw, Waldorf, and Hazan 2010).[5] These issues, and others of this kind, have been communicated to me numerous times during my fieldwork. For northern Uganda, some have proposed that localized non-state forms of transitional justice are preferable to international criminal justice (see Baines 2010; Meier 2013). Others are skeptical of the potential advantages of such local and traditional transitional justice measures (Allen 2007; Branch 2014).

Mainly based on the work of Sally Engle Merry, anthropologists have understood the interplay of global international law and its entanglement with the local as a matter of legal translation (Merry 2006a). Merry and others have highlighted that when international law manifests in different places, it must be *translated* into the local context and that in this translation it is also, to a certain degree, shaped and transformed. Human rights talk and "legalese" hence become "vernacularized" into local discourses (Levitt and Merry 2009). The direction and degree to which human rights concepts are transformed in this process of translation into the vernacular vary greatly. Merry (2006b) ascribes the role of *translators* to those intermediaries who facilitate the transposition of global international law into local contexts (and the other way around). A fundamental idea of the translation concept is that some core ideas of international law concepts such as human rights remain intact even after translation into the vernacular (Merry 2006c).[6]

Translation is thereby used in a twofold way: First, in a narrower, more straightforward sense, namely, that a linguistic translation is conducted from English and French as the languages of international law into non-European languages in many of those places where international law is implemented. In northern Uganda, these are mainly Acholi and other variants of Luo. Second, in a broader, more metaphorical sense, translation is used "to explore how the meanings attached to concepts and principles such as human rights shift as they travel from one historical and cultural setting to another" (Englund 2012, 71).[7] This can also be evidenced in northern Uganda. The ICC outreach team and their collaborators from local NGOs do the work of translators to make the workings of international criminal law understandable to local audiences. And, indeed, many of the members of local massacre survivors' associations I talked to framed their claims for recognition and reparations in terms of international law and human rights.

This is particularly relevant in the Ongwen case, as northern Uganda's transitional justice landscape also provides alternative normative systems to address the atrocities of the past. In this sense, northern Uganda clearly represents a case of legal pluralism (Griffiths 1986; Benda-Beckmann 2002). The ICC, as the main actor of international criminal law,[8] competes with other transitional justice forums.[9] The most relevant contender is the Acholi legal system, which is dominated by traditional leaders. Additionally, there is a strong system of religious moralities, dominated by local religious leaders, that emphasizes forgiveness and reconciliation. Both of these other normative orders claim, not unlike international criminal law, to provide an adequate normative frame for assessing justice and injustice and for coming to terms with past violence in a productive way. Actors in northern Uganda are constantly faced with a number of choices regarding which of these normative orders might be the most appropriate for dealing with the past and for ultimately achieving a sense of justice. In Chapter 5, I will delve more deeply into these navigations of normative pluralism.

To compete against these other normative alternatives, the ICC engages in legal translation work, using outreach events like the one I attended in Abok as its primary means. In addition, the church and the traditional leaders also organize public gatherings.[10] The numerous traditional Acholi rituals and the many public prayers structuring everyday life for many people in northern Uganda represent spatialized events and are similar to the ICC outreach events I describe here.

Building on these insights in the need to translate international law into the local context, this chapter analyzes how the ICC attempts this kind of translation in its outreach work. For the sake of this analysis, I suggest further complicating the category of "the local" and conceiving of it not merely as an abstract space that is culturally constructed in relation to the global (Appadurai 1990); "the local" is also as a set of very concrete places in which it is not only linguistic utterances and discourses that have an impact on how things work out, but the copresence of bodies also figures very powerfully into the equation. In Chapter 1, I elaborated on the role of atmosphere for international criminal law and described the courtroom as an affective arrangement. In this chapter, I am making a similar argument about outreach events.

AN ICC OUTREACH EVENT AS AN AFFECTIVE ARRANGEMENT

Although outreach events resemble courtroom proceedings, especially as the events in the courtroom in The Hague are often live-streamed via a video link, there are significant differences. Most obviously, while outreach events such as the one I attended in Abok are clearly structured, they are less regulated by procedural rules than a court hearing. They are, moreover, far more highly publicized than the regular court hearings. I spent many months visiting the visitors' gallery at the ICC in The Hague, and most of the time I sat there alone. Outreach events are also directed toward a broader public and a larger group in a way that the ICC's hearings are not; in this sense they resemble public rituals. Any analysis of the role of atmosphere for outreach events must take account of these differences.

The role of atmosphere in public rituals is well explored in the anthropological investigation of ritual and collective emotion. Emile Durkheim (1915) described how the gathering of people in a certain place during a ritual creates an affective intensity he calls *collective effervescence*. Building on this insight, Victor Turner (1969) argued that in affectively charged collective rituals, an enhanced sense of community emerges, which he calls *communitas*. A still prominent interpretation of the affective dimension of rituals is the idea that they provide emotional release by allowing the participants to discharge accumulated emotional distress in a collective catharsis (Scheff 1977). I, however, agree with those who argue the opposite. Instead of providing a forum to release bottled-up feelings, rituals produce affect through emotional arousal and create, transform, and cultivate specific affective and emotional dynamics (Kapferer 1979; Mahmood 2001; Bonhomme 2008). The affective dimension of ritual induces reflexivity in the participants (Berthomé and Houseman 2010), which enhances memory and cultural transmission (Whitehouse 1996). Because of this affective and emotional dimension, public gatherings such as these outreach events can be seen as a crucial device for creating group ties and social cohesion, reifying group symbols, generating values, and creating social spaces and belonging through a common affective experience (Urban 1988; Csordas 1997; Dilger, Mattes, and Kasmani 2018; Dilger et al. 2020).

It has been pointed out recently that many accounts of the emotional workings of collective gatherings lack a theoretical approach to the microworkings of how exactly people are emotionally affected and collective emotions are elicited (Röttger-Rössler 2012; Scheve 2012). I argue that analyzing public gatherings such as those that occur at ICC outreach events as collective ritual gatherings structured by affective arrangements can provide the necessary nuance to explore in more detail how the atmosphere created results from the co-presence of bodies in space.

The organizers of transitional justice events try to engineer the atmosphere at the event so as to influence the processes of collective emotion and feeling. They do so by designing an affective arrangement in which the various human and nonhuman bodies are placed in relation to one another and moved around in a certain way. The potential of collective gatherings to transform collective emotions is the key here. In their normative dimension, such outreach events aim at the participants' *sense of justice*. Generally speaking, the sense of justice is "a general moral competence that consists of a bundle of affective and cognitive capacities" (Dubber 2005). The sense of justice develops as a moral sentiment, a feeling of what constitutes justice; it is felt at an individual level, but also shared collectively with others (Bens and Zenker 2019). The sense of justice can be investigated empirically by focusing on how people make assessments of the legitimacy and justice of specific phenomena and how they justify these assessments (Bens and Zenker 2017a). In this sense, outreach events are designed to influence how people perceive justice and injustice with regard to past violence by tapping into the affective and emotional dimensions of collective gatherings. On a more general level, I argue that the law creates atmospheres as a basis for changing sentiments.

This is, of course, a difficult task for those who organize outreach events. Andreas Philippopoulos-Mihalopoulos, who has elaborated on the role of atmosphere in legal settings, has observed that for any atmosphere to be stable, it must make invisible the fact that it is engineered (Philippopoulos-Mihalopoulos 2015, 144). From the perspective of those who arrange it, an atmosphere is successfully engineered to the degree that it feels natural to the participants. Participants must be able to immerse themselves in the event. As I will describe, the ICC personnel are not always able to create the atmosphere they envisage, mainly because they are not able to arrange the bodies in the way they intend to.

DAY 1

On the day we went to Abok, and on the following day as well, the ICC was in session in The Hague. The Court was conducting the opening of the trial against Dominic Ongwen. During these two days, the OTP, the representatives of the victims, and the defense team gave their opening presentations.

About one hour after our arrival, at least two thousand people had gathered. There was no specific introduction by the organizers; the two small televisions were simply switched on. People carried on loud conversations even after the broadcast had started. Apparently, the official ICC delegation had not yet arrived. We had expected that there would be a live feed from the courtroom in The Hague, but instead the televisions showed NTV, a Ugandan news channel. The proceedings were broadcast nationwide with intermittent interruptions of the newscast. While people were watching the images, the clear majority of those in attendance did not understand English well enough to follow proceedings as technical as this one. The local language in Abok is Leb Lango, a Western Nilotic language of the Luo group that is quite similar to Acholi – the language of the neighboring district, as well as of Dominic Ongwen and the LRA. Only those with several years of formal education speak fluent English, the national language of Uganda.

Shortly after the proceedings had been opened in The Hague, the seventy counts of crimes against the accused, Dominic Ongwen, were read out by the court clerk in the courtroom. The people in Abok seemed to realize that something important was going on, but the looks on their faces and the frequent discussions among the viewers indicated that they could not fully fathom what it was. Instead of sitting quietly and following the proceedings attentively, people frequently engaged in conversations or left their seats and moved around in the tents. The excitement that was in the air before the televisions were switched on seemed to have dissipated. Instead, people behaved as they would while waiting for something. The crowd appeared to be suffering from the same mixture of boredom and unease one generally observes at, for instance, a bus station – people were there of their own accord but not to engage in any kind of activity beyond waiting.

While the charges were being read to Dominic Ongwen in The Hague, the registrar of the Court arrived in Abok in a motorcade comprising several white SUVs – accompanied by some ICC personnel and embedded journalists (Figure 2.2). Except for me, the very few whites who were present at this event had been transported there in one of these SUVs. Shortly after their arrival, the registrar began his speech. Many people looked interested and paid attention to the official, but most of them, not being fluent in English, could not understand the content of what he said. At one point he said, "In my fifteen years working for the ICC, I have never seen anything of this magnitude regarding community engagement in a proceeding." It took a little time for an interpreter to translate the ICC official's words into the local language. Then people applauded.

After the registrar had ended his speech, he called for questions. One village official started by telling the ICC official that many in the

Figure 2.2 A television journalist from a Kenyan news channel standing amid the crowd during an ICC outreach event in Abok, northern Uganda, December 6, 2016. (A black and white version of this figure will appear in some formats. For the color version, please refer to the plate section.)
Source: Jonas Bens

community had not had the opportunity to fill in the forms necessary to formally participate in the trial. He was referring to the fact that in a trial before the ICC, the victims of the accused can be legally represented as a group and thereby formally participate in the trial proceeding. These victim groups then serve as a third party alongside the prosecution and the defense. The local official asked, in the local language, if it would still be possible for those who had not yet filled in the form to participate in the trial. People applauded loudly – about as loudly as before.

The ICC official answered in English. He replied that he could not do anything about the forms, as there had been a deadline before the start of the trial, which had already passed. But he wanted to reassure people that they could nevertheless take part in the trial and see justice be done by participating in screening events like these, accompanied by discussions. This magnificent event would be an example of such victim participation. After his reply was translated, many villagers started whispering among themselves. There was no audible applause.

At the time I had the strong impression that something significant had transpired here, although I was not yet sure what. Having listened closely to what people were saying, I had already detected some kind of irritation. The local official had asked a question, and the ICC official had not answered in the affirmative without reservation. It only became fully clear to me that this was a significant exchange when the collective mood seemed to shift after the ICC official's second statement. His second statement ("this magnificent event") was semantically not very different from his first statement ("I have never seen anything of this magnitude … "). But while his first statement elicited applause from the crowd, his second statement was met with doubtful hesitation on the part of the villagers. Something had changed; the atmosphere had shifted. Before, the bodies of the audience members were oriented toward the speaker, applauding; after, they were directed toward each other, discussing what had been said. The speech acts and the description of the atmospheres alone do not seem to be enough to settle the question of what exactly happened, let alone why. I argue that in this moment, something was enacted that went beyond the scene and even beyond the whole event; it was a performance that related to sentiment.

In the question and answer session after the ICC registrar's speech, the local official referred to past as well as to future events. He spoke of the fact that a number of community members had not been able to fill in specific forms in the past, and also expressed the wish for the future that participation in the trial would still be possible. On the level of the affective and emotional perception of actors present at an event, storytelling in the form of pre- and reenactment reminds people of feelings and can thereby elicit emotional responses. In such cases, pre- and reenactments serve as frames within which actors normatively assess the present situation and form opinions about the event's legitimacy and relevance (Bens 2017).

In the question and answer session, the ICC registrar answered the question put to him by offering a notion of participation that differed from that of the local official. While the local official was talking about the formal participation of victim groups in the trial, the ICC official was referring to a more informal participation of villagers attending public screenings of the trial. Inscribed in this exchange are differing sentiments of justice.

Although this exchange was seemingly about victim participation, contextualizing it within other bodies of data collected during ethnographic fieldwork reveals that the local official was anticipating the time after the end of the trial and alluding to the issue of reparations. The villagers were concerned that only by formally participating in the trial proceedings would they become eligible for individual reparations through the ICC's Trust Fund for Victims. If Dominic Ongwen ended up being convicted, then the Trust Fund for Victims might give money to his victims.[11] Interviews I have conducted with grassroots victim organizations in northern Uganda show that sentiments of restoration and reparation heavily influence people's perceptions of justice (Bens 2017).

Whether knowingly or unknowingly, the ICC registrar did not react to this allusion. He instead pointed to the current event as an example of effective victim participation – implying that formal participation in the trial was not necessary to see justice in action. He was assuming that the villagers were motivated by a sentiment of retribution in which the successful punishment of the perpetrator is to be desired as a just outcome.

These competing sentiments of justice structure many different debates on transitional justice. In transitional justice scholarship, this is framed as the debate between retributive justice and restorative justice (see, e.g., Clark 2008). Retributive justice points to retribution and punishment of perpetrators in order to come to terms with large-scale violence (Moore 2010).[12] Restorative justice focuses on repairing the damage done by this violence, be it in the form of monetary reparations or some other kind of efforts to heal broken social relationships (Menkel-Meadow 2007).[13] These competing sentiments were inscribed into the outreach event and were performed in its affective arrangement. Sentiments not only influenced the speech acts as such but also the atmosphere of the event. The atmospheric irritation resulted to a large degree from partial incompatibilities between sentiments that were structurally and processually embedded rather than spontaneously produced during the event. The atmospheric irritation again reinscribed these sentiments into the discourse and hence to some degree reproduced them.

While the registrar was present at the outreach event in Abok, Dominic Ongwen made his statement in the courtroom in The Hague. Remarkably, although he spoke in Acholi, NTV only broadcast the English translation. The LRA had committed heinous crimes, Ongwen conceded, but, referring to his abduction as a child in the 1990s, he said, "I am not the LRA." Only a minority of community members were able to follow this important moment in the proceeding.

People quickly became bored with staring at the same image of a prosecutor presenting evidence on the tiny television screen. Many started speaking loudly, left their seats, and gathered in groups inside and outside the tents.

The presence of representatives of international news organizations provided an additional distraction. On a number of occasions, journalists jostled through the seated crowd to get themselves in position for dramatic video shoots. Figure 2.2 shows a television journalist standing in the midst of the crowd (the audience of the first degree) and broadcasting to his television viewers (the audience of the second degree), in this case the viewers of a Kenyan news channel. Through him and his bodily presence, the international media audience influenced to some degree the atmosphere of the event.

The language in which the proceedings were screened was a crucial component of the affective arrangement. Harri Englund (2006, 47-69) has pointed to the salient empirical problems that occur when the language of international law is translated into African languages and dialects. In this case, people were obviously not able to follow the legal proceedings in a language they did not understand. The international media audiences could not, however, realize this. These atmospheres did not translate into the images that were being broadcast from Abok to the rest of the world. The television viewers saw masses of people coming together and participating in a transitional justice event.

From the perspective of the ICC outreach personnel, this prioritization of the media audience over the audience present at the event had its logic. They were under severe funding constraints due to recent budget cuts and were much more dependent on the support of international elites watching BBC Africa than they were on Dominic Ongwen's victims. The fact that the proceedings were transmitted in English instead of Acholi was another instance in which the international media audience was brought into the affective arrangement of the outreach event, at the expense of the local villagers.

But apart from this problem of translation in the narrow linguistic sense, the lack of semantic content had a profound influence on the affective setup of the event. Sara Ahmed has highlighted the role of language in the production of affect (Ahmed 2004b). In her analysis, which is inspired by affect theory, words are circulated in what she calls "affective economies" (Ahmed 2004a). Such affective economies can stick words to bodies, which not only marks and names them in the linguistic sense, but also shapes people's experiences in the co-presence of other bodies in space. The atmosphere of confusion, boredom, and indifference at the outreach event is a good indicator that the words, which are presumably of central relevance in court proceedings, did not "stick" with the present bodies in Ahmed's sense.

Berg and Ramos-Zayas (2015) have recently argued that the manner in which affect is experienced by individual bodies and collectives is deeply racialized. The deep history of racism and colonialism in Africa is not only a macro discourse that forms the background of concrete situations, but inscribes itself into the micropolitics of affect that are manifest in spatialized events such as the one I describe here. The discourse on the ICC as a neocolonial institution that I alluded to at the beginning of this chapter exemplifies the degree to which the current politics of international criminal justice are enmeshed in the racialized colonial history that connects Africa and Europe.

Within the framework of her "phenomenology of whiteness," Sara Ahmed has highlighted the racialized ordering of the movement of bodies in space (Ahmed 2007, 161). While the white body is free to move, the non-white body is obstructed. In her view, "whiteness" is not an essential or substantial "thing in the world," but more of a structuring principle for bodies in space. The movement of white bodies in expensive SUVs even as most black bodies were shown sitting on cheap plastic chairs can be read as if it were a metaphor from Ahmed's theoretical writings. The presence of white bodies in an African village shapes the atmosphere of the events taking place in such a way that the arrangement of bodies is determined at least to some degree according to racialized orderings: white bodies (the registrar) talk, black bodies (the villagers) listen; white bodies move (in SUVs), black bodies are stationary (on plastic chairs), and so forth.

During my fieldwork in northern Uganda, I realized in my conversations with ICC outreach officers that they are very conscious of the fact that the presence of a *muno* (the Luo word for white foreigner) disturbs the atmosphere of an outreach event. All of the members of the ICC outreach team highlighted to me the importance of recruiting local NGOs and civil society members to organize the events. These efforts to "localize" transitional justice measures are, on the one hand, the result of a lack of funding for the ICC outreach unit, which would not be able to afford to pay foreign personnel to do the work even if it wanted to. On the other hand, the members of the ICC outreach team understand that local mediators are more readily accepted by the local population and confer legitimacy upon the outreach work. One can also read this reliance on local translators as the attempt to make invisible the fact that the atmosphere of being so close as to be able to "touch justice" in these events is the product of a purposeful production process. If the events appear engineered by foreign personnel, this atmosphere will not emerge.

Long before the end of the court day in The Hague, it became clear that NTV would not broadcast the trial any longer. People began to leave by the hundreds, and some men began loading hundreds of white plastic chairs onto a truck. We also decided to leave and to return the next day to watch the continuation of the trials.

DAY 2

When we arrived in Abok the next day, we were in for a surprise. The tents in front of the administration building had vanished and, at first glance, nobody was to be seen. We asked an official who was working in the building that just the day before had been the center of the huge space with tents and televisions and thousands of people. He directed us to a small community center down the road, where the second day of the trial opening would be screened. On arrival we saw that the place was a small courtyard with benches where some forty people were already sitting and watching NTV (Figure 2.3). A telenovela from Latin America was on – dubbed in English (an enchanting white woman was trying to seduce a dashing white businessman and initiate him into her evil plots; the attempt failed).

No ICC official was to be seen. On the second day, only local organizers from the village were present, and I was the only white person there. On this day, NTV screened a little more of the trial opening than the day before. With only a one-hour delay, the oral submissions by the OTP were broadcast in part. Instead of using NTV's English-language audio feed, the organizers had tuned into MegaFM, the Acholi-language radio station, which was transmitting the Acholi translation of the proceedings. They were getting the feed directly from The Hague, where the trial was being translated into Acholi for Dominic Ongwen.

The smaller room was now equipped with photocopied "Case Information Sheets" translated into Acholi. These one-page documents contained basic information about the case and the participants and were also available in The Hague in English and French. Obviously, they had been left there by the ICC personnel the day

Figure 2.3 An ICC outreach event on the second day of the trial opening, Abok, December 7, 2016. (A black and white version of this figure will appear in some formats. For the color version, please refer to the plate section.)
Source: Jonas Bens

before when the registrar visited Abok. Many people took one of these leaflets before taking a seat. By the time the proceedings began, the hall had filled up with some 250 people, an audience about one-tenth the size of the day before. No ICC officials came to Abok that day.

This alternative arrangement on the second day felt different not just to us, but apparently to the villagers as well. People were calm and serious; the mood was tense. If people talked at all, they did so quietly and in small groups. People mostly stayed in their seats and seemed to be following the event attentively on the screens. The majority of people there seemed to understand what was going on. When the prosecution was describing Dominic Ongwen's crimes, one could see reactions in people's faces. At one point, Benjamin Gumpert, the senior trial lawyer for the prosecution, described in detail how Dominic Ongwen had ordered his men to rape an underage girl whom the LRA had abducted after she had refused to have sex with him. A number of older women shook their heads and looked away from the screen. That seemed to hit a raw nerve. Their sense of justice seemed to have been triggered one way or the other.

This time, both the audio feed of the proceedings and the case information sheets (two examples of the role of nonhuman bodies in the affective arrangement) were in the Acholi language. What was being said during the proceedings could be incorporated into an "affectctive economy" (to come back to Ahmed's term) with the bodies present at the event. The story of the young rape survivor was conveyed in such a way that it stuck with people. As to whether it actually had a similar impact on everybody is doubtful, however. The affective arrangement cannot program how linguistic and discursive utterances are experienced, but it can be set up in such a way that at least some kind of affective economy emerges.

The atmosphere was different because the relationality of bodies in the affective arrangement had changed. While the first day was characterized by the hectic industriousness of the ICC staff, paired with boredom and confusion on the side of many of the local participants, on the second day, the atmosphere was calmer and more focused.

Actors involved in producing these affective arrangements demonstrate a high degree of sensitivity to the aesthetics of arranging bodies so as to be able to engineer the right atmospheres and effectively leverage their "immersive power" (Mühlhoff 2018), in this instance, specifically with the aim of addressing people's sense of justice. On the first day, it seems, the ICC had problems arranging the bodies in a way to create an immersive atmosphere of transitional justice. It is a truism that infrastructural arrangements such as the strategic positioning of nonhuman bodies (television screens, radios, and sound systems) determine to a large degree the atmospheres of any kind of event.[14] In the case of this first day of the outreach event, the ICC failed to effectively organize this technical infrastructure, another important reason why the event seemed hectic and even boring on the first day.

If we agree with Philippopoulos-Mihalopoulos's proposition (2015, 144) that for an atmosphere of any kind to be stable and immersive, the fact that it is being actively engineered must be rendered invisible, then the atmosphere on the second day was clearly more effective and "worked better" than on the first day. As Rainer Mühlhoff has argued most convincingly, the ability to immerse people in an affective arrangement is in itself a form of power (Mühlhoff 2018, 355–373). This leads to the somewhat paradoxical insight that the ambiguous atmosphere on the first day could be attributed to the overattentiveness of the ICC's staff, which made their efforts to engineer the affective arrangement visible. People were not fully immersed in the event. The

ICC brought many different bodies together at the event, including the foreign journalists and the registrar of the ICC, all of whom were unfamiliar to the villagers. The attendees at the event were aware that the ICC outreach unit was putting on a show for the registrar and the international press, and this awareness disturbed the transitional justice atmosphere for other bodies (the villagers). Another important aspect of the first day of this event was the multiple publics the ICC outreach unit was trying to address: the local population, their direct superiors in the Court hierarchy, their donor base, and the international media audience, to name a few.

***

In the literature on transitional justice, many have tried to come to terms with the question of why and how transitional justice fails. Could it, for instance, be because the models of transitional justice formats (especially criminal trials) do not fit the local context? Critics of the "translational turn" in the anthropology of international law and transitional justice make exactly this kind of argument: that the translation analysis remains blind to a real mismatch between the global and the local.

Harri Englund, for instance, sees the concept of vernacularization as an attempt to circumvent the problematic tensions between universalism and relativism so characteristic of the anthropological critique of human rights. In Englund's view, these tensions remain and are only made invisible by the translation metaphor. The metaphor of vernacularization obscures important insights into dissident movements against human rights ideas and is not able to conceptualize the local "as a possible origin for fresh travels," by which Englund is referring to local actors' ability to bring into the debate their own normative ideas that go beyond those already enshrined in the international conception of human rights (Englund 2012, 72).

Kamari Clarke has criticized the idea of vernacularization as well as the not dissimilar notion of "friction" (Tsing 2005) by pointing to those "cases in which convergence and negotiation are not an option, when meanings of justice are so incommensurate that they cannot be understood in terms of each other because they are defined against (or in contradistinction to) each other" (Clarke 2009, 32). She therefore focuses on what she calls the *politics of incommensurability*, which "cannot be explained in terms of particular forms of norm internalization or straightforward attempts to supplant vernacular forms, nor can they be understood as simply vernacularization or even as an emergent relation of 'friction'" (Clarke 2009, 32).

In anthropology, there are three ways to conceptualize this mismatch of (global) transitional justice and (local) reality on the ground. A culturalist and postcolonial conceptualization of the global/local mismatch articulates the idea that those who are the "targets" of transitional justice measures in Africa have conceptions of legality, justice, and responsibility that are different from those inherent in transitional justice. Actors on the ground experience the use of these Euro-American legal concepts as a form of neocolonial imposition (Clarke 2009; Meier 2013).

A political-economic analysis sees the mismatch on the level of what transitional justice should actually be about. Although large-scale violence, such as a civil war, is based on political-economic structures of inequality and is, therefore, a political matter, the law is mobilized to deal with it and individualizes a complex problem, reducing it to either the guilt or the innocence of individual persons. Terms such as "judicialization of politics" (Comaroff and Comaroff 2007) and "legal encapsulation" (Clarke 2019) are mobilized to shed a critical light on such processes.

A third line of analysis refers, not unlike a broader critique of humanitarianism (Fassin 2012; Ticktin 2014), to the temporal bias of transitional justice processes. Transitional justice implies a crisis, a short-term moment in which transition must be facilitated. The mismatch occurs when people on the ground experience problems not as transitory but as permanent – a phenomenon transitional justice measures cannot address and tend to ignore or sweep under the rug (Anders and Zenker 2014a; Macdonald 2017).

Such contributions on the mismatches between global expectations and local perceptions have provided many insights into the workings and failings of transitional justice on the ground. But what they all have in common is that they refer to the mismatch as cognitive and purportedly rational. In these views, the local/global mismatch results from the conscious views that people hold about the incongruity between their expectations and what transitional justice offers. It might be that people often say, "That is not our culture; that is your culture." "It is not about law; it is about money, power, and politics." "You speak of exceptionality and crisis, but this is my everyday life." But I have tried to show in this chapter that this might not be the whole story.

Deploying an analysis based on the production of atmosphere means paying attention to the myriad of unconscious, emotional, and affective dynamics that emerge between co-present bodies in space and that relate to people's sense of justice. Perceptions of justice are not only produced on the level of translations of abstract norms into local understandings. There is also an everyday materiality and affectivity to the production of justice. The material and affective microworkings of these processes of justice-making shape to a large degree what people feel is right and just. What may, at first sight, appear to be petty questions about how bodies are arranged in concrete events can have just as much of an impact on the success or failure of transitional justice projects as international discourses of justice. To better understand the workings of transitional justice, one must investigate how law – in this instance international law – is translated and shaped in the interplay of the global and the local by paying close attention to how these translation processes are carried out in concrete affective arrangements.

PART II

SENTIMENTS

3

THE SENTIMENT OF PLAUSIBILITY

Affective Framing and the Production of Legal Truth

> *In the system of Plato the soul is considered as something like a little state or republic, composed of three different faculties or orders. The first is the judging faculty, the faculty which determines not only what are the proper means for attaining any end, but also what ends are fit to be pursued, and what degree of relative value we ought to put upon each. This faculty Plato called, as it is very properly called, reason, and considered it as what had a right to be the governing principle of the whole. Under this appellation, it is evident, he comprehended not only that faculty by which we judge of truth and falsehood, but that by which we judge of the propriety or impropriety of desires and affections.*
>
> Adam Smith, *The Theory of Moral Sentiments* (1759)

Legal proceedings are presumably about finding the truth.[1] When judges must assess whether somebody committed a crime, they first have to find out what happened: the who, what, where, when, how, and why. This is no easy task, and in most legal proceedings – criminal or otherwise – the greatest amount of time and effort is spent on trying to establish "what actually happened." Normally, versions of "what actually happened" compete with each other in the course of a trial. The different parties might agree on some facts and disagree on others when they speak about the relevant past events. In the end, somebody, usually the judges or, in an Anglo-American system, the jurors, must decide which version of the past they find the most plausible. This chapter is about this highly important, but often neglected, notion in law (and, of course, beyond): plausibility.

It is my argument that plausibility is best understood in terms of sentiment. To find something plausible is to make a judgment about the truth of certain facts about the world. People make these judgments, like any judgment for that matter, while subjectively experiencing the world at the same time. Something cannot simply *be* plausible; it must always be *experienced as* plausible by somebody. Or to phrase it differently: in social reality, nothing *is* plausible if it does not *feel* plausible. It is this rather banal insight that opens the door to my exploration of the sentimental dimension of plausibility.

When social scientists, particularly those interested in language, ask why people believe one thing and not another, why they are convinced of this fact but not of that fact, they will often use the notion of "framing." Framing refers to the idea that specific propositions and individual statements cannot be understood simply on their own terms. They must be analyzed as embedded in other statements and propositions that frame them. The way a statement or a proposition is framed plays a major role in how it is understood by an audience. Framing is an indispensable but also rather mysterious concept that people often use but seldom clearly define. On the following pages I will explore the notion of framing and propose analyzing frames in terms of affect, an idea I will call *affective framing*. Affective framing, I contend, is a key process in understanding plausibility.

DOMINIC ONGWEN AND THE QUESTION OF PERSONAL GUILT

The case *The Prosecutor* v. *Dominic Ongwen* is to a large degree about personal responsibility. Ongwen was undoubtedly a ruthless and effective military commander, and his alleged crimes encompass, among others, mass murder of civilians, abduction, rape, sexual slavery, forced marriage, and pillaging. But his biography is also complicated. When Ongwen was a young teenager in the early 1990s, he was abducted by the LRA. Like many other children in northern Uganda, the LRA forcibly recruited him into their ranks. The military strategy of conscripting and using child soldiers was a key component in the LRA's fight against the Ugandan government (Ehrenreich 1998; Eichstaedt 2009; Beard 2011; Preston 2015; Oloya 2018). Studies estimate that between 1986 and 2006, the LRA abducted between 54,000 and 75,000 people, including 25,000 to 38,000 children (Pham, Vinck, and Stover 2008). When Ongwen grew older, he went through the ranks of the LRA, eventually becoming a middle rank and then quite quickly a top commander in the early 2000s.

In the 1990s Dominic Ongwen was a victim of an already ongoing military conflict. Being himself a child, he was abducted and forced to fight and kill. In this respect he is not very different from thousands of other children that were forcibly recruited during the long and bloody conflict. It is probable that his socialization inside the LRA during his formative teenage years significantly altered not only the course of his life, but also his inner self: his understanding of the workings of the world, his values, and his conception of right and wrong. How can you judge a perpetrator like this? How can you measure the degree of his personal guilt in light of his actions? As such, these questions are at the center of this case. In an attempt to capture the complexities of Dominic Ongwen's biography, Erin Baines (2009) has argued for fully acknowledging the role of "complex political perpetrators" in order to understand the war in northern Uganda and what kind of justice can be brought in its aftermath. Naturally, the questions that emerge regarding Dominic Ongwen's guilt go far beyond judging one man for his crimes. This problem has many theoretical implications that touch on theories of the formation of the self, of the relationship between structure and agency in times of war, of crime and punishment, and of the relationship between law and politics. In practice, none of these theoretical problems is ever resolved to the satisfaction of all. Instead, actors constantly navigate these conundrums and try to manipulate them to their own advantage. The Dominic Ongwen case is no exception.

Two major opposing narratives characterize the discourse on Dominic Ongwen's guilt. There is Dominic Ongwen, the war criminal: ruthlessly ambitious, willing to do anything to get ahead in the LRA and to amass power. And there is Dominic Ongwen, the child soldier: abducted by force, brainwashed by a religious cult, too afraid and too disoriented to know any better. During my research I found these two narratives everywhere. Of course, they were performed in the courtroom. But they were also brought up in conversations I had in Europe and Africa, in small villages and big cities, in highly official settings, and in private and informal contexts. They were represented in all kinds of different international, national, and local media. When I heard people present these two narratives, they sometimes portrayed them in their black-and-white versions; other times, their interpretations were imbued with the shades of gray that open up between the two extremes. It was necessary for everyone involved to assess the degree to which Ongwen was guilty of the atrocities he committed, and people did that by placing him somewhere on a spectrum with guilty war criminal on one extreme and innocent child soldier on the other.

I began to be interested in how the people I listened to made sense of these opposing narratives and reached the point – if only for a moment – where they found one at least a bit more plausible, a bit more convincing than the other, and how they performed the narratives in ways intended to convince others. Right from the beginning of my research I was confronted with these two narratives and realized something quite astonishing: In order to assess Dominic Ongwen's guilt or innocence for his actions, different people tended to invoke the same biographical facts, but would use them to reach very different, even opposing conclusions.

Regarding Ongwen's guilt or innocence, one question in particular stands out: Why did he not run away? Of the thousands of child soldiers the LRA recruited in the twenty years it fought in northern Uganda, a majority did not stay with the rebel group. In 2000, the Ugandan Parliament enacted an Amnesty Act that granted freedom from prosecution to any LRA fighter who left the bush voluntarily and registered in a government reception center.[2] The Amnesty Act, which had been lobbied for by many in northern Uganda, can be seen as an attempt to deplete the LRA of their most precious resource: their fighters. But even before the Amnesty Act, many LRA soldiers took whatever opportunities that presented themselves to desert.

In fact, desertion was such a serious problem for the LRA that it implemented a number of severe measures to prevent it. Most importantly, young children were strictly disciplined inside the LRA, and desertion was punished severely, often by death.[3] It was also an established practice to force new recruits to commit atrocities to their own family members.[4] After doing so, the children felt that they had been irredeemably severed from their family and kinship ties and were afraid to go back to their villages, where they feared they would face violent retribution by neighbors and family members. But the spiritual order of the LRA also played a major role. The LRA's leader, Joseph Kony, is a spirit medium, an *ajwaka* in the Acholi language. Being possessed by spirits who confer supernatural powers upon him makes Kony an even more powerful military leader.[5] The LRA fighters were led to believe that they were under constant surveillance by the spirits, who were in direct contact with Joseph Kony, even if he was not present in person. Because of this, Kony would know if they were planning to run away.[6] Despite such measures, thousands of children managed to leave the LRA, such that recruitment and maintaining troop numbers remained a key problem for the rebels throughout the course of the conflict.

Unsurprisingly, the defense and the prosecution answered the question of why Dominic Ongwen did not run away quite differently. According to the child soldier narrative, put forth in its purest form by the defense, Ongwen "had no choice in joining the rebel ranks and remained in rebel ranks against his will" and that "Dominic Ongwen was just an instrument."[7] Ongwen did not try to leave the LRA because he feared for his life. He was constantly being watched and was forced to obey the orders given to him. As his defense lawyer put it:

> Your Honours, throughout the turns and twists in the armed conflicts between the government of Uganda and the LRA, Dominic lived his life under duress. Left to the vagaries of life in the bush, and knowing that he had no home to return to, as his mother and father and perhaps his entire family were no more, Dominic succumbed to the so-called Stockholm syndrome. He had to adapt to the realities of his misfortune and develop acute survival instincts. He recoiled into existentialist living until such a time an opportunity would avail itself for him to escape. And that only came on 21 January 2015 or thereabout. The all-knowing and all-seeing Joseph Kony instilled institutional ethos that required complete compliance and discipline. This exactitude, your Honours, was so stultifying to the young minds of child soldiers that it had made an indelible mark, indelible mark on their minds for the rest of their lives in captivity.[8]

The prosecution in the trial insisted that although Ongwen was abducted as a child, he was only charged with crimes that he committed as an adult in his mid-twenties. Even after he had grown up and had seen so many of his fellow child soldiers desert, he himself did not leave. He wanted to get ahead in the rebel group, and the way to get ahead was to prove himself as a ruthless and effective fighter. This was, according to the war criminal narrative, why Ongwen did not leave the LRA. This, the prosecution argued, was because he liked being in the LRA. In the courtroom the prosecution elaborated on this narrative:

> The assertion that children in his position become dissociated, that they live in an environment without education and, as a result, performed unspeakable acts are nothing to the point. It is not, as the Defence suggests, in direct contradiction with international criminal law for Dominic Ongwen to be tried for any of the 70 crimes in the Document Containing the Charges. The Defence's argument, frankly, is one more of the heart than of the head. The logical result of the argument is that for those who are abducted and conscripted as child soldiers, there is an immunity from prosecution for any crimes they may subsequently commit. That's not good law, it's not good sense. The Prosecution recognizes

> that to launch wholesale prosecutions of rank and file LRA fighters abducted as children, who merely did the minimum to avoid extreme disciplinary measures would be a questionable way of proceeding, but Dominic Ongwen doesn't fit that description. He rose through his own murderous efforts to the highest ranks. He enthusiastically embraced the LRA's policy of targeting civilians. You've heard him say as much. He led, planned and ordered attacks where hundreds of people lost their lives. And he took the lead in satisfying the demand of LRA commanders for young girls to be their wives.[9]

As one can already gather from these courtroom transcript excerpts, these two narratives – "Ongwen the child soldier" and "Ongwen the war criminal" – so eloquently put forth in the courtroom in The Hague, provide fertile ground for an analysis of affect and emotion. But these narratives, which try to address the question "Why did he not run away?" extend far beyond the courtroom. They are at the core of the debates revolving around Dominic Ongwen's guilt and innocence.

During my time in northern Uganda, I had many conversations with former child soldiers. Given the incredible number of LRA abductees, it is highly likely that anyone you talk to of a certain age was in the LRA at some point in their lives. Usually, my conversation partners, who were in the LRA for very different lengths of time, deserted at some point when the opportunity presented itself. Still, surprisingly, their assessments of Dominic Ongwen's personal guilt varied widely. Some saw him as yet another child soldier who, like themselves, was forced to fight and therefore saw him as a victim rather than a criminal. Others highlighted the difference between Ongwen and themselves and saw him as a criminal rather than a victim. I was struck even more by the fact that my interlocutors frequently referred to Ongwen's status as a high-ranking LRA commander either to add to his guilt or to excuse him. Some people told me that, because Ongwen was a high-ranking commander, it would have been easier for him to desert than for a simple foot soldier, and that his responsibility was all the greater for not having done so. Others told me that, because he was a high-ranking commander, it would have been much more difficult for him to desert than for a simple foot soldier, and that his responsibility was consequently diminished.

In the first line of argumentation Dominic Ongwen, as a high-ranking commander, was portrayed as being in a position of authority. In this position he commanded troops who were obliged to obey his orders. It would have been easy for him to create a situation in which he had an opportunity to desert, and even to order some of his subordinates to leave with him. My interlocutors often illustrated their argument with a hypothetical scenario. I was asked by one of my interview partners in northern Uganda to imagine Dominic Ongwen in the bush commanding a small unit of LRA soldiers on some mission. The scenario went something like this:

> Ongwen is lying in the tall grass, maybe close to a road. Only loyal soldiers to each side. A convoy of the Ugandan army is approaching on the road; the LRA unit is in hiding. Ongwen hears the vehicles nearing. At this moment, Ongwen can make the decision to desert. He would simply have to ask his unit to lay down its weapons, take a few steps from the bush onto the road, and surrender to the UPDF troops. The danger is minimal. Ongwen can be held responsible for not making this decision, for not taking these few steps necessary to end his murderous career. Because he remains in the tall grass, so to speak, he is a guilty man.

In the second argument, Dominic Ongwen is portrayed as a high-ranking commander, under constant pressure and permanent surveillance. A simple foot soldier, another former child soldier told me, can much more easily fall back during an ongoing raid, leave the camp under cover of darkness, or hide during long walks in the bush in order not to be found. As a commander, Ongwen could never do that. The hypothetical scenario went something like this:

> Ongwen is in a camp. He is always surrounded by people, many of whom are fiercely loyal to the LRA leadership around Joseph Kony. Kony himself may often be elsewhere, but he is always present on the radio standing close by. When there is a raid or a long march through the bush, Ongwen is, as a commander, always the center of attention. Never being unobserved, how can he decide to run away? The risk is enormous, the fear of being caught overwhelming, because it is so probable. It is immensely dangerous and, therefore, not so easy to hold him responsible just for not taking these risks.

These narratives, "Ongwen, the child soldier, in the LRA camp" and "Ongwen, the war criminal, in the tall grass," ran like a common thread through all the different places I visited and the different conversations I had with people. What puzzled me then and what still puzzles me is that I feel somewhat drawn to both versions of Ongwen's life. If we take Baines's (2009) concept of the "complex political perpetrator" seriously, then it follows that Dominic Ongwen is to be located somewhere between the war criminal and the child soldier, somewhere between complete guilt and complete innocence. In a way, the inability to come to a definitive answer regarding Ongwen's guilt leads us to yet another, maybe even more interesting question. Assuming that many people find it similarly difficult to decide who Dominic Ongwen is, what practices and strategies do they employ to render these competing narratives plausible to themselves and to others – sometimes in a ways so successful that both can seem convincing? I believe a perspective on sentiment can shed light on this.

FRAMING, PLAUSIBILITY, AND AFFECT

That the same piece of information can be used to support very different, even contradictory conclusions is in itself not surprising to the social scientist. How the information about events can be understood depends on how it is *framed*. The term has so thoroughly colonized academic language and is used so widely and casually that it is important to remember that the idea of "frame" and "framing" first entered the vocabulary of the social and cultural sciences in theoretical writings by ethnographers as they put forth their ideas gained from ethnographic research. Curiously, nowadays, the notion of framing seems to be more popular outside anthropology. I argue for taking a look back at some earlier works to reappropriate the term for anthropological research.

Gregory Bateson proposed the concept of "frame" in his essay "A Theory of Play and Fantasy" (1972, 177–193). In this essay, Bateson reflects on how it happens that people, and certain animals, have the ability to distinguish between genuine events and their playful imitations. In many instances, people instinctively grasp the difference between a real attack on their life and one that is only jokingly acted out as an ironic gesture. They are able to make this distinction because they can convey and interpret linguistic and paralinguistic signals that establish a frame. They can communicate: "This is real." "This is just a joke." "This is meant ironically." These signals that frame an event and an action can be very subtle. Most of the time it is not necessary to explicitly utter the words, "I'm just kidding." In fact, people utter these words mostly in cases when other, less explicit signals are felt to have failed already. And still, most of the time, the other person gets what is going on.

In *Frame Analysis* (1974), Erving Goffman took up Bateson's term and developed out of it a sophisticated theory of the production of meaning. Goffman assumes that in their everyday lives people are always posing to each other the question, "What is it that's going on here?" (1974, 8), and people are only able to answer this question in reference to a frame. Are they experiencing a genuine event or one of its many permutations: a fabricated event in the course of which people are deceived, be it jokingly or with harmful intent? A put-on event, for instance, on a theater stage? For Goffman, *frame analysis* is a method of determining how people give sense to and make sense of the reality of actions and events. Frame analysis in Goffman's version means to investigate how people produce the frame to communicate the degrees to which actions and events are genuine and real, how they set the scene for a casual conversation, a solemn heart-to-heart, a genuine compliment, or a silly joke. Frame analysis also entails investigating how people manipulate the frame to deceive other people about the degree of reality of an event: How they set the scene for a polite lie, an elaborate con, a surprise party, or a devious intrigue. For Bateson and Goffman, framing is a social practice through which people signal to others and determine for themselves the difference between truth and lie, genuine and fake, actual and imagined. Frame analysis is the research practice of investigating how exactly people determine the degree of how real an action or an event is, or when and why they fail to make these determinations correctly.

The concept of framing has since been significantly broadened. It has, for instance, had a career in media and communication studies, and – as often happens – has become a much more generic term in the process. In a prominent article from the early 1990s, media studies scholar Robert Entman (1993) conceived of framing as a "fractured paradigm." Often the idea of frame analysis is taken quite literally. If one analyzes a newspaper article, for example, one identifies a sentence containing specific information. The sentences before and after are then treated (even quite literally in its visual appearance) as the "frame" of the information. I do not doubt that even in this broad sense, the term "frame" has some analytical potential, but with such overuse the term eventually becomes almost synonymous with the "context" of an utterance.

When I use the term "framing" in this chapter, I insist on conceiving of its function beyond giving context to an event, an action, or a piece of information. My conception is to understand framing as the social practice of determining how "real" things are on the broad spectrum between fact and fiction – whether it is to make these determinations for themselves on the basis of available evidence, or to try, as part of a rhetorical strategy, to determine what others will perceive as "reality" on the basis of one's selective presentation of evidence. While all people across any sociocultural context can be observed to make these determinations on the degree of reality of an event, an action, or a bit of information, it is equally clear that people make these determinations according to a myriad of different, often competing standards. In other words, while all humans have some notion of reality, not all humans use the same (even vaguely similar) criteria to determine how real things are.

Obviously, the question of how real things are is at the heart of any legal proceeding. Criminal law, or any normative order for that matter, is about ascribing legal significance to actual events that have occurred. One person orders the killing of civilians in a military conflict, and the judge in court qualifies this action as a war crime. To come to a proper legal conclusion, it has to be established how exactly the events transpired. The different parties usually disagree about that. Hence, the main task of a criminal trial is to compare all the different and competing versions of past events and to establish "the truth." The degree to which the narration of past events in court is all about framing has already become clear. All parties in a criminal trial have an interest in establishing that their version is a more accurate reflection of the actual past than that of their competitors. Consequently, all have to work on signaling to their audiences the degree to which what they say about the past actually happened. In other words, they frame.

Sometimes social scientists seem to believe that lawyers deal with truth in an extremely essentializing way. The story goes that anthropology and law were two distinctive manners of imagining the real (Geertz 1983, 184), that the two disciplines have completely different ways of conceiving facts and the degree to which they are socially and culturally constructed. In other words, lawyers have a naïve understanding of essential and universal truth – "facts are facts," so to speak – but anthropologists know better. I believe this claim of an epistemological divide between law and social science to be largely exaggerated (Bens 2016). In my experience, legal actors know very well that the process of truth-finding is a highly constructive endeavor. Because it is not possible to travel back in time and because people experience events sometimes radically differently, one can never know the truth about the past. It is for this reason that the law deals with narratives of the past in terms of "plausibility."[10] A court proceeding establishes a plausible version of past events, and judges apply legal significance to this plausible past.

This is how the law approaches truth through plausibility. The terms are, of course, connected. Actors believe (and the law depends on this belief) that the truth is plausible and that, as a rule, it can be assumed that what is more plausible is also closer to the truth. As an anthropologist one must, however, be skeptical of this assumption. *Being* plausible is not an objective condition in social reality. To have an impact in a court proceeding, something must *appear* plausible to specific actors. People's perceptions are influenced by many things, and it is difficult to empirically ground the assumption that people perceive the truth (even if we assume there is any truth beyond human perceptions) as any more plausible than even a blatant lie. As such, an ethnographic approach to plausibility should concentrate on the practices and perceptions of how people make sense of past events and how they determine whether a narrative of the past is plausible, and – indirectly – whether it depicts reality, actual events, and the truth.

What I argue, therefore, is that there is a connection between framing (as a practice of determining the degree to which something is real) and plausibility (the degree to which something appears to reflect actual events, actions, or situations to specific audiences) in legal proceedings. Courtroom actors constantly frame when they narrate past events. They attempt to frame their own narratives as depicting reality to a very large degree and the narratives of the opposing side as depicting reality to a significantly lesser degree. Courtroom audiences also frame when confronted with the competing narratives of the past. In order to determine the degree to which the narratives that are presented depict reality, they either follow the frames the courtroom actors offer to them or they reject them and establish frames of their own. One can deploy Goffman's idea of frame analysis to investigate how courtroom actors manipulate the frame to manage how real they want certain things to appear to courtroom audiences and how courtroom audiences make their own determination in the context of this rhetoric. With the idea of plausibility, we are able to specify that analysis. Actors aim to manipulate the frame in order to create plausibility with their audiences, and audiences frame to determine plausibility for themselves. Plausibility as a concept hence connects the social practice of framing directly to the subjective perception of the degree to which a narrative reflects reality.

Although people usually perceive the experience of plausibility as located in the inner self, close analysis shows that the creation of plausibility is actually embedded in complex social-relational processes that transcend the inner self and the outer world. Plausibility as "felt reality" is created inside affective arrangements. In fact, I argue that affective arrangements regularly serve as frames for the creation of plausibility. This is what I mean by the term "affective framing": the practice of evoking affective arrangements in such a way that an action or an event is *felt* to be more or less plausible.

EVOKING AFFECTIVE ARRANGEMENTS

A key component of affective framing is the narration of affective arrangements. Things appear plausible to audiences when speakers describe and thus performatively construct through their speech an affective arrangement, in which the bodies in that arrangement resonate with each other, avoiding the perception of dissonance.

In this respect, I believe we can learn from anthropological studies of discursive power relations in rape trials. Anthropologists have shown that the discursive structures of trials shape specific gendered representations of the relevant events that systematically marginalize female voices in the courtroom (Ehrlich 2001), amounting to a revictimization of rape victims (Conley and O'Barr 2019). Specifically, rape trials tend to reproduce "the patriarchal logic of sexual rationality" by creating a specific framework within which to determine what is a "rational," hence plausible, way for women to behave in certain situations (Matoesian 1998, 70). Lawyers tend to try to discredit female witnesses in rape trials by creating "a patriarchal inconsistency through poetic representations of space and time" (Matoesian 1998, 70). In his ethnography of the widely publicized William Kennedy Smith rape trial in the 1990s, Matoesian reproduces this excerpt from the trial transcript by way of example (2001, 71–72):

> Cross-Examination of Ann Mercer (AM) by Defense Attorney (DA) Roy Black

DA: So you went into the house is that correct.
AM: Yes.
DA: Into the house where the rapist is right?
AM: I guess you could say that yes.
DA: It's dark in there.

AM: Yes.
DA: You go through the kitchen right?
AM: Yes.
DA: Into this little hallway.
AM: Yes.
DA: It's dark in this hallway, isn't it?
AM: Right.
DA: You meet up with this man who your friend says is a rapist, isn't that correct.
AM: I was not afraid of him, no. I was not afraid of him.
DA: That's not my question Miss Mercer, you understand my question? My question is did you meet this man who your friend says is the alleged rapist?
AM: Yes.
DA: In this dark hallway is that right.
AM: Yes.

In this example, the criminal defense attorney tries to discredit the witness. He is hoping to present the witness's story in such a way that the court finds it implausible. Why would you go into a dark house when you know that a rapist is waiting there for you? That is not plausible. Matoesian's analytical focus for this scene is how the defense attorney creates "a chronologically segmented, sequentially organized, and ultra-detailed matrix of space, time, and motion" (2001, 71–72). I would like to shift the analysis and focus on the kind of affective arrangement the defense lawyer works to establish through his narrative strategy.

The lawyer's description of space, time, and motion evokes an arrangement of bodies that create a specific atmosphere: a woman alone, night, dark house, dark hallway, rapist around the corner. In this affective arrangement, the witness's story appears implausible because, within the confines of the dominant patriarchal matrix, any female body in such an affective arrangement should feel afraid and would not enter such an arrangement voluntarily. It would be much more plausible if the affective arrangement were in fact quite different, that is, if there was no need to feel afraid because she had consented to the sexual intercourse and concocted the rape charge later; or if her friend had never told her about the accused having raped her; or if something else in the witness's story was not true, because it does not feel plausible.

The witness obviously realized that her emotions were the key determinant in this game because she interrupts the lawyer, saying, "I was not afraid of him." This discursive strategy is very dangerous for the defense attorney because it disturbs the affective arrangement he wants to evoke. By saying this, the witness redefines an important component of the defense lawyer's arrangement, namely, the affective relational position between the bodies of the witness and the accused. For that reason, the defense lawyer tries to regain control of the narrative by reprimanding the witness: "That was not my question."

These kinds of strategies to create plausibility, very common in rape trials, exemplify what I mean by affective framing. Actors want to create plausibility with audiences. They do this by framing events or actions into an affective arrangement. When the affective arrangement and the version of the event or action affectively resonate with each other, it is possible, even probable, that an audience will find that version of the past plausible.

During my research on the Dominic Ongwen case, I found actors constantly engaged in affective framing, both inside and outside the courtroom. In 2016, I made my first visit to the village of Lukodi, about forty-five minutes by bus from the town of Gulu in northern Uganda. The small trading center has a few little shops, a school, and an administrative building. In the late 1990s and the early 2000s, when the violence increased significantly, people no longer felt safe living at their homesteads scattered across the area because of the threat of being looted by LRA or UPDF troops or even abducted. More and more, therefore, people began to move to the trading centers, first voluntarily and later under threat of violence by the government. At the high point of the conflict, Lukodi had thousands of inhabitants living in dire conditions. The small village had been transformed into an IDP camp. Just as happened at the Abok IDP camp I introduced in Chapter 2, Dominic Ongwen's troops looted the camp and massacred civilians. This took place on May 24, 2004.

On my first visit I met a few villagers who were involved in a massacre survivors' association. This association had taken upon itself responsibility for memorializing the massacre of 2004 and the terrible times when Lukodi was an IDP camp. They coordinate with international and local NGOs that support such politics of memory; they are also the main communication conduit to the International Criminal Court and its trial against Dominic Ongwen. They told me that they support the trial not least because they hope to receive reparations for the loss of life and property they suffered during the armed conflict, whether it be out of funds from the ICC Trust Fund for Victims or from other sources.

As Lukodi is relatively close to Gulu, this community has had the most regional, national, and international visibility of the four massacre sites that figure in the Dominic Ongwen case. When the ICC's OTP first put together its case, they favored the strategy of including only the Lukodi massacre in the charges against Dominic Ongwen – access to evidence and witnesses would be the easiest there, and the prosecution felt that it needed to limit the scope of the charges to keep the case manageable in light of the many years that international criminal trials can take in any case. Only after several other communities bitterly protested and demanded not to be left out of the case did the OTP change its strategy. This is only one example that underlines the degree to which victims' groups in northern Uganda feel that they are engaged in a competition for public visibility and recognition.

It was, therefore, no surprise that my interlocutors saw my first visit also as an opportunity to convey to me their version of the past violence. One of the leading figures of the massacre survivors' association, who is also the local school teacher, asked me if I wanted to take a walk around the village and visit the memorial they had put up to remember the massacre. When we began our walk, he talked about the time when Lukodi was still an IDP camp. Stretching out his arm he showed me how far the camp extended into the now vacant surrounding areas. There, at that tree, stood the barracks where the UPDF soldiers were stationed. That was the direction from which the LRA fighters attacked that night. When we arrived at the memorial, a modest concrete stele with a cross mounted on the top (see Figure 3.1), he paused and gave me some time to immerse myself in the affective arrangement he had created for me. The school teacher had not only narrated for me the past by evoking an affective arrangement, but he had also mobilized all kinds of nonhuman bodies, including the memorial and other landscape features, to create an affective frame for the kind of past he wishes to be publicly recognized – a past of violence and loss, a past that demands reparation.

After having visited the memorial, my guide led me to the other side of the school, to the place where the barracks had been. He told me about the attacks on May 19, 2004, and how the UPDF soldiers, afraid of being massacred as well, abandoned their posts and left the camp population to their own devices. In fact, during the attack Ongwen commanded that day, not one government soldier was killed. We then

Figure 3.1 A memorial for the massacre on May 19, 2004, in the village of Lukodi. (A black and white version of this figure will appear in some formats. For the color version, please refer to the plate section.)
Source: Jonas Bens

arrived at a small building at about the same place where the barracks had been in 2004. It is now used as a small documentation center to store documents pertaining to the Lukodi massacre. A mural on its wall describes the story of the massacre; a list of names commemorates the dead (Figure 3.2).

Only after we had finished our walk did we sit down for a longer conversation. My interlocutor had first established a larger affective frame in order to create plausibility for the kind of past he wanted to present to me. He and I were both bodies in this affective arrangement of bodies. He had lived in Lukodi for more than twenty years and had survived the attack. Now I too had become part, if only for a moment, of this arrangement. My conversation partner hoped to create plausibility with me for his demand for recognition, visibility, and reparation. It was very rational to act in this way, but this rationality only becomes plausible when it is situated within an affective arrangement.

Many other victims' groups in the countryside in northern Uganda deployed similar strategies of affective framing. Building memorials

Figure 3.2 A mural commemorating the massacre on May 19, 2004, on the wall of a small documentation center in the village of Lukodi. (A black and white version of this figure will appear in some formats. For the color version, please refer to the plate section.)
Source: Jonas Bens

such as those in Lukodi was one component of this strategy. In fact, after the LRA conflict, many memorials were set up in northern Uganda (Edmondson 2018). The ICC case against Dominic Ongwen and the opportunity presented by heightened national and international interest intensified the politics of recognition and the affective framing it demands. Massacres in four former IDP camps – Lukodi, Abok, Odek, and Pajule, all of which I visited during my research – are formally included in the charges against Dominic Ongwen. In Lukodi, the memorial had already been there for a few years. In the case of Abok, which I mentioned in Chapter 2, I was present for the dedication ceremony of a new memorial. In Odek, the victims' group had just started construction of a new memorial. And in Pajule, they had just started debating whether to construct one or not.

In Pajule I was invited to attend a ceremony commemorating the massacre of October 10, 2003. The event took place on October 26, 2016, a little more than a month before the opening of the trial against Dominic Ongwen in The Hague. The festivities began at the local school and included a peace walk to the area where the ceremony itself would take place. It was a very large setup. Tents had been erected to protect against the sun and hundreds of plastic chairs were assembled. During the opening of the event, one representative of the massacre victims' group felt that it was necessary to address a perceived misunderstanding. He said that some might assume or suggest that this commemoration day was only organized because of the ongoing proceedings against Dominic Ongwen at the ICC. That, however, was not their intention, he said. This commemoration was to further peace and memory in Pajule, not about a case in The Hague. It is understandable, he continued, how people could get the impression that the ICC case had induced this kind of politics of memory. The fact is, however, that there had already been commemoration days in Pajule for the 2003 massacre, but only two times, and those were in the years immediately following the massacre. The funding to hold another such ceremony only materialized in light of the ICC's case in 2016.

Besides many official greetings by local dignitaries, the ceremony also included witnesses' accounts of the massacre in 2003. One woman explained, in her own words, how she experienced the massacre, how people suffered, were abducted, hurt, and killed. One speaker, the Anglican bishop, put into words a sentiment that became clear throughout the ceremony: "To understand these things you need to listen to your heart." The commemoration ceremony itself, as well as the building of memorials in general, can be understood as an attempt to evoke affective arrangements in order to make plausible the need for recognition and reparations. For the people engaged in a politics of remembering and reparation in northern Uganda, it is not only about becoming visible but about being able to provide the affective framework in which a certain version of specific actions and events appears plausible.

FINDING THE TRUTH BY COMPETING FOR THE AFFECTIVE FRAME

Let us revisit the narratives about Dominic Ongwen's responsibility. The question of why Ongwen did not desert from the LRA before 2015 emerges as the key to the assessment of his personal responsibility for his crimes. These narratives evoke affective arrangements in which Dominic Ongwen is relationally positioned with other bodies, but the affective arrangements differ significantly. To convince their audiences, to create plausibility for the veracity of their version of the past, actors need to establish an affective frame for their claims about the past. How the affective arrangement evoked frames the claim determines the degree to which audiences might be seduced into finding the narrative plausible.

The first narrative, "Ongwen, the war criminal," locates Dominic Ongwen in the tall grass. He is conducting a military operation, commanding a unit in the bush. The speaker creates a specific arrangement of bodies in which Ongwen is embedded. He is surrounded by loyal soldiers who are under his command, obliged to obey his orders. There is the grass in which they hide and which provides safety for them. While they can see the military convoy of the Ugandan army approaching on the road, the UPDF soldiers cannot see them. It is their choice to walk onto the road and confront the vehicles. In this hypothetical scenario, the bodies are arranged so as to evoke how it must feel to be in Ongwen's shoes. It cannot be narrated without eliciting memories of feelings audience members had in arrangements similar to those described, and the listeners are invited to speculate on the feelings the actors might have had in this same situation. The idea of surrendering to the UPDF feels somewhat possible in this situation. The loyal soldiers and the tall grass convey a feeling of relative security from which Ongwen could have decided to surrender. And, as a consequence, he could be held responsible for making a different decision. It appears plausible that he might not have wanted to surrender, that he wanted to remain with the LRA out of his own free will.

The second narrative, "Ongwen, the child soldier," locates Dominic Ongwen in an LRA camp. The arrangement of bodies in which Ongwen is embedded is markedly different. The human bodies that surround him are not described as obedient subordinates but watchers and potential spies loyal to the LRA's leader, Joseph Kony. One false move and Ongwen will be immediately reported to the top. Kony is never far away. Either he is physically co-present, or he is there over the radio, a nonhuman body that is never far away. Usually, the radio is kept in Dominic Ongwen's tent or close by. There is no tall grass in which Ongwen can hide, but a camp full of people. He is never unobserved. The "in-the-camp scenario" feels quite different from the "in-the-tall-grass scenario." The speaker conjures up an arrangement of bodies in which feelings of insecurity are evoked. Could one be held responsible for not deserting when one feels so insecure all the time? Here it feels plausible that Dominic Ongwen might have wanted to leave the LRA but was too afraid to attempt it.

This is the kind of affective arrangement that Ongwen's defense lawyer favored during the trial, and one can see in the short excerpt from his remarks represented above how he evokes the affective arrangement of the LRA camp. He speaks of the "vagaries of life in the bush," where Ongwen was under constant surveillance by the "all-knowing and all-seeing Joseph Kony." He clearly elaborates how it felt for Ongwen to be in this arrangement. He had to "adapt to the realities of his misfortune and develop acute survival instincts"; he was "stultified" and had to succumb to the "complete compliance and discipline" of the camp.

The prosecution argues their case quite differently. They also provide descriptions of how Ongwen felt during his time in the LRA: he rose through the ranks in the LRA through his "murderous efforts," which he "enthusiastically embraced." Interestingly enough, though, the prosecution elaborates far less on the concrete affective arrangement surrounding Ongwen. This does not mean, however, that they engaged to any lesser degree in affective framing. Again, here we can learn from the anthropological analysis of rape trials that decontextualization plays a key role in diminishing plausibility (Ehrlich 2012). If actions or events are not explicitly framed by the speaker, the affective frame is nevertheless supplied by the audience. In these cases, it is probable that broader, more commonly held sentiments that largely govern the meaning-making of audiences do the work for the speaker. It is likely that, left to their own interpretations, audiences apply mainstream understandings of gender roles, racial ideologies, and conceptions of class to the case at hand, often to the detriment of marginalized people (Eades 2008). This is the reason why decontextualization and insinuation mainly work for the powerful, as they mobilize already existing and already hegemonic understandings of how people act in a plausible way.[11] Hence, it is not surprising that the prosecution does less explicit affective framing than the defense. In light of Ongwen's atrocities and the popular damnation of the LRA, they have to do less affective framing work in the courtroom. They let the larger, more widely accepted affective frames work for them.

***

I began this chapter with the question of truth in the law and proposed that sentiment provides an analytical lens through which to understand it. Sentiments, as I have defined them at the beginning of this book, are the evaluative regimes of meaning that govern the judgments of people as embedded in and colored by affective and emotional dynamics. What, then, is the relationship between sentiments and the truth? Some might believe that sentiments lead away from the truth. That is a position that one might attribute to the legal ideology of the rational (meaning *unemotional*) law. Others have the contrary opinion. They argue that sentiments do lead one closer to the truth, that people are guided by a moral sense, and that one can feel the truth. That is a position occupied famously by the Scottish moral theorists such as David Hume (1751) and Adam Smith (1759). They believe that people have a sense of justice, an inner feeling that guides people to natural law, and that moral sentiments are a guideline to the truth.

From an anthropological perspective, I would reject both approaches. The law is not about truth. Not in this world, at least. The law is about plausibility. As cynical as this might sound at first and despite the fact that it is often decried, this view would be widely supported by legal professionals. There is a connection between sentiments and plausibility. The legal proceeding is all about a competition to make things plausible. What I hope to have shown in this chapter is that this is a competition to establish an affective frame to assess whether a certain action appears plausible in light of the affective arrangement in which it has taken place. Emotions and affective dynamics play a key role here: only that which creates affective resonance with the arrangement in which it is embedded feels plausible. Plausibility hence comes into being through affective and emotional relational dynamics. It is itself a sentiment: a regime that governs how people assess the truth of an event or an action by and through affect and emotion.

4

THE SENTIMENT OF OBJECTIVITY

Arranging Objects and Subjects in the ICC Courtroom

Pour le colonisé, l'objectivité est toujours dirigée contre lui.[1]

Frantz Fanon, *Les damnés de la terre* (1961)

Law exists to regulate judgments. Judgments pervade all facets of human existence, because when people feel that they are confronted with choices, they have to decide what to do.[2] People can mobilize all kinds of criteria to help them arrive at these decisions. While these criteria vary widely from person to person, every human decision is made according to some rules – be they rather implicit or rather explicit, rather flexible or rather strict, rather informal or rather formalized. A judgment is hence always the result of a process of applying rules to a problem. The legal proceedings, the trial, is one manifestation of such processes.

One pervasive characteristic of legal proceedings is their relative complexity. This complexity often manifests itself in time-consuming procedures. The Dominic Ongwen trial, for instance, was approaching its fifth year and still not finished at the time of this writing. While international criminal trials are infamous for taking many years, even ordinary legal proceedings can last for days, weeks, and months. This is not only the case in Western legal systems; legal anthropologists have presented accounts of sometimes very lengthy legal proceedings from a great variety of cultural contexts.[3] The law provides a framework for ensuring that decisions are not made on a whim but in a thoughtful and reflected way. And while people frequently complain that the wheels of justice turn very slowly, they are also wary when legal proceedings go very quickly. There is a certain suspicion that an all-too-quick decision might not be all-too-just. It is, after all, one important function of the law to guarantee that the entire process is deliberate and carefully considered as a way of ensuring that a correct, appropriate, and just decision will ultimately be reached.

In Western legal thought, the law's concern that the proper amount of thought and deliberation go into a decision is encapsulated in the concept of objectivity. Legal proceedings must pass the test of objectivity to make sure that decisions are more likely to be right. What objectivity means, generally and in every single instance, is, of course, the subject of a great controversy that far surpasses the boundaries of the courtroom or even the law itself. Objectivity is at the very core of modernity. On the most general level, all major areas of contemporary global society – capitalist economy, democratic politics and the rule of law, and scientific research, to name but a few – claim to rely on objectivity in one way or another.

In this chapter, I take on the concept of objectivity. I challenge the assumption that objectivity is somehow antithetical to affect and emotion, an assumption that is widely communicated in legal education (Flower 2014). My argument is that the contrastive pair objectivity–emotion is a misconception. The opposite of objectivity is not emotion but subjectivity. From this very simple claim, I derive an alternative conceptual relationship between objectivity and the realm of feeling. Indeed, I argue that objectivity is itself a sentiment and that this sentiment is actively produced by actors in the courtroom. They assemble and arrange bodies, turning them into either objects or subjects, to support their claims and serve their agendas. The result is an affective arrangement of bodies, both physically and discursively, that creates objectivity in the subjective experiences of their audiences.

ONE VIDEO AND TWO BOOKS

On January 22, 2016, I was again seated in the visitors' gallery of courtroom one at the ICC in The Hague. In their presentation of the evidence against Dominic Ongwen, the prosecution played a short video that had been recorded by Ugandan army investigators shortly after the LRA had attacked the Lukodi IDP camp on May 24, 2004. The prosecution lawyer who introduced the video did so in a particularly dispassionate manner. Her face showed no sign of emotion. Her tone of voice was calm and monotonous. Her whole performance appeared distanced to me, even cold. Her lack of emotional expression contrasted sharply with the propositional content of her speech:

> As in Pajule, Odek and Abok, the civilians of Lukodi who fell victim to the LRA were living their day-to-day lives and were not taking active part in hostilities. The number of murdered and wounded civilians, the brutal nature of the crimes, the ages and identities of victims and the extent of destroyed civilian property all demonstrate that Ongwen's soldiers attacked the civilians of Lukodi deliberately. Your Honours can observe this in the video footage taken during a local investigation in the aftermath of the attack. A government pathologist, P-36, exhumed and examined 25 bodies revealing the identities of victims and the manner in which they died. Parts from this video were played to you by Mr Gumpert during his opening submission. On the screen now is the video. I have to warn members of the public that the video fragments I'm about to show are disturbing. You will see bodies of small children, some as young as three.[4]

After this introduction, the video was played. The video, which lasted just under one minute, depicted several dead bodies, some of them children, mutilated and partially burned. After the video stopped, the prosecuting attorney did not display any indication that she had been moved by the gruesome images. Instead, she went on to speak in the same "unemotional" manner as before: "The LRA fighters killed more than 45 civilians, including 12 children. They were shot, stabbed, strangled, burnt, and beaten to death. In contrast, not even one government soldiers was killed in the attack."[5]

When I witnessed this performance in the courtroom, I immediately thought, "This is what objectivity is." In the face of horror, the "objective" lawyer is not emotionally moved, but remains calm and cold, focused only on the mechanical, almost robotic application of the law. It is exactly at this point where the traditional critique of law-and-emotion scholarship starts. This strand of scholarship is based on the notion that there is an overarching, hegemonic legal ideology that needs to be exposed and debunked, namely that "the sphere of law admits only to reason; and vigilant policing is required to keep emotion from creeping in where it does not belong" (Maroney 2006, 120). In countering this claim and in an effort to come to a better understanding of the law, law-and-emotion scholarship very deliberately takes account of emotions in legal proceedings (Abrams and Keren 2000, 2009; Bandes and Blumenthal 2012, 162). From this perspective, the prosecution lawyer's strange performance can be easily explained as an attempt to conform to the "feeling rules" (Hochschild 1979) of a criminal trial, which allow for emotional displays only in certain situations, of which this presumably was not one.[6] She produced objectivity by suppressing emotion, or at least that is how it might appear.

About one year later, on January 16, 2017, after having spent several of the intervening months in northern Uganda, I sat once again in the courtroom in The Hague. In the meantime, the judges had decided that there was enough evidence to try Dominic Ongwen. That day, the prosecution presented its first witness: an anthropology professor specializing in northern Uganda. Having produced two books on the armed conflict and the LRA specifically, he was there to provide insights into the workings of the rebel militia and to contextualize Dominic Ongwen's crimes. When the expert appeared in the witness box, his two books were already there, prominently displayed on the table in front of him. As the prosecution lawyer, Benjamin Gumpert, began questioning the witness, he asked him to tell the court something about the two books and what was written in them.

QUESTIONED BY MR. GUMPERT: [9:36:41]

Q.	[9:36:43] One preliminary of my own, Professor . . . . You came into court with a binder and a couple of books I observed. Would I be right in thinking that the binder is a selection of documents, some 14 in number, which you were given during the course of the familiarisation process?
A.	[9:37:06] Yes, that's correct.
MR GUMPERT:	[9:37:07] Your Honours, I believe that all three members of the Bench, all three Judges have that binder. And indeed, I've caused copies to be printed so that we're all literally on the same page for Defence and Legal Representatives and indeed the interpreters and transcribers. Normally speaking, if I can just speak generally for a moment, when a witness comes into the witness box, there will be on every occasion a similar binder, but normally I wouldn't put it in front of the witness because we would be showing the witness document by document on the screen. But with an

expert witness like [the] Professor . . ., it struck me as highly likely that at some stage he might say in answer to a question: "Well, yes, that's right, but can I take you to tab 3 or 4," and we will be thereby better informed.

Q. I think also you've got two books. Are those books that you have either written or edited?

A. [9:38:10] Yes.

Q. [9:38:10] I'm grateful. I'll come to them in just a moment.

A. [9:38:14] Yeah. I just thought I might forget something I'd written, yeah.

Q. [9:38:18] An anxiety which I share often. Professor . . ., let's start with that title. Where are you a professor and in what discipline?[7]

This seemed to me to be another example of trying to create objectivity in the courtroom. A distinguished professor, having written well-researched books, providing expert knowledge to the court, knowledge that is properly annotated in documents for later reference. When I thought about this a bit more, however, it struck me that this kind of objectivity seemed not to be as "unemotional" as the earlier example. At the very beginning of the anthropology professor's testimony, he already appears to be joking with the prosecution lawyer. Asked about the books he had with him in the courtroom, he says that he brought them in case he forgets what he had written. The prosecution lawyer takes up the joke and adds that he himself is also often plagued by this fear. In fact, over the course of the two days in which the professor was questioned, he regularly made jokes, and the prosecution as well as the judges seemed to be amused from time to time.

This performance of the anthropological expert witness can be related to a debate in anthropology about the role of expert witnessing in legal proceedings.[8] Whether anthropologists can or should have a role in providing courts with expertise began to be broadly debated in US anthropology in the 1950s and 1960s, when anthropologists first started to be regularly called upon as expert witnesses, often in claims brought by indigenous communities in North America (Bens 2016). At that time, the notion of objectivity was at the core of the debate. While anthropologists initially were very much in favor of anthropological engagement in court cases, beginning in the late 1960s, it became more common among anthropologists to believe that the epistemological differences between the ideal of legal objectivity and the reality of anthropological knowledge production were so great as to be insurmountable and that communication between anthropologists and lawyers would inevitably lead to chronic misunderstandings and misrepresentations (Geertz 1983; Rigby and Sevareid 1992; Assier-Andrieu 2015). Anthropologists were simply not able to give the kind of yes-or-no answers to complex questions on cultural issues that the law demanded (Clifford 1988, 321–322). More recently, some (including myself) have criticized the vehemence with which anthropologists claim a deep epistemological divide between law and anthropology (Edmond 2004; Good 2004; Bens 2016; Zenker 2016), focusing on the power differences between law and anthropology instead of the epistemological differences (Höhne 2016). In a study of anthropological expertise in international criminal trials, Richard Wilson (2016) has recently rejected the view that anthropological accounts had less impact and carried less weight in court proceedings than more hard-science-based evidence using quantitative data. In fact, he argues that the opposite is the case. The ethnographic evidence of anthropological expert testimony, which generally relies on accessible narrative styles, is more convincing to judges and juries than numbers in tables and graphs (Wilson 2016, 731).

The impact of the performance of the anthropology professor in the Dominic Ongwen trial confirms this claim. In fact, the anthropologist was a very effective witness for the prosecution and seemed to relate well to the judges. It seems the courtroom might not, after all, be the modernist machine populated by robots, as some envision it. In fact, the emotionally relaxed atmosphere that both the witness and the prosecution lawyer were trying to establish did not seem antithetical to the witness's claim to scientific objectivity or legitimacy.

What are we to make of this, then? How can we understand objectivity in a new way, different from the predominant view that it is something that emerges when emotion is left out of the picture? In this chapter I argue that objectivity is something that is *felt* by actors and that they use it to guide their decisions. In other words, objectivity is a *sentiment* that emerges, as I have argued in this book, out of the affective relationality of bodies.

OBJECTS AND SUBJECTS IN THE COURTROOM

To approach the question of objectivity, one should be mindful of the courtroom's temporality and spatiality. The time and place of the acts in question and the time and space of the court proceedings do not overlap. Because of this, court proceedings are basically performances in which the past must be reenacted in the present. In these courtroom performances, actors must bring in evidence that makes the past materialize in the present proceeding. This is a profound act of constructing and producing legal knowledge. Humans play, of course, a critical role in that – particularly witnesses performing an oral account of past events. But nonhumans are similarly important: the bloody murder weapon, the videotape on which the crime is captured, the perpetrator's fingerprints made visible with powder on a piece of paper, the results of a DNA test saved in a PDF file. The trials at the ICC are no exception (see Figure 4.1). When ethnographically investigating the courtroom, one must take seriously not only the prosecution lawyer but also the video film she shows; not only the anthropology professor but also his documents and books.

From the perspective of affect theory that I have described so far, both human witnesses and nonhuman evidence in the courtroom can be construed as bodies. Bodies, in the way I have introduced the term in

Figure 4.1 A showcase in the foyer of the International Criminal Court in The Hague exhibiting the kinds of material evidence that are often of relevance in the ICC's criminal trials. (A black and white version of this figure will appear in some formats. For the color version, please refer to the plate section.)
Source: Jonas Bens

Chapter 1, include all entities that have the "power (or potential) to affect or be affected" (Massumi 2002, 15). The courtroom is an arrangement filled with human and nonhuman bodies, material and immaterial bodies. To understand the production of evidence in the courtroom, one should focus on the specific ways in which bodies affect and are affected by each other in court.

In such a view, an ethnographic approach to the courtroom assumes that affective dynamics constantly pervade courtroom performances, even in those moments when the performance would appear to be at its most "unemotional," and even from the viewpoint of the actors themselves. When a performance is described as being void of emotions, it indicates more a shift in affective dynamics than the absence of affective dynamics. A law-and-affect approach, then, operates from a different angle than a more traditional law-and-emotion focus. One does not look so much for emotional expressions in legal proceedings: the shouting, the crying, the righteous indignation. One rather tries to sketch out in a more exploratory manner how the relational dynamics between bodies might affect what happens in court. This opens up other affective dynamics for investigation that are usually not categorized as emotional episodes. The analysis then focuses on different questions: the positioning of the prosecution lawyer in relation to the video and how this moves other bodies in the courtroom are issues that become more interesting. Whether the prosecutor presents it in an "emotional" or an "unemotional" way becomes a secondary concern. In fact, moments in which emotion might, on the surface, not be performed by courtroom actors become relevant. If an expert witness is arranged in the courtroom with other nonhumans, such as his books, the ethnographer focuses on this as an affective dynamic, and the question becomes how the prosecution and the defense try to modulate these relational dynamics between bodies. In their courtroom performances, opposing actors compete with one another in an effort to establish the most plausible version of what has transpired and how these past events can be assessed legally. The actor who most successfully evokes the sentiment of objectivity wins the competition.

I argue for thinking of objectivity as an affective dynamic between bodies. To that end, I build on Loraine Daston and Peter Galison's (2007) work on the history of objectivity and propose to differentiate between two kinds of bodies in the courtroom: subjects and objects. Daston and Galison have shown that the history of scientific objectivity is characterized by a process of differentiating subjects and objects from each other. How this differentiation is achieved by the scientific community is subject to historical change. According to Daston and Galison, the dominant paradigm of mechanical objectivity, which is shared throughout the natural sciences and is the foundation of the objectivity paradigm of modernity, emerged in nineteenth-century Europe with the invention of photography. In this view, subjects and objects are conceptualized as antithetical. Science becomes the process through which subjects (researchers) investigate their objects of study. The ideal of scientific objectivity is to represent the object *inter*-subjectively, meaning that everyone – that is, all the *subjects* – can conceive of the object in the same way. The photograph seemed to approximate this ideal: it represents the object of science "as it is."

As I have already indicated above, anthropologists do not uncritically accept this ideal of mechanical objectivity. As early as the 1960s anthropologists across the board began to reject the separation of subject and object as the starting point of their investigations. In 1964 Jacques Maquet argued in his *Current Anthropology* article "Objectivity in Anthropology" that the decolonization of Africa showed the degree to which the discipline of anthropology, conceived in nineteenth-century Europe, had been inextricably entangled with colonialism and how its findings have been colored by it. According to Maquet, this clearly demonstrated how much the researcher's perspective matters in anthropological research. He highlights

> the fact that the anthropologist perceives the social phenomena he studies not from nowhere but from a certain point of view, which is his existential situation. To define adequately an anthropological study, it is not enough to indicate its object, e.g., "the social structure of the Mundang"; one should add "as seen by an anthropologist belonging to the socioeconomic middle stratum of the white colonial minority."
>
> (Maquet 1964, 51)

This has, for Maquet, clear ethical implications. "Societies studied by anthropologists have tended to view the attention of this discipline as a sign of implicit discrimination; to be an object of research is never pleasing, and if one feels, as many educated Africans do today, that selection for study by the 'science of savages' expresses the European conviction of difference and superiority, the unpleasantness becomes painful" (Maquet 1964, 51).

The consequence is that anthropological knowledge emerges not from the separation of subject and objects, but from their convergence: "How can an anthropologist verify what another has written about a certain society if the description or analysis is determined not only by the object (the society studied) but by the subject (the anthropologist) as well?" (Maquet 1964, 50). Maquet still argues for objectivity, but an objectivity that comes about through a dialectical relationship with subjectivity: "A perspectivistic knowledge is not as such nonobjective; it is partial. It reflects an external reality but only an aspect of it, the one visible from the particular spot, social and individual, where the anthropologist was placed. Nonobjectivity creeps in when the partial aspect is considered as the global one" (Maquet 1964, 54).[9] The approach to objectivity that Maquet described in the early 1960s had become mainstream in anthropology by the late 1980s and early 1990s, when the methodological programs for ethnographic research that are still dominant today were popularized: reflexivity (Marcus 1991) and the explicit acknowledgment of the ethnographer's positionality (Abu-Lughod 1991) in ethnographic writing.

What we can learn from this debate is that objectivity is a phenomenon that relationally emerges through the interaction between objects and subjects. Anthropologists have a problem with legal proceedings because legal "objectivity" focuses too much on objects, to the exclusion of subjects. Actors try to produce objectivity by bringing human or nonhuman, material or immaterial bodies into the courtroom and positioning them in relation to each other *as objects*.

Another lesson we can take from the objectivity debate is that bodies are turned into objects by denying their subjectivity. The object is to be looked at; the subject looks at the object. While the subject has intentionality, the object does not. While the pure subject has a free will, the pure object has no agenda – no *agency* – of its own. In reality, these pure forms of subject and object do not exist. In fact, actors constantly disagree on the degree to which bodies have intentionality and where the border between object and subject lies. This question is especially decisive in criminal trials, where guilt or innocence must be determined. Actors in the courtroom therefore struggle to mobilize bodies and to define them as object or subject in the way that best suits their agenda. To produce objectivity, bodies in the courtroom have to be objectified, which – as its flipside – entails stripping them of their subjectivity.

ARRANGING OBJECTS IN THE COURTROOM

Let me revisit the two short scenes I introduced at the beginning of the chapter to illustrate what I mean. First, there is the anthropological expert witness who was questioned with his books placed on the table in front of him. While the anthropologist was a human body in the affective arrangement of the court, the books themselves had a very prominent role. Sometimes, they even seemed more important than their author. Over the course of two days, the expert witness was time and again referred to specific passages from these books, both by the prosecution and the defense. The expert would regularly answer these questions by paraphrasing parts of his books, sometimes even reading a few sentences out loud. It appeared as if the books themselves were being questioned, and the author was there only to lend them his voice.

The fact that texts are brought into the courtroom to serve as evidence, even if their authors are present, is in itself not unusual. In a criminal trial, prosecutors and defense lawyers must always narrate those events of the past that are relevant to the guilt or innocence of the accused. They narrate a version of the facts that furthers their agenda, either to accuse or to defend the person on trial. To that end, they not only narrate freely but also read texts out loud. They quote from investigation reports and the reports of forensic experts. But often they also read out from summaries that they themselves have written and put into the file. This is a rhetorical strategy known as "quoting from the case file" (D'hondt and Houwen 2014). Trials are densely intertextually structured communicative events, and the performative power of criminal proceedings depends on discursive strategies to link different texts to one another. The larger the number of texts that can be mobilized in this context, the better; they can be woven into the intertextual web and take on a certain power independent of their author.

My point is similar. But beyond being describable as an intertextual web, the courtroom is also an affective arrangement of bodies. Texts, like human witnesses, books, or bloody murder weapons, change the affective arrangement when they are brought into the courtroom as bodies. Typed up in files, displayed on computer screens, or printed in books, texts can easily be brought into the courtroom as a specific kind of body: as objects.

To be clear, the fact that a book is a thing rather than a person is not what determines its status as an object. There are a few complications we have to introduce before we can make this determination. First, we have to be mindful that the distinction between persons and things is not a cultural universal. In fact, which bodies are categorized as persons and which as things depends very much on the cultural context, as anthropological studies have revealed time and again (Strathern 1988; Latour 1991; Viveiros de Castro 1998; Descola 2005). The law has its role in creating and maintaining the systems that determine this distinction between persons and things (Pottage and Mundy 2004). The courtroom itself can be the space where these determinations are made, particularly through the manipulation of affective and emotional dynamics (Bens 2018b).

The second complication is that the divide between person and thing is not coterminous with the divide between subject and object. As I have argued above, subjects and objects are differentiated from each other by their relational position. Subjects investigate objects. As such, the degree to which a body is imbued with intentionality determines the degree to which it can be subject or remains object. One can relate to a thing *as* an object or *as* a subject, and one can relate to a person *as* an object or *as* a subject. In practice, all four of these categories can be in flux; while one might think of the systems distinguishing persons, things, objects, and subjects as relatively stable, the courtroom is a space where there is a constant struggle between the parties to effectively ascribe these categories to the bodies in the affective arrangement.

Our anthropological expert witness is not alone in the courtroom; he is accompanied by two books. Three bodies, one would think: one person and two things, one subject and two objects. But this, I argue, is only the result of a careful production process designed to create specific affective dynamics – and it is not an uncontested result. The prosecution wanted these books to enable a certain narrative about the LRA and the context of the conflict to unfold, and to establish that narrative as the objective basis on which to judge Dominic Ongwen's crimes. To realize their full potential as objects testifying to an objective reality, these books need to be arranged in such a way that they appear to be not too closely related to the subject that made them. They need a certain independence and to take shape as bodies in and of themselves. As the court transcript presented at the beginning of this chapter shows, the expert is asked to introduce the two books and describe them separately, which he does extensively. In the course of being questioned by the prosecution, the books – one a monograph, the other an edited volume – are mentioned over and over again. As can be evidenced from the court transcript, the prosecution makes reference to these books no less than twenty times in the course of the six-hour court day.

The prosecuting attorney wanted to make the books appear as independent objects. To do so he has to create separation between the books and their author. While the anthropologist has an academic agenda with regard to the LRA conflict and his own specific ideas about how to interpret the armed conflict in northern Uganda, the books must be perceived as independent of this subjective intentionality of the expert. They must be able to speak independently and to aid the expert in his testimony by recounting scientific facts. Here the distinction between object and subject is far from simple, clear-cut, or dichotomous; rather, it is a spectrum or a continuum along which one can assess the degree of intentionality, and therefore the degree of subjectivity, a person or a thing has. The books can help the prosecution's case if the prosecutor can successfully make them appear to be more of an object to courtroom audiences than the expert. This, then, makes the entire arrangement of bodies appear more objective.

These attempts to establish an objective arrangement did not go unchallenged. It was in the defense's best interests to make the books appear as subjective as possible. The best way to achieve this is to relate them closer to their author, to make the books entirely dependent on their author. The defense wanted to establish an affective arrangement in which the two bodies are merged: one witness, one voice, one subject, one opinion among many.

How did the defense try to achieve this? The lead council of the defense team, a seasoned criminal lawyer and former member of Parliament from northern Uganda, also made reference to the books right at the beginning of his performance. But he did so mockingly, smirking sarcastically all the while. As a running gag, the defense council used the phrase "that celebrated book of yours" when he talked about the expert's monograph on the armed conflict in northern Uganda,[10] and he asked the witness several times to read out passages from his own book. The running gag obviously stuck, because the presiding judge took it up ironically when he admonished the defense lawyer for overdoing it a bit with his insistence on having the expert read aloud from his own book:

A:	. . . Do you want me to continue reading, to continue reading? Or that's enough?
PRESIDING JUDGE. . . :	[12:00:59] I think we should not entertain now reading of the celebrated book in its entirety. I would really appreciate it if we could now come up with a question that refers to the passage that [the] Professor . . . has just read out.
MR ODONGO:	[12:01:20] I am much obliged for your guidance.
Q:	[12:01:31] Professor, what would you make of that narrative?[11]

In an important respect the defense lawyer's emotional display, interjecting ridicule and irony, was surely an attempt to disturb the emotional mode of earnest solemnity and gravitas that contributes to the appearance of professional expertise. However, I read this also as an attempt to manipulate the affective arrangement by changing the relationality between the expert as a subject and the books as objects. The phrase "this celebrated book *of yours*" is a way of emphasizing that the author and the books are not so much different bodies, witnessing independently of each other, but that one is only the other's proxy. The rhetorical strategy of having the witness read out long excerpts from his books relates the bodies closely to each other, creating an intimate, unbreakable link between them and imbuing the books with the subjectivity of the author.

In his cross-examination of the anthropological expert witness, the defense lawyer further attempted to change the affective arrangement by transforming yet other bodies from objects into subjects: the spirits.

In northern Uganda spirits play a major role in everyday life. They are part of both Christian beliefs, especially in the many Pentecostal churches that dot the northern Ugandan landscape, and traditional religious forms that preceded colonialism and are still practiced today. As mentioned in Chapter 3, how one approaches the spiritual aspects of the LRA is of great importance in assessing the degree of Dominic Ongwen's guilt. The LRA leader, Joseph Kony, is an *ajwaka*, a spirit medium. It is widely reported by former fighters in the LRA that Kony's power over the spirits translated into power over his fighters. The spirits with which Kony was in contact constantly surveilled the members of the LRA and told him about any insubordination. It was even widely believed inside the LRA that because of his special relationship to the spirits, Kony could read minds and knew if fighters were making plans to run away.[12] Highlighting the role of spirits in the order of the LRA is key to the defense's strategy of arguing that Dominic Ongwen was under duress during his time in the LRA, an approach the prosecution disparagingly referred to as the "brainwash defense."

This difference between the defense's and the prosecution's respective assessments of the importance of spirits mirrors a discussion in the scholarly literature on the role of religious beliefs in the LRA. Some studies argue that spirit beliefs play an important role for the LRA and its precursor movements (Ward 2001; Cline 2003) and have attempted to understand the internal logic of these beliefs (Behrend 1993). Others have forcefully emphasized that the LRA is first and foremost a rebel militia with a rational political agenda (Branch 2005; Finnström 2008; Allen and Vlassenroot 2010a) and are interested in its religious component only as an instrument that the LRA uses to advance its rational agenda (Titeca 2010). Translated into the discussion in the courtroom, nothing less than what kind of perpetrator Dominic Ongwen represents is at stake in this debate. And it is at its core a question of affect: Is Dominic Ongwen a rational political actor following a rational political agenda, or is he an actor under duress, constantly surveilled by supernatural actors – something that would, from a modernist perspective, be categorized as a premodern irrational belief.

The defense lawyer pressed his point by asking the anthropologist to differentiate between the different kinds of spirits present in northern Uganda. He was particularly keen on pressing the expert on the difference between *jok* and *cen*. The kind of spirit that would possess a spirit medium such as Joseph Kony would usually be called *jok* (Behrend 1999, 22–23). The concept of *jok* goes back to precolonial times and denotes spirits that are deities, sometimes tied to a specific place, which do not necessarily originate in the world of the living (Atkinson 1994, 88; P'Bitek 2011 [1971], 35–38). The concept of *cen* is different. In northern Uganda, many believe that people who have died in a violent way leave behind traces of their spirit in the world of the living. These *cen* can haunt those whom they see as responsible for their violent deaths. To get rid of *cen*, people must undergo specific rituals that are presided over by religious specialists and which often include paying reparations to the family of the deceased. This is highly relevant in the context of the armed conflict, where many people have died violent deaths.

In his answers, the anthropological expert described *cen* as a kind of spiritual pollution or emanation rather than as the more or less personified remnant of a dead person. At this point the defense lawyer claimed that the expert had an insufficient understanding of the spirits in northern Uganda. On the surface, the defense lawyer was only testing the expert's knowledge in the hope of exposing gaps in his expertise. And indeed, there was a certain discrepancy between the anthropologist's explanation and what I had learned. During my research in northern Uganda, the concept of *cen* often came up. Many of my interlocutors noted that it is very dangerous even to be near people who have been closely associated with violent death and have not undergone the necessary cleansing rituals. Based on how most people described *cen* to me, I would also characterize it quite clearly as the soul or spirit of a dead person rather than as an unspecified spiritual pollution (Behrend 1999, 25).

But this kind of rhetoric served yet another purpose beyond disputing the witness's interpretation of Acholi religious beliefs. The defense lawyer was trying to shape the affective arrangement of the trial. By invoking the spirits, he brought into the courtroom another kind of body and attempted to relate to them as subjects rather than as objects. The prosecution brought in the anthropologist in order to portray the LRA as first and foremost a political movement. International media coverage had often highlighted the religious and spiritual aspects of the LRA by calling it a "cult" rather than a "rebel force." The expert disagreed with that characterization. In his view, the spirits were objects, not subjects. The LRA leaders used them as mere instruments; they had no agency of their own.

The co-presence of spirits in the affective arrangement of the courtroom disturbed this narrative. Acknowledging the fact that people in northern Uganda experience spirits not only as a social fact in their lives, but also as actors imbued with intentionality, hence as subjects rather than objects, changed the perspective on the intricacies of criminal responsibility. Many of the young recruits in the LRA were forced to kill very soon after their abduction. The fact that the *cen* of their victims would haunt them made them dependent on the religious cleansing rituals performed inside the LRA.[13] Bringing spirits into the courtroom as subjects rather than objects was meant to turn the relative plausibility of the versions of the past that have been presented in the favor of the defense. The presence of spirits mitigated Dominic Ongwen's personal guilt for his crimes; in fact, the accused might still be haunted by the *cen* of his victims. The prosecution's arrangement of objectivity is radically disrupted when spirits appear to be imbued with subjectivity.

With this perspective on the prosecution and the defense entangled in a game of relating objects and subjects in mind, we can also revisit the scene in which the prosecution lawyer introduced the gruesome video. Her performance was surely intended to bring the video in as an object depicting images of dead children as facts. The clip itself should not have an agenda of its own. This objectivity is potentially disturbed by the subject who introduces the object, the prosecution lawyer herself. One can read her performance not as the attempt to create objectivity by suppressing her emotions, but as the attempt to make herself as a body – as much as possible – into an object. To that end she suppressed any emotional display – not because emotion or affect in itself hinders objectivity, but because the display of emotion could give the appearance of too much intentionality in introducing the video footage. She was more interested in presenting herself as not too subjective than as not too emotional.

Attempts can also be made to turn human actors, despite being persons with a presumption of free will, intentionality, and subjectivity, into objects in the arrangement of bodies in the courtroom. The "self-objectification" by the prosecuting lawyer is one example. But it can also be advantageous to turn opposing witnesses into objects rather than subjects – particularly in courtroom settings more adversarial than the ICC, such as in Anglo-American courts, where strict turn-taking rules between defense and prosecution are enforced and judges have little control over witness examinations. Linguistic anthropologists have investigated how lawyers in the Anglo-American court system assert discursive hegemony over witness testimony through certain questioning techniques, including micromanaging witnesses' accounts through leading yes/no-questions during cross-examination (Matoesian 1998) or disturbing the narrative flow of the opposing witness through constant objections (Matoesian 2018). These strategies of sabotaging witnesses' attempts to take control of their own narrative can also be interpreted as an attempt to de-subjectify them as bodies in the courtroom.[14]

The performance of the prosecution lawyer making herself into an object in the Dominic Ongwen trial nevertheless remains striking. The video is expected to produce great emotional intensity in the viewers. This emotional reaction would likely be further intensified if it were mimicked by the human being introducing it. This, however, would arrange the two bodies – the video and the lawyer – in close proximity to each other and create an identification of the one with the other. This, however, is not necessarily in the best interests of the prosecution. This becomes understandable when one accounts for the highly contentious nature of this particular piece of evidence. The video was shot by the Ugandan army, one party in the armed conflict in northern Uganda. As I mentioned in Chapter 1, the trial against Dominic Ongwen is the only one regarding the conflict in northern Uganda being prosecuted at the ICC. Although many claim that the Ugandan army likewise committed war crimes, no indictments have been brought against its commanders. Moreover, the prosecution relied heavily on materials provided by the army as evidence against Dominic Ongwen. The resulting legitimacy issues regarding the case are severe.

The video represents these dilemmas. The images show the destruction of a camp and its casualties, but they do not provide any proof as to who commenced the attack and who killed the children. A representative of the victims in northern Uganda later told me during my fieldwork that this particular video was not very helpful because many people believed that Ugandan army forces themselves sometimes killed civilians and then later blamed the LRA for the attack (Bens 2019a). Many people in northern Uganda, including some who are sympathetic to the ICC's efforts to bring charges against Ongwen, are highly skeptical when it comes to evidence provided by the Ugandan army. When these perspectives are added to the equation, it becomes that much more difficult to convincingly present the video as having no agenda of its own, that is, as an object and not a subjective piece of evidence.

The prosecution lawyer was hence well advised to be careful with the video. Its affective power was significant, but clumsily arranged it could backfire. If the prosecution lawyer were to relate herself too closely to the video, her own power to affect the courtroom could be diminished. Better to create an affective arrangement in which there is a certain distance between herself, on the one hand, and the video and those who provided it – the Ugandan army – on the other hand. The carefully staged unemotional display now appears more like a measure to shape the affective arrangement by managing the relational positions of subjects and objects within it.

***

Objectivity is a tricky thing. In the perspective I am advocating in this book, the courtroom is not a space for an objective proceeding that is made possible by cleansing it of all emotion. The contrary is the case. Objectivity is a sentiment. It must be felt by the participants of the trial. They can feel that a certain version of the past is objective if courtroom actors have skillfully managed to curate the affective arrangement of bodies in such a way that it creates this sentiment of objectivity which, like all sentiments, can only be created in affective relationalities.

Actors in the courtroom constantly try to manipulate the affective arrangement of the trial in order to let certain bodies relate to other bodies in specific ways. As one party attempts to affectively produce a relationship of bodies, another party usually aims at sabotaging this attempt. In these acts of sabotage as well as attempts to establish alternative arrangements, both emotional displays and more tempered, "rational" rhetoric can be observed. But both modes – the "emotional" as well as the "rational" – are affective in the sense I have laid out here. The process of producing objectivity before court can therefore be characterized as the participants' attempt to produce specific affective dynamics, and not as an effort to cast aside affect and emotion altogether. The production of objectivity can be seen as the attempt to mobilize objects and to relationally entangle them in an affective arrangement. To create these affective dynamics actors in a courtroom constantly compete to mobilize objects – de-subjectifying some bodies when it is in their interest to do so, and subjectifying other bodies when doing so might undermine the interests of their opponents.

One is tempted to think about this competition over the most plausible narrative as a game of allocating "credibility points" to, or withdrawing them from, individual bodies. The perspective of objectivity as dependent on the relational position of objects and subjects breaks with this rather simplified assumption. Bodies, be they persons or things, objects or subjects, have performative power, not because of the "credibility points" they accumulate as individual entities, but with respect to the relational position they occupy within an affective arrangement. Actors in the courtroom compete with each other by attempting to introduce bodies and by relating and positioning them in specific ways. The degree to which they are able to manipulate the affective arrangement to their advantage determines their chances of successfully establishing an "objective" version of the past.

5

THE SENTIMENT OF JUSTICE

Navigating Normative Pluralism in Northern Uganda

At one extreme, cash; at the other, love.

E. P. Thompson, *Whigs and Hunters* (1975)

What is the relationship between law and justice? The answer to this question, which might easily be categorized as one of the more exciting and mysterious questions in the theory of law and politics, is, unsurprisingly, complicated. To answer it, we should bring to the fore the complications it entails.

The first complication we have to introduce concerns the basic premise of the question. It is already based on the assumption that law and justice have a relationship, meaning that they are not the same thing, nor are they completely separate from each other. They are somehow related and I would argue (perhaps contrary to others) that they cannot exist independent of each other, that they are mutually interdependent.

On the one hand, law exists, presumably, to bring about justice. As such, the law is a tool, an instrument used to judge actions and events as just or unjust according to the rules, processes, and methods it sets up. This is in accord with the self-understanding of most legal practitioners. They conceive of the law as a "means to an end" (Riles 2004), and the end is justice. On the other hand, the law seems never to be able to guarantee that it can deliver on its promise to bring justice. The rules and processes that are aimed at bringing justice do not always succeed. As Jacques Derrida (1989) has convincingly reminded us, any legal process guided by rules ultimately cannot circumvent the moment of judgment. And a judgment – according to Derrida's simple claim – can always go one way or the other. If there is no alternative there is no judgment, only a simple mechanical operation. A judgment always entails a choice, and a choice cannot circumvent the moment of indeterminacy, the moment when it could go either this way or the other way. It is the moment of judgment, the moment of indeterminacy, that separates law from justice.

I think it is impossible to approach the question of the relationship between law and justice without investigating the moment of judgment, because that is where law and justice interact and where their boundaries become porous. The moment of judgment is always concrete; it has a time, a place, a social and cultural context. It involves bodies – persons, things, and all the other kinds of bodies I have discussed in the preceding chapters – that are arranged and related to each other. To pick up on the terminology I have developed in this book, judgments are always embedded in affective arrangements and embroiled in atmospheres. In this chapter, I argue that justice itself is a sentiment: an evaluative regime of meaning embedded in and colored by affect and emotion. Without understanding the sentimental dimension of justice, it is difficult to grasp the moment of judgment.

But we have to introduce a second complication. In social reality, law and justice do not exist in the singular. People sometimes vehemently disagree about the content of justice, and they also disagree about the normative systems according to which one determines what is just and what is not. Legal anthropologists have always criticized the idea of "legal centrism," namely, that there is only "the law" and that it is the law of "the" state. They have argued, rather, that "legal pluralism" is the norm, not the exception, meaning that people's lives are governed by a plurality of normative orders – official and unofficial law, national and international law, formal and informal law, secular law and religious law, written law and customary law, to name a few of the categories one can use (Griffiths 1986; Merry 1988; Benda-Beckmann 2002; Benda-Beckman and Turner 2018).[1] If we take this plurality of normative orders seriously, it means that there is also a plurality of imaginaries of justice, something like a "justice pluralism." And because there is a complex relationship between law and justice, the plurality of normative systems and the plurality of imaginaries of justice are connected. Specific kinds of law are connected to specific kinds of justice, albeit still quite loosely connected.

If we take up both of these complications in the relationship between law and justice, we can approach the problem in all its complexity. People make judgments about justice according to a specific set of legal rules, although this set of rules does not predetermine the decision. But people also choose a specific set of legal rules in the first place according to which they want to make their judgment about justice. In other words, people not only regularly switch between different imaginaries of justice, but also between different normative orders that guide and frame their judgments about justice. Sometimes they choose the normative system that best serves the kind of justice they imagine. Sometimes the normative system they are attached to shapes the kind of justice they are able to imagine.

The relationship between law and justice must, therefore, be approached by investigating how people navigate the pluralism of normative orders and of imaginaries of justice that they are confronted with. They navigate this plurality not in a mechanical way, but as feeling bodies. Sometimes they consciously decide for or against a normative order, for or against a certain kind of justice. Sometimes they feel drawn to and are seduced by a certain normative order or conception of justice; other times they do not think about it at all because it feels as if it is their only choice. How one can describe this navigation using of the idea of sentiment is the topic of this chapter.

A CONVERSATION ABOUT JUSTICE IN NORTHERN UGANDA

In the month of August 2016, I was seated in the relatively spacious town hall of Pajule, a village in northern Uganda about one and a half hours by bus from the town of Gulu. Four members of the community had agreed to discuss their feelings about the Dominic Ongwen case, which had just that year been brought before the International Criminal Court in The Hague. In the early 2000s, the village was the location of a camp for internally displaced persons. On October 10, 2003, Lord's Resistance Army fighters under the command of Dominic Ongwen attacked the Pajule IDP camp, looted it, abducted men, women, and children, and killed many civilians. The four community members I talked with that day were engaged in organizing a day of commemoration for this 2003 massacre that was scheduled to take place about two weeks later. I had come to ask them about the Ongwen case and the ICC because I wanted to know if they felt that the ICC was a legitimate institution and if they supported its case against the former LRA commander.

When I had this conversation, I had already spent quite some time in northern Uganda. During this time, and again when I returned for another fieldwork phase at the beginning of 2018, it was my goal to investigate the local workings of international criminal justice, particularly regarding the Ongwen case before the ICC. One goal was to investigate the ICC's outreach work in the region through ethnographic observation, work which I have described in Chapter 2. Another was to come to terms with how people in northern Uganda – a region which was heavily affected by the war – assessed the justice or injustice of the transitional justice measures that were instituted by the ICC and other actors. To that end I conducted several dozen interviews in which I asked people about different aspects of their perceptions and assessments of transitional justice measures in northern Uganda. An important component of my research strategy was extended group interviews in villages that had hosted IDP camps in the early 2000s and were heavily affected by the violence – including all four villages where massacres were formally among the charges against Dominic Ongwen. With the help of MA students from the Peace and Security Studies Program at Gulu University, I also collected ninety short interviews in three villages that were differentially affected by the violence to get a sense of how opinions differed relative to people's personal involvement with the events under scrutiny at the ICC. In addition to these conversations with people in the countryside, I also conducted about twenty audio-taped conversations in English with local activists, politicians, and traditional and religious leaders, most of whom resided in Gulu. I selected these conversation partners because they were representative of important societal groups. Many of them also have, as individuals, a significant impact on public opinion as it is discussed in the local and national media.

In addition to the numerous informal chats I had over the course of my fieldwork, I draw heavily from these interviews in the course of this chapter. The conversation I had on that August day in Pajule was quite typical of many others I had with massacre survivors' associations in rural northern Uganda. My interlocutors told me that they supported the ICC proceedings. They said that they and many others felt a need for "justice" in the community, and they hoped that the ICC might be able to deliver it. But they also highlighted the normative pluralism that governs the transitional justice landscape in northern Uganda.

International Criminal Law

This positive attitude toward the ICC is not the mainstream view in northern Uganda. The Ongwen trial is only the latest focal point in a long-standing discussion about the ICC's transitional justice intervention in northern Uganda (Allen 2006; Branch 2011). In the early 2000s, shortly after the Court started its operations, it was the Ugandan government under President Yoweri Kaguta Museveni that had referred the case of war crimes in northern Uganda to the ICC. At that time, many people in northern Uganda perceived this as a move by the government to recruit the international community in its fight against the LRA. Many in the north feared that the ICC might impede the peace process and were therefore deeply suspicious of Museveni's motives. At that time a majority of people in the north were critical of the ICC's indictments of the top five LRA commanders, including Dominic Ongwen, and many still are.

There is a broader background to this debate in northern Uganda. At the time of my conversation in Pajule, there was a massive crisis in the ICC's perceived legitimacy in Africa (Werle, Fernandez, and Vormbaum 2014; Clarke, Knotterus, and de Volder 2016). The ICC's investigations and proceedings were openly criticized as a form of neocolonialism. Although most African states were initially in favor of the establishment of the ICC, in 2009 the winds shifted among the African Union member states that are signatories to the Rome Statute. That year the Court put out an arrest warrant for the then sitting and since ousted president of Sudan, Omar Al-Bashir, for war crimes in the Darfur conflict. This moment is believed to be the turning point when the relationship between the ICC and the African states started to deteriorate (Jalloh, Akande, and Plessis 2011; Cole 2013). Since then, the African Union has criticized the indictment practice of the ICC in several decisions and resolutions.[2]

Recently, the Ugandan government has been at the forefront of this "pan-Africanist pushback" (Clarke 2019). After he had won his fifth term in office, President Yoweri Museveni invited Omar Al-Bashir to his inauguration ceremony. Instead of arresting the Sudanese president, as would have been his obligation under the Rome Statute, Museveni officially recognized Al-Bashir in his speech and welcomed him in Uganda. In his remarks, he referred to the ICC as "a bunch of useless people."[3]

When I asked my conversation partners about Museveni's criticism of the ICC, they looked at each other and smiled ironically. Some shook their heads. In their opinion, Museveni had his own motives for criticizing the ICC. His ICC bashing had to do with his position in the African Union, where he wanted to raise his profile. Then there was his relationship with Kenyan President Uhuru Kenyatta – also a target of an ICC investigation. In any case, Museveni's new opinion of the ICC had little to do with northern Uganda, they implied. His flip-flopping with regard to his support of the ICC was evidence enough that his motives were sinister. In our conversation it became obvious that Museveni's newfound anti-ICC rhetoric and his anti-colonial sentiment did not resonate well with my interlocutors.

In fact, my conversation partners displayed little, if any, trust in the Museveni government. In the late 1980s and the early 1990s, when Museveni, who is from southwestern Uganda, had just overthrown his predecessor, Tito Okello, and therefore ended northern dominance of the country's government, there was much popular support for several rebel movements against the new government – among them the LRA. After years of violence, however, little sympathy remained for the LRA in the north. Nevertheless, suspicion against Museveni's government remained strong. Election results for the National Resistance Movement (NRM), Museveni's party, and the president himself are exceptionally weak in the north relative to other parts of the country.[4] In the early 2000s, when Museveni called in the ICC, most northerners were opposed to the Court, not least because Museveni supported it. Although this attitude is still prevalent, I met some people during my research who argued along the same lines, only the other way around now: if Museveni does not like the ICC anymore, then perhaps Court might not be so bad after all.

National Criminal Law in Uganda

There are several other options to come to terms with the violence of the past that could serve as alternatives to trials before the ICC. Although I had already learned that my interlocutors supported the ICC, I was still curious about how they felt about those other options, so I asked them how they would feel about a national criminal trial against Ongwen.

There already exists a structure to adjudicate LRA fighters in Uganda, which was born out of the peace negotiations that took place between the LRA and the Ugandan government from 2006 to 2008.[5] During these talks, questions of accountability and reconciliation were discussed, the so-called agenda item three. These issues were, of course, contentious because they dealt with punishment of criminal acts by LRA and UPDF fighters. At that point, the ICC had already indicted the five LRA commanders, among them Joseph Kony, the LRA leader, and Dominic Ongwen. Many thought that fear of being prosecuted in The Hague would keep the LRA from signing a peace deal. It was therefore agreed that a special division of the Ugandan High Court, the International Crimes Division (ICD), should be established to adjudicate war crimes committed during the conflict.[6] As the Rome Statute, which governs the jurisdiction of the ICC, includes a strict complementarity clause whereby the ICC can step in only if national courts cannot or will not adjudicate the crimes enumerated in the Statute, it would have been up to the ICD to ensure that the top LRA commanders were tried before a Ugandan court (El Zeidy 2008).[7] In the end, Joseph Kony, the leader of the LRA, did not sign the peace deal, but the ICD was created nonetheless. Since its establishment in 2008, the ICD has had only one case: against the former LRA commander Thomas Kwoyelo (McNamara 2013; Macdonald and Porter 2016).

My interlocutors were wary of the idea of having Ongwen tried in Uganda. When I mentioned the Thomas Kwoyelo case, they were hesitant to talk about it and looked at each other as if they hoped they would not have to be the first to reply. Finally, one of them gave a diplomatic answer. He said that the Kwoyelo case was special in many ways and that they did not know too many details about it. Generally, my conversation partners said that it was also an advantage that Ongwen was tried in far-off The Hague. The situation was still somewhat volatile, they said. It was still possible that some relative of Ongwen's might show up to call for revenge. A local trial would give too much visibility to the details of who said what against whom. Moreover, on a general level, they talked about a distrust of the Ugandan court system, which served the interests of the government more than the interests of the LRA's victims in the countryside. As such, they were somewhat relieved that the case was not adjudicated in the courthouse in Gulu.

Customary Law

As the conversation progressed, I asked the four community members about traditional justice mechanisms – particularly the Acholi system of customary law – as a proposed alternative to a criminal trial in The Hague.

Like many African legal systems, one of the general features of the Acholi customary legal system is that it is more communally oriented, especially in comparison to Western legal systems (Woodman and Obliade 1995). The most important political unit of Acholi traditional society is the clan, a kinship group that consists of several family subgroups, headed by a clan elder, the *rwot*.[8] When individuals breach Acholi law (including acts considered criminal offenses by the national legal system, such as the killing of a person), it is seen as the responsibility of the individual's clan. If the offense has occurred within the clan, the clan elders are responsible for delivering judgment. If the offense has occurred between members of different clans, the clan elders of the two clans come together to meet and engage in negotiations. While clan elders can punish members of their own clan, they cannot punish the member of another clan without fear of retaliation. Because of this, these interclan negotiations are directed toward reparations rather than the punishment of the perpetrator. After the clan elders have agreed upon the amount of reparations, a series of rituals is conducted. First, the offender must engage in truth-telling, that is, he or she must truthfully admit to having committed the offense. Then, the agreed reparations are exchanged. Finally, a formal reconciliation ritual, the *mato oput*, is conducted.[9] Afterwards there is a feast. If all has gone well, the matter is considered settled. Retaliation against clan members is no longer allowed and would be seen as a breach of the law.[10]

During and particularly after the LRA conflict, many saw the traditional Acholi legal system as an alternative to other transitional justice measures such as criminal trials (Baines 2007; Anyeko et al. 2012; Lenhart 2012).[11] There was a hope that conducting customary law proceedings could contribute to a project of "Africanizing" transitional justice instead of just importing Western law measures. However, to serve as a tool of transitional justice, the traditional clan-based Acholi legal system had to undergo transformations. The sheer number of offenses committed during the conflict made it necessary to conduct *matu oput* rituals *en masse* in central locations instead of handling every single case individually in the respective village. The question of paying compensation, a necessary precursor for a traditional *matu oput* ritual, was reduced to mere symbolic reparations if, indeed, it was addressed at all. This provoked severe criticism. Adam Branch (2014) has pointed to the discontent that accompanied such "ethnojustice" measures in northern Uganda. In fact, these "ethnojustice" measures were rituals that may have been inspired by the traditional Acholi legal system but were also shaped by forces beyond what could be called "traditional justice" – usually determined by the funding agendas of international donors.[12]

While my conversation partners took Acholi customary law quite seriously, they were nevertheless acutely aware of its shortcomings in the context of the conflict. I asked them if they felt that the trial before the ICC was a suitable alternative to Acholi customary law – assuming that it would replace the customary legal measures. The response of one of my interlocutors somewhat surprised me. He replied that, in his opinion, Ongwen still must come back to the community and undergo *mato oput* when the trial is over and after he has served his time in prison. "So, you don't see a contradiction between the ICC trial and the *mato oput* ritual?" I asked. They shook their heads. "Also," another of my interlocutors added, "for *mato oput*, Ongwen must tell the truth first. I have not heard him confessing before the ICC. Without truth-telling, there can be no *mato oput*." They all agreed that the criminal trial in The Hague and Acholi customary law, including the *mato oput* ritual, were two different things. One did not necessarily preclude the other.

Religious Ethics of Forgiveness

The discussion took a different turn when we began talking about forgiveness – a most prevalent term in transitional justice discussions in northern Uganda. In the days prior to this meeting, I had spoken to several religious leaders who belong to an organization called the Acholi Religious Leaders' Peace Initiative (ARLPI), which brings together clergy from all congregations, including Anglican, Catholic, Evangelical, and Muslim. They espouse a religiously grounded ethic based on the need to forgive the offenses committed during the conflict. I was particularly impressed by a meeting with the local *sheikh*; he was a Muslim cleric and the Islamic law judge (*khadi*) of the Muslim district of Gulu, and he played a major role in the ARLPI. His message was that only reconciliation could guarantee peace for the war-stricken region. At the very beginning of our talk, he quoted Sura 42, Verse 43 from the Quran: "[A]nd verily whoever shows patience and forgives – that would truly be what is commended by God." He then went on to explain his, and hence the ARLPI's, political stance:

> As religious leaders under the Acholi Religious Leaders' Peace Initiative, we – together with the cultural institutions – advocated for alternative

> justice mechanisms as the best mode of justice that would really bring an everlasting and holistic peace . . . . [I]t's holistic in the sense that we apply amnesty – and amnesty was actually what came out of the Acholi Religious Leaders' Peace Initiative.

There are two important points in this brief statement. First, like other religious leaders, the *sheikh* saw the political manifestation of his religious views in the law granting amnesty to all LRA fighters who voluntarily return from the bush. The Ugandan Parliament enacted this law in 2000, and the ARLPI was one of its most vocal proponents. The ICC indictments against the top LRA commanders represent a sharp departure from the amnesty rule; prior to that, many had hoped that Kony, Ongwen, and the others might still give up their fight voluntarily. Since then, the religious leaders have been largely critical of the ICC's intervention (Apuuli 2011).[13] The second point refers to the idea that forgiveness is not only a religious policy but also largely in accord with Acholi customary law. The *sheikh* stressed that the ARLPI worked hand in hand with the "cultural institutions," by which he meant the clan leaders.[14] Still, this perspective in which religious and traditional views are largely in accord is not always as coherent on the ground as its proponents might wish.[15]

The ARLPI's agenda of forgiveness was also extended to Dominic Ongwen specifically. When Ongwen was captured in 2015, the religious leaders' peace initiative put out a statement arguing against sending him to the ICC.[16] In the course of my research, I had a conversation with the Catholic archbishop of Gulu. When I asked him about the Dominic Ongwen case, he said that he would like to see the amnesty law extended to Dominic Ongwen and the case against him in The Hague closed:

> Ongwen claims to have surrendered. He was not captured on the field of battle. They also say that that he pleaded for amnesty. So, we were asking, could he be given some room there in that area, because he came out voluntarily, and he also requested amnesty? And for us the argument was . . . some . . . of his predecessors who were also high ranking, with Joseph Kony, they were given amnesty. Why couldn't this be also considered?

My conversation partners had already told me that they had invited these religious leaders to lead prayers during the day commemorating the 2003 massacre that they were organizing. I asked them how they felt about the religious leaders' view that Ongwen should not go to trial in

The Hague, but that he should come back to northern Uganda, be forgiven, and reintegrated into the community. My question was, of course, provocative, because it put a finger on the fact that they had invited the religious leaders, who seemed to have a diametrically opposed view on the Ongwen case, to play a prominent role in the massacre commemoration day.

After my question, there was silence in the room. It lasted for several seconds. My four conversation partners began to look at each other. Finally, one of them broke the silence, saying, more to her peers than to me, "Well, it is just another way of thinking." The others began nodding. Another one added, "That is how religious people think." And he also said that he did not disagree with that kind of thinking. The group did not present me with a solution for this apparent contradiction. When I attended the massacre commemoration day about two weeks later (see Chapter 3), I met both the religious leaders and the community organizers. Both "ways of thinking" seemed to be able to coexist.

What struck me in this conversation and in many others I had had during my research in northern Uganda was the plurality of normative orders my conversation partners were confronted with – international criminal law, national criminal law, traditional justice, religious ethics. What I found particularly surprising was my interlocutors' ability to navigate this normative plurality and find some kind of position for themselves – while being aware of all of these logics and often also of their contradictions. When I came to northern Uganda, I was keen to find out how people assessed the ICC's legitimacy. It became clear, though, that the question was more complex than I had expected, and it quickly turned into a question of how people navigated a plurality of normative logics and assessed their legitimacy within this plurality.

JUSTICE, LEGITIMACY, AND SENTIMENT

In recent years, some anthropologists interested in legal matters have taken to focusing their attention on the concept of justice, giving rise to an "anthropology of justice" (Clarke and Goodale 2010; Brunegger and Faulk 2016; Johnson and Karekwaivanane 2018b). In many ways, this chapter contributes to this emerging field of study. For the case that this book has focused on, the work of Kamari Clarke is most formative. In her book *Fictions of Justice* (2009), Clarke analyzes the debates on the ICC in Africa as embedded in competing imaginaries of justice that are carefully produced by actors. In her most recent book *Affective Justice* (2019), Clarke builds on this work to show the role of affect in the production of such imaginaries of justice. She is particularly critical of a kind of imaginary of justice that equates law and justice in such a way that it denies the political basis for justice in the midst of structural violence. In a way, Clarke sees the project of forcefully broadening legal anthropology into the anthropology of justice as a way of provincializing law to the benefit of justice.

In some ways, this approach resonates with anthropological approaches to transitional justice (Wilson 2001; Ross 2003; Eltringham 2004; Allen 2006; Doughty 2010; Zenker 2014; Anders 2014a). Most of these works have been similarly critical of all-too-legalistic approaches to coming to terms with past violence. The anthropology of justice seems to be about casting aside legalistic approaches to justice and exploring the dynamics that emerge when people actually assess the justice or injustice in particular situations.[17] As Alexander Hinton remarks in the introduction to an influential edited volume on the topic, anthropologists should "explore the local justice dynamic by considering what justice means and how it is negotiated in different localities where transitional justice efforts are under way (or related rhetorics and processes are in play) after genocide and mass atrocity" (2010a, 2).

In a recent edited volume on the anthropology of justice in Africa, Jessica Johnson and George Karekwaivanane feel the need to remind the field that law and justice – as much as they are not the same – are also not antithetical to each other:

> [The anthropology of justice] is promising in its expansiveness, its ability to hold together disparate topics, time periods, and locations, and its broad appeal to scholars, policy makers, and ordinary citizens across Africa and beyond. There is an instinctive sense in which justice is greater than human rights and more capacious than law. And yet they are related in practice as they are in (legal) imaginaries.
>
> (Johnson and Karekwaivanane 2018a, 1)

I would like to engage with this insight and even amplify it. There is a relationship between law and justice. And while it is perfectly possible to have law without justice – a fact that anthropologists of justice have amply demonstrated – it is not possible to have justice without law. To be clear, I am not making a plea for liberal legalism here. By "law" I do not only mean the regulations grounded in liberal contractualist

Western theory to govern the modern state but, much more broadly speaking, the whole array of rules and processes people set up in order to decide what is right and what is wrong. Without such normative orders, there is no frame of reference within which to decide if an action, an event, or a decision is just or unjust. People constantly struggle to find justice. But the concrete work they are mostly concerned with is to find the right kind of law, the right kind of normative order, on which to base their assessment of justice.[18] In the case of my interlocutors in northern Uganda, they have at least four normative orders to choose from: international criminal law, Ugandan criminal law, Acholi customary law, and religious ethics. As such, the question of justice cannot easily be separated from the question of how people assess the legitimacy of these normative orders.

Justice as Legitimacy

But what can such an anthropology of justice, which takes shape as an anthropology of the perceived legitimacy of normative orders, look like? Let us analyze the approaches that social scientists have developed to explain the most obvious crisis of perceived legitimacy of the International Criminal Court in Africa, in northern Uganda particularly. There are basically three approaches.

The first approach is often taken by the above-mentioned anthropologists, who criticize the criminal justice component of transitional justice (Clarke 2009; Mamdani 2009) or, more generally, the "judiciaialization of politics" (Comaroff and Comaroff 2006).[19] They make a quite general argument that combines cultural analysis with a political economy perspective. These authors are critical of international criminal law, with its insistence on individual criminal responsibility, for being mainly a Western theoretical construct. Imposing it on Africa produces two problems: First, it obscures the structural, not least of all economic, root causes of violence by unduly focusing on a few bad people (i.e., the political economy perspective). Second, it ignores the local specificities of traditional African kinship-based justice systems, which are oriented toward reconciliation and restoring social relationships instead of individual punishment (i.e., the cultural analysis perspective). Because of this, people find the ICC in Africa illegitimate.

A second approach is represented by a number of on-the-ground studies, mainly interview-based studies, some semi-quantitative in design, of how people perceive the legitimacy of punishing war criminals in the ICC (Ford 2012; Macdonald and Porter 2016). These studies tend to come up with a kind of mapping of societal groups that are more or less in favor of an emphasis on punishment and hence find the ICC more or less legitimate. Although these studies provide a great deal of empirical insight, they seem predestined to identify three groups: (1) the camp of the victims, which finds criminal justice measures and the ICC legitimate; (2) the camp of the perpetrator, which finds the criminal trial illegitimate because it acts against their interests; (3) the majority of people, who do not really care, but because of their general skepticism of the criminal justice system, they tend to find the ICC illegitimate.[20]

A third approach is represented by a number of studies from legal sociologists in the tradition of the sociology of perceived legitimacy and legal compliance (Henham 2007; Cassese 2012; Sarkin 2012; Takemura 2012; Conti 2016). They follow the approach of Tom Tyler, who defines perceived legitimacy as "the belief that authorities, institutions, and social arrangements are appropriate, proper, and just" (2006, 376). Such studies identify several factors that seem to influence how legitimate the ICC is perceived to be: the process of the Court's creation and the trial procedures that are followed (Ramji-Nogales 2010); the Court's location (Burke-White 2003); the ethnic composition of the Court's staff (Higonnet 2006); the Court's institutional structure (Dickinson 2003); and the Court's outreach activities (Stromseth 2007). What these factors have in common is that they are all more or less directly connected to how the Court itself conducts its business, therefore follow the concept of "procedural justice" – the idea that objectively fair procedures translate into subjectively perceived legitimacy (Rawls 1971; Tyler 1990; Habermas 1996).

All three approaches tell us a great deal about the phenomenon of the perceived legitimacy of normative orders, and their results provide compelling explanations of why the ICC lacks legitimacy in Africa. Still, in my view, all three have limits when it comes to better understanding the various exceptions from the rules they set up. When we think about my four conversation partners in Pajule, northern Uganda, they did not conceive of Western justice and African justice as quite as incompatible as many critiques from approach one would predict. Being in the camp of the victims made them candidates to find the ICC legitimate, as the proponents of our second approach propose, but they were far from steadfast in this assessment. Forgiveness likewise seemed to appeal to them, and their distrust of the courts was more directed toward Ugandan courts under the Museveni government in particular. It was not just "punishment" they were after, but a specific legal procedure. And while they found the ICC a legitimate forum, most of the factors the studies of our third approach named, such as how the ICC came into existence, the ethnic composition of its personnel, or its specific procedures, did not really matter to them. In fact, the Court's location in The Hague was even seen as an asset rather than an impediment to the Court's legitimacy.

In my view, all three approaches tend to undertheorize two dimensions of perceived legitimacy: First, they undertheorize how deeply the problem of legitimacy is embedded in a pluralism of normative orders and the ability of actors to switch between them. Second, they undertheorize what one could rather technically call the psychosocial interface – either by relying on crude rational choice models or by assuming that structural factors more or less directly translate into actors' perceptions. Let me explain what I mean by focusing in greater detail on the second approach: the studies on perceived legitimacy and procedural justice.

Pluralizing Legitimacy

Tom Tyler's famous book on legitimacy is called *Why People Obey the Law* (1990). In my view, the title poses the wrong question. It should rather be phrased "Why People Obey *Which* Law." If the study of legal pluralism has taught us anything, it is the very basic insight that people always abide by some kind of normative system. The question, then, is which one. When my interlocutors in northern Uganda do not find the ICC legitimate, it is not that they do not "obey the law"; it is that they orient their assessment of what is right and wrong for them according to a normative order other than the one provided by international criminal law – religious ethics, for instance, or Acholi custom. It is, therefore, important to pluralize the notions of perceived legitimacy and compliance to account for the fact that, rather than "not obeying *the* law" in the singular, people switch between different normative frameworks. Pluralizing the notion of legitimacy means highlighting the fact that people assess the legitimacy of normative orders relationally. The assessment of the legitimacy of one of these normative orders necessitates an assessment of the others. Perceiving legitimacy means navigating normative pluralism.

As noted earlier, in northern Uganda there are a number of normative options for people to choose from. One is international criminal law in the form of the ICC. Another is the national criminal legal system in the form of the ICD of the Ugandan High Court. The amnesty law enacted in 2000 for LRA fighters returning voluntarily from the bush is yet another normative system, one that at least partially conforms to religious (Christian as well as Muslim) moralities of forgiveness and reconciliation. There is also the traditional dispute settlement system with the *mato oput* rituals at its center. The members of the Pajule massacre survivors' association I introduced at the beginning of the chapter have a very differentiated view on the legitimacy of these normative orders in relation to dealing with Dominic Ongwen. They see the ICC's criminal trial as the most legitimate option. They accept that the Ugandan national criminal justice system is then precluded from coming into effect, not least because they perceive the Ugandan courts as less legitimate than the ICC. They also see the traditional legal system and *mato oput* as a legitimate normative order to deal with past violence, but they do not believe that the ICC's trial necessarily precludes *mato oput* from taking place later. They believe in the legitimacy of the ICC with its strong emphasis on punishment, but, evidently, they also find the logic of confession and forgiveness very powerful. They acknowledge this dissonance, but they do not seem to be particularly bothered by this logical contradiction.

For my interlocutors, the perceived legitimacy of the ICC is profoundly interconnected to the other normative orders. They know the normative plurality fairly well. Sometimes they can switch registers to assess legitimacy. Sometimes they follow one logic and not another. Sometimes they seem to follow two or three without seeing any contradiction between them. And then again, they see several normative orders as legitimate and just tolerate the emerging contradictions.

This way of assessing the legitimacy of normative orders is typical of many of the people I met during my fieldwork. I met people who supported one or another of the above-mentioned normative systems as the *only* legitimate option to deal with past violence. Some traditional chiefs insisted that only African justice can deal with African violence. "Everything else is foreign to us," one of them said to me. Some religious leaders suggested that the logic of forgiveness is the only legitimate option for northern Uganda. Everything else would "open half-healed wounds," as one of them said to me, and hence endanger the fragile peace in the region.[21] ICC advocates promoted punishment of those most responsible by international law as the only legitimate solution, as the "culture of impunity" – a phrase often used – would never allow northern Uganda to heal. Others said the same thing about the Ugandan criminal legal system. All these actors assessed the legitimacy of "their" normative order in relation to the other options. And then again, there were others who switched normative logics all the time, sometimes several times during a single conversation.

In a classic text on legal pluralism, Keebet von Benda-Beckmann (1981) elaborated on one way to navigate different normative systems – through what she calls "forum shopping." When people have a dispute, and when they have a choice regarding which forum to bring that dispute to, they will choose the forum (and hence its associated legal order) that they believe is most likely to provide the best outcome for their specific case. The dispute settlement institutions themselves have an interest in attracting cases to adjudicate; as such, they appear to disputants as "shopping forums" and compete for disputes to settle.

In some respects, the question of navigating normative pluralism I am proposing here is much broader. On the one hand, when it comes to perceived legitimacy, people do not necessarily have a case of their own in which they have a stake. One can also assess the legitimacy of a normative order from a distance. On the other hand, people do not necessarily conceptualize the assessment of legitimacy as a choice, like choosing a dispute resolution forum. Often, they just find it legitimate or not without having made a conscious decision in that regard. But Benda-Beckmann's analysis, slightly reframed, can also work for the assessment of the legitimacy of normative orders: people probably find those normative orders legitimate that seem to further the kind of justice they imagine for a particular situation. Conversely, normative orders and their practitioners likewise actively advocate the kind of justice imaginaries "their" normative orders imply.

Sentimentalizing Legitimacy

Such a conception is quite different from the widely influential concept of procedural justice. As its basis, Tyler (1993) has theorized a "procedure–legitimacy–acceptance connection." The idea goes like this: if normative orders and their organizations are consistent in following their own procedural rules, and if these rules are rational and fair, people will perceive these organizations and the normative orders they represent as legitimate and accept being governed by them. From the perspective of anthropology as a discipline and ethnography as a research practice, the "procedure–legitimacy–acceptance connection" is somewhat questionable from the outset because to argue a connection between rational procedure and people's perception of that procedure as legitimate means crosscutting one of the most basic epistemological features of the ethnographic endeavor: the emic/etic distinction (Harris 1976). An analysis of certain procedures within a normative order as rational and fair is an etic description, and the legitimacy, to the degree that it is defined as a *perception* of people, is an emic category.[22] In other words: for procedural justice to work, *etic fairness* (rational procedure) and *emic fairness* (perceived legitimacy) must be the same. But that is rarely the case.

Anthropologists usually conduct ethnography in contexts where there is a remarkable divergence between emic worldviews and the various competing etic narratives that they can mobilize to explain them. Anthropologists take people's emic conceptions seriously; they do not assume that those who are being analyzed see the world in a way that is even vaguely similar to the way the analyzer sees it. Hence, an ethnographic approach to legitimacy must take full account of people's subjective experiences. That means taking seriously precisely those conceptions that procedural justice – with its basis in liberal contractualist philosophy and its strong emphasis on rational fairness – regularly casts aside: the role of affect and emotion in the assessment of the legitimacy of normative orders. It means *sentimentalizing legitimacy*.

Sentimentalizing legitimacy requires challenging, on a very basic level, the rational choice models that underlie many conceptions of perceived legitimacy. That is not only because it might very well be that many people do not make choices within the kind of rationality framework that the analyst assumes. It is also because making choices is only a part, sometimes a rather small part, of human action. Human practice is often habitual; most things people do are determined by structural forces, and they often do not realize that they could act differently (Bourdieu 1972). Ethnography is not only about explaining human action but about finding out in the first place what kind of forces are at work when individual people act (Latour 2005). As I observed earlier, actors on the ground often do not conceptualize their legitimacy assessments as a choice. But even if they do, the most efficient choice, the most rational decision in a given situation, can only be made along the lines of a fairly coherent normative logic. And this normative logic, of which there are always several others around to choose from, is often not consciously chosen.

I believe it is methodologically indicative that when I asked the people I met during my fieldwork in northern Uganda to elaborate on why they find something just or unjust, they tended to illustrate their legitimacy assessment by presenting biographical and historical narratives in which emotions were encoded. I propose that listening to people's justice assessments on their own terms, using their emotional experiences as a starting point to delve into the production, maintenance, and transformation of sentiments, is a methodologically sounder approach than all-too-hastily distilling their answers into "rational" motives for conscious decision-making. One should take these emotional narratives seriously as an integral component of people's process of assessing legitimacy. Emotional utterances indicate that people attach a heightened relevance to the content of their talk. Through the life course, emotions are an integral part of forming, remembering, and mobilizing normative assessments. I argue that through emotion, people, as well as collectives, construct normative repertoires, in other words, *sentiments of justice* (Bens and Zenker 2017b).

Such sentiments of justice are multi-scaled. On the micro level, they can include very personal biographical stories. On the meso level, institutionalized discourse arrangements, for example, church, political group, or clan, contribute to such repertoires. On the macro level, all kinds of local and national discourses, such as the north–south divide in Uganda or current developments of political regimes in East Africa, can become part of normative emotional repertoires, as can global and deep, historically grounded macro discourses such as colonialism and the anti-colonial struggle. When people actively assess the legitimacy of a normative order, they draw from these repertoires. But these assessments are not scripted in the sense that only one justice imaginary is possible. They depend on which parts of the repertoire are actively reenacted. By following the sentiments, one can follow the twists and turns actors take in navigating a plurality of normative orders in order to find out for themselves which is more likely to deliver the justice they imagine.

SENTIMENTS OF JUSTICE: NAVIGATING COMPETING NORMATIVE LOGICS

What I argue in this chapter deviates from much of the literature on emotions and transitional justice. In transitional justice research, which is still dominated by legal studies approaches, some have argued that transitional justice must be "rehumanized" by taking stock of people's emotions rather than focusing merely on cold legal proceedings (Halpern and Weinstein 2004). Mass atrocity, according to this notion, evokes intense emotions, particularly out-group hate and anger (Volkan 1988), and transitional justice must provide a forum to deal with these emotions after the violence has ended (Brudholm and Lang 2018). Inherent in this line of thinking is that there is a "symbolic politics" that cannot account for the "emotional politics" on the ground and sees the exorcising of "negative emotions" as crucial for the creation of the necessary "positive emotions" (Kaufman 2006). Others criticize the way in which specific emotions such as anger are pathologized and argue for a more inclusive model (Pupavac 2004; Mihai 2016).[23] Not unlike the broader law-and-emotion scholarship, these approaches assume that legalized forms of transitional justice are based on the systematic exorcism of emotions, which ultimately yields harmful results. This strand of literature tends to argue against legalized forms of transitional justice. Nonlegal forms such as truth and reconciliation commissions, it is argued, allow for the public expression of emotion and are better able to deal with it (Minow 1998).

While these studies have rightly insisted on taking emotions seriously in transitional justice and have also contributed to analyzing their workings, this kind of literature is still based on the basic distinction between rational modes of action and emotional modes of action, and they continue to attribute rationality to the law and emotionality to other nonlegal forms such as reconciliation procedures. The concept of sentiment crosscuts this distinction. Rational legal proceedings are no less affective than seemingly emotion-laden truth commissions. People experience and imagine transitional justice as bodies in affective arrangements. Their assessments of the legitimacy of normative orders and the kind of justice they promise to deliver entail the full range of subjective judgment – both cold calculation and heated passion are emotion-laden, felt experiences.

This also means that rational choice models do not always fail to explain actors' perceptions of justice. Ongwen's victims, my interlocutors in the conversation at the outset of this chapter, often told me that they are hoping for reparations out of the Victims' Fund at the International Criminal Court. In many years and if Ongwen is ultimately convicted, the Victims' Fund should implement some form of reparations – something these villagers cannot hope for from any other forum. In one of my many conversations with villagers in massacre survivors' associations, I was told that they do hope for tangible reparations:

> If Ongwen is . . . found guilty, we believe that the Court will facilitate . . . reparations, whether individual or collective, . . . based on the

> properties, the lives ... that were destroyed. My worry is they may not. The Court may not get the story, but they should try as much as possible to give what's appropriate to the victims. Because as I speak right now, ... they are counseling some of the victims here. But people normally feel that they should have tangible things in their hands. Those counseling services that are provided, those are lip service; they are not enough. Indeed, they are trying, but I feel that the Court should deliver something out of the trust fund to the victims – that's my recommendation to the Court.

Other actors also have tangible interests with which one can explain their assessments of the legitimacy of normative orders. The traditional leaders I have talked to, who are, for the most part, vocal proponents of traditional justice mechanisms such as *mato oput*, are also the same people who conduct these rituals. That puts them in a position of power they might not want to give up to other forums (Behrend 1993; Branch 2010; see, more generally, Mamdani 1996).[24] It might, therefore, be no surprise that one traditional leader I talked to – the prime minister of *Ker Kwaro Acholi*, the organization of traditional leaders – completely denounced the competing normative order of international criminal law and human rights and made a plea for Acholi customary law:

> And remember, the Acholi socialize themselves in the collective. That is, what happens to one person happens to all; what affects one person affects everybody in that collective. It could be the collective, it could be a family, it could be a clan. So, we live in the collective, and that influences what people think. ... We are living in traditional societies. Sixty, seventy percent of our people are traditional; they don't understand these complexities of advancement, they don't! They don't understand. You talk of human rights, you talk of governance, you talk of all these ... That does not matter for them.

But if we apply only such a relatively crude rational choice model in order to understand how people perceive the legitimacy of normative orders and how they imagine justice, it would also mean dismissing many other things people say about justice. The massacre survivors I have spoken to also often talked about "justice" in the abstract and told me stories of dead relatives and terrible experiences as abductees in the bush. "People are just looking for true justice to be served to Ongwen," one villager, a member of a massacre survivors' organization, told me. He looked me steadily and somberly in the eye and said, "Yeah, at least he has to suffer for those crimes he has committed. Even if the reparations do not come, he has to answer for his crimes." The Muslim *sheikh* of whom I wrote at the beginning of this chapter not only explained the rationality of prioritizing reconciliation over retribution to stabilize the security situation in northern Uganda, but he also passionately quoted passages from the Quran to me. The Catholic bishop told me a moving story about how he recently met a group of women who had been forced to become the wives of LRA fighters and who now faced the desperate plight of being ostracized from their communities. The Acholi prime minister also talked to me about the frustration he felt about NGO interventions being more trouble than they were worth and about the indignity of a people being subjected to foreign help. "There was a time we had over 400 NGOs, international, local, and all these, so every person has at least been touched by an NGO." And then he started to laugh out loud and said, "Our lives are project-like; we are governed in a project-like life."

In the end, the question is: Does one cast aside these affective-emotional utterances as mere rhetoric to justify decisions people have already made based on instrumental rationality? Or does one take them seriously as an integral part of their assessment of the legitimacy of the normative order they are following? Sentiments of justice lure, seduce, and attract actors, leading them to assess one normative order as more legitimate, more apt to the situation, more just than another normative order. From the perspective of actors, it seems far more important for the normative logic they apply to *feel* legitimate. Questions of procedure play a role in this, as do instrumental rationality and economic interests. But terms such as "fair process" or "vested interest" can have very different meanings depending on the normative logic one *feels* is the legitimate logic to apply. Sentiments of justice are therefore deeply entangled with those considerations. Approaches to perceived legitimacy based on merely *rational* models prevalent in socio-legal research, such as procedural justice or forum shopping, cannot conceptualize this.

SENTIMENTS OF JUSTICE AND AFFECTIVE FRAMES: RETRIBUTION VERSUS RECONCILIATION

I argue that sentiments of justice can be observed in actors' perspectives by analyzing the affective and emotional dimension of the narratives they produce to justify their assessment of legitimacy. Emotion research has shown how rules and values are learned by being inscribed into emotional memory and how, consequently, normative orders are deeply connected to affect and emotion (Quinn 2005; Benei 2008; Scheve 2011; Röttger-Rössler, Scheidecker, and Funk 2015). People appraise actions and events on the basis of such normative memory (Assmann 1995), which is learned and embodied (Scherer, Schnorr, and Johnstone 2001).

But "emotional arousals" not only inscribe normative orders into the bodies of people; they also lead to re-evaluations of already embodied normative orders: people constantly relearn their embodied normative frames (Quinn and Mathews 2016). Indeed, anthropological studies show how any kind of narrative storytelling both makes sense of and creates emotional experience (Capps and Ochs 1995). Emotional appeals in storytelling play a key role in the creation of individual as well as collective identities (Ramaswamy 1997). In these contexts, people create and recall memory emotively (White 1999; Cattell and Climo 2002; Carsten 2007). Anthropological scholarship has described how collective memory is emotionally embodied in ritual contexts in Africa (Berliner 2005; Argenti 2007).

This suggests that to identify and comprehend the sentiments of justice people are drawn to, one must be attentive to the normative statements that are implied in their narratives of legitimacy. People actively encode sentiments in the stories of past events that they bring to the fore to justify their assessments of legitimacy. But at the same time, they also attempt to convince themselves and their audiences of the plausibility of these assessments. As I have shown in Chapter 3, affective framing is a key practice in creating plausibility with audiences. People not only imply sentiments of justice in their narratives, but they also evoke affective arrangements in which these sentiments feel plausible.

Of the many competing normative logics in northern Uganda, the demand for punishment in an international criminal trial in The Hague and the religiously motivated demand to forgive past crimes may mark the two extreme ends of a spectrum. These two opposing logics of retribution and reconciliation can be fruitfully described as sentiments of justice. On a logical level, they may be very difficult, if not impossible, to reconcile. But as the conversation with massacre survivors I reported at the beginning of this chapter shows, they can feel similarly – and simultaneously – plausible to one and the same actor.

The religious leaders who belong to the religious peace activist group ARLPI were very outspoken in their promotion of an ideology of forgiveness and positioned themselves largely against the ICC. When I asked some of them why reconciliation was the kind of justice they imagined for northern Uganda, they would tell me a story from the time of the high point of the conflict in the early 2000s, when people had to live in IDP camps under the worst possible conditions. Religious activists' narratives referred to the unbearable life in the IDP camps, the "bad surroundings" (Finnström 2008) during this time. Nobody can want to go back to that terrible situation. The preference for peace and reconciliation over punishment then feels like the only possible measure to prevent another armed conflict and ensure ongoing stability and security in northern Uganda.

Others, especially the massacre survivors' associations in the villages, told me other stories. They told me that in 2006, they wanted nothing but to get out of the camps. Now, ten years later, they have been forced to realize that they will never get their lost childhoods back, never be able to complete their interrupted educations, and will never have the livestock they lost – the source of their livelihood – returned to them. They are now starting to think that, maybe, if their children, husbands, wives, or parents were still alive, they could have helped them get through the financial difficulties they have been mired in; that maybe it is unfair that they still live in such "bad surroundings" while amnestied LRA commanders have good lives in the town – some are even officers in the Ugandan army. Such were the stories and histories that they were tapping into to justify their – generally unpopular – support for the ICC. As one former civilian leader of an IDP camp and now a victims' activist told me,

> Our people know who did what to them. Because we have got children who were taken into captivity and these children were able to know that this is so-and-so who was behind this attack. They know, so it is so-and-so who killed my father. In the event that this person comes back what should I do? My father is no longer there, my mother is no longer there. That kind of thing comes into the minds of people. ... Can those commanders be convicted instead of setting them free? So, this religious peace team and the cultural leaders, before they come out with their findings, they should first look out for the interests of the victims – the real people who suffered.

Such historical and biographical narratives, both those put forward by the religious leaders and those presented by the massacre victims, diverge in the affective arrangements that they recall. In the religious leaders' narrative, the time in the camps reminds the listener to fear for his or her bare survival. The narrative induces indignation against anyone who might prolong or risk resurrecting the anguish of life in the camp. One of the most persuasive arguments against the ICC in the years leading up to and during the Juba peace talks was that the ICC investigations might prolong the plight of the internally displaced persons in pursuit of hollow justice. This is known as the "peace versus justice" debate (Armstrong 2014). All normative imperatives that endanger peace and threaten to reinstate the conditions that lead to the existential fear for one's bare survival appear illegitimate in light of these narratives of IDP camp life.

The affective arrangements of the massacre victims' narratives are different. They tell stories of people's lives after the camps were dismantled. The emotions they evoke are indignation about perpetrators going on with their lives unharmed and anger and frustration that comes from the realization that the losses suffered during the conflict – in life, property, and relationships – will never be regained. A normative logic that does not ignore personal responsibility, that recognizes that somebody must pay retribution for all this, feels more legitimate in the light of such narratives.

***

Understanding justice as a sentiment means taking seriously the insight that people decide right and wrong as feeling bodies, with the whole range of subjective experience that implies. As we have learned from the conversation I laid out at the beginning of this chapter, sentiments of justice are not necessarily exclusive. Their workings are multifaceted, and they unfold in a world of normative pluralism. People can follow one normative logic in light of certain emotional arousals and others in light of other affective arrangements. I started this chapter with the question of the relationship between law and justice. My argument was that how people imagine justice and how they assess the legitimacy of normative orders are inextricably intertwined. It is feeling that connects law and justice. Affect and emotion do not distract from justice, as some political theories might suggest; rather, they make justice possible in the first place. With affect and emotion people navigate the plurality of normative orders that provide them with the guidelines to conceive of justice. With them they overcome the moment of indeterminacy that is immanent in every decision regarding justice or injustice. There is no normative legitimacy and no imaginary of justice that is not embedded in and colored by affect and emotion. Focusing on how people produce, maintain, and challenge sentiments takes us a long way toward understanding how they struggle for justice.

Figure i.1 *The Gift*, a sculpture by Navid Nuur in front of the permanent premises of the ICC in The Hague
Source: Jonas Bens

Rules
ICC Premises

You are entering a court of law and are requested to observe appropriate standards of conduct.

Audio recording, filming, or photographing is prohibited within the Court's building.

Please dress appropriately for a Court; insignia or images that could be considered disruptive or offensive are not allowed.

Abusive or inappropriate conduct, including loud noise, is strictly prohibited.

Wear your Visitor's Badge visibly and return it at the end of your visit.

Drinking and eating is only allowed in the Visitor's Restaurant.

Entry under the influence of narcotic substances, including alcohol, and use of such substances is not allowed.

Smoking is only allowed in designated areas outside of the building, before going through security.

Personal belongings can be stored in lockers and must not be left unattended.

The Court accepts no responsibility for any loss, damage to, or theft of, personal possessions within the Court building.

All visitors must follow the directions of ICC staff members at all times.

Rules
Courtroom Gallery

Coats, bags and all type of electronic devices are not allowed in the Courtroom Gallery. They shall be stored in lockers.

Persons under 16 years of age are not allowed in the Courtoom Gallery whilst Court is in session, without prior written authorization of the relevant Chamber.

Follow all directions given by the Chamber in relation to the Courtroom Gallery.

Visitors must rise at the opening and closing of a Court session.

Reading, talking, pointing or gesturing at anyone seated in the Courtroom is not permitted.

During closed sessions, no visitors are allowed in the Courtoom Gallery.

The above is derived from the Presidential Directive regulating visits to the building of the Court which can be consulted at the information desk. Visitors not abiding by the applicable rules may be subject to measures and sanctions, including expulsion and/or exclusion from the Court's building.

Figure i.2 Rule sheet for visitors to the ICC
Source: Jonas Bens

Figure i.3 A public gallery in the ICC
Source: ICC-INT

Figure 1.1 The ICC courtroom with IT workspaces including monitors and the audio system for simultaneous translation (foreground). The elevated booths where interpreters sit are visible in the back of the room. Cameras are positioned on the walls
Source: ICC-INT

Figure 2.1 Public screening of the first day of the Dominic Ongwen trial before the ICC, December 6, 2016, Abok, northern Uganda
Source: Jonas Bens

Figure 2.2 A television journalist from a Kenyan news channel standing amid the crowd during an ICC outreach event in Abok, northern Uganda, December 6, 2016
Source: Jonas Bens

Figure 2.3 An ICC outreach event on the second day of the trial opening, Abok, December 7, 2016
Source: Jonas Bens

Figure 3.1 A memorial for the massacre on May 19, 2004, in the village of Lukodi
Source: Jonas Bens

Figure 3.2 A mural commemorating the massacre on May 19, 2004, on the wall of a small documentation center in the village of Lukodi
Source: Jonas Bens

Figure 4.1 A showcase in the foyer of the International Criminal Court in The Hague exhibiting the kinds of material evidence that are often of relevance in the ICC's criminal trials
Source: Jonas Bens

Figure 6.1 The Al Jazeera television studio for the program *UpFront–Arena* on the topic "Is the ICC biased against African countries?" with former ICC Chief Prosecutor Luis Moreno Ocampo (left) and anthropology professor Mahmood Mamdani (center) from March 12, 2016

Figure 6.2 Paolina Massidda (left), Principal Counsel of the ICC's Office of the Public Counsel for Victims, in the courtroom

Figure 6.3 Krispus Ayena Odongo (right), Dominic Ongwen's defense counsel, in the ICC courtroom

PART III

POLITICS

6

THE POLITICS OF ATMOSPHERE AND SENTIMENT

International Criminal Justice in Africa and Competing Indignation Regimes

> *Krieg den deutschen Zuständen! ... Mit ihnen im Kampf ist die Kritik keine Leidenschaft des Kopfes, sondern sie ist der Kopf der Leidenschaft. ... Sie gibt sich nicht mehr als Selbstzweck, sondern nur noch als Mittel. Ihr wesentliches Pathos ist die Indignation, ihre wesentliche Arbeit ist die Denunziation.*[1]
>
> Karl Marx, *Zur Kritik der Hegelschen Rechtsphilosophie: Einleitung* (1844)

Law and politics are often conceived of as opposites. Politics is dominated by power and interests, driven by passionate argument, and aims at implementing the practical. Law is dominated by rules and processes, driven by dispassionate judgment, and strives for the ideal.

This conception of the divide between law and politics is shared by quite different theoretical streams. What they mostly disagree about is whether a society is better off placing the emphasis on politics or on law. Theorists of law and politics inspired by Marxist thinking, for instance, have highlighted the degree to which any legal order is determined by political operations, that law is basically a tool to further the interests of the powerful (Paschukanis 1929; Althusser 1970). They argue for prioritizing the political over the legal and for the need to politicize the law and make its political workings visible in democratic discourse (Mouffe 2013). The clearest elaboration of this argument in anthropological thought is the Comaroffs' critique of the "juridification of politics" (Comaroff and Comaroff 2006). On the other end of the theoretical spectrum are theorists of law and politics inspired by liberal contractualism. They argue that the law has the potential to tame the more disruptive modes of political processes (Rawls 1971; Habermas 1992). For liberal thinkers, "juridification of politics" are not fighting words, but a necessary strategy to set the ground rules for meaningful deliberation in democratic societies.

Implicitly, and sometimes explicitly, this law-and-politics debate emerges in the form of a debate about regulating affect. What the two sides in this debate disagree on is which affective mode is more conducive to the political process: excited deliberation or calm deliberation. While liberals are more on the side of calmness, Marxists tend to be more on the side of excitement. These leanings tend to correspond to respective preferences for more or less law. Consequently, whether you are on the side of the law or on the side of politics, a mixing of the two modes becomes problematic. That the division between law and politics is based on the distinction between reason and emotion is a distinctively modern notion. It also, not coincidentally, corresponds to the distinction between the West and the Rest.

The perspective on the affective life of law and justice that I have been developing in this book questions this division in a very basic manner. It asks: Is there any way to conceive of law and politics other than as characterized by, respectively, cold rationality and heated passion? Can a perspective on the myriad of entanglements between the legal and the political and between law and justice change our understanding of both law and politics? I argue that taking careful stock of the production of atmospheres and sentiment both in law and politics has the potential to do that. Both concepts – atmosphere and sentiment – crosscut the reason–emotion divide and the law–politics divide. In social reality, people form opinions and judgments as bodies within affective arrangements. They are not robots – neither in the sense of biological robots that are determined by their emotional programs nor in the sense of mechanical robots that are determined by their rational programs. They make sense of the world as people, and one is well advised to pay careful attention to how they do that on their own terms.

This chapter analyses a specific debate that looks on the surface as if it were a simple recapitulation of the law and politics divide introduced above: How legitimate are the International Criminal Court's interventions in Africa? ICC proponents argue for the priority of law above politics and say the ICC must enforce international criminal law, whether it is politically convenient to do so or not. ICC critics argue for the primacy of politics over law, insisting that political problems need political solutions. It will become clear that, in fact, all parties in this debate argue in favor of some normative orders and against others, for specific imaginaries of justice and against others. It is not law and politics that are being pitted against each other, but different sentiments.

What I aim at describing here is a *politics of sentiment*. A politics of sentiment is directed toward the production and maintenance of what I will call *indignation regimes*, by which I mean a specific discourse formation that is based on a narration of the past in which various collective and individual bodies are arranged so as to affectively produce indignation when it is used to evaluate the present and the future.

Indignation is a powerful emotion that is able to create political mobilization and allegiance.[2] As such, indignation regimes always imply moral communities and function to produce, maintain, and transform them. I use the term *moral community* to denote those collectives of bodies that are bound together by imagining a common kind of justice and a shared normative order to bring it about. As I have shown in Chapter 5, different normative orders are in constant competition against each other, as are different imaginaries of justice, and people tend to switch more or less freely between them as they navigate normative pluralism. Moral communities are, therefore, not fixed entities; rather, they emerge in the political process. As they depend on the stability of the indignation regimes to bring them into existence, they sometimes emerge and dissipate quickly, and sometimes remain stable over a long time.

The production, maintenance, and transformation of indignation regimes can be analyzed by focusing on how actors narrate historical actions and events to assess the justice of present or future actions and events. Actors tell these histories to remind their listeners of certain moral emotions. As such they always imply processes of belonging to certain moral communities (Mattes et al. 2019). Such historical narratives affect listeners by suggesting that they follow a certain logic of justice and pledge allegiance to a certain moral community. A politics of sentiment is successful to the degree that it manages to crystallize such narratives of justice and injustice into stable indignation regimes and, therefore, to partially stabilize political discourses on justice and belonging.

ATMOSPHERE, SENTIMENT, AND THE ICC IN AFRICA

Many African governments were initially in favor of the establishment of an International Criminal Court and ratified the Rome Statute in the late 1990s and early 2000s. But when the ICC indicted the president of Sudan, Omar Al-Bashir, while he was still in office, it triggered a discussion inside the African Union. The Union has criticized the indictment practices of the ICC in several decisions and resolutions.[3] A discourse in which the ICC is portrayed as an instrument of neocolonialism became more and more prevalent. In the May 2013 session of the African Union, Hailemariam Desalegn, African Union chairman and prime minister of Ethiopia, said in his closing remarks that the ICC's process of investigating and trying international crimes "has degenerated into some kind of race hunting."[4] These criticisms of the ICC led the African Union to initiate a process to establish an international criminal chamber within the African Court of Justice and Human Rights, which would serve as an African alternative to the ICC. The legal instrument to achieve this is the so-called Malabo Protocol (Matasi and Bröhmer 2012).[5] Kamari Clarke (2019) has presented an extensive analysis of this "pan-Africanist" pushback and highlighted how the deployment of affect plays a major role in this setting.

The connection between affect/emotion and political processes has been analyzed in anthropology and beyond. Studies of emotions and political rhetoric in linguistic anthropology have shown that emotion, language, and power are intertwined at all scales: the expression of emotion plays a major role in creating an affective connection between politicians and their constituencies (Duranti 2006); emotional rhetoric is crucial in creating commotion and scandal (Kulick and Klein 2003); and national subjectivities are created through the narration of emotionalized, sometimes personalized stories (White 2004). Similar insights have come out of the scholarship on media and mass communication. The public space in mass media democracies is in important respects characterized by "affective publics" (Lünenborg 2019). The "economies of attention" (Franck 1998) that govern these public spaces can be described as affective economies (Lehmann, Roth, and Schankweiler 2019). Both the political space and the private space are created through affective and emotional processes, a dynamic that I have called the "affective co-production of the political sphere" (Bens et al. 2019).

It is therefore crucial to thoroughly investigate affect in discourse practice (Bens 2019b). The microevents in which discourse is practiced are always affective in the sense I have laid out in this book. Anthropological studies of the development of international law regimes, especially human rights regimes, have exactly this perspective. They highlight how various micropractices produce new global justice and truth regimes and investigate these micropractices ethnographically (Riles 2001; Tsing 2005; Merry 2006b; Goodale 2009). Global justice regimes are brought into being through micropolitical interactions within different spheres of legal power (Clarke 2009). The "theatre of the rule of law" (Humphreys 2010) demands a "spectacularization of justice" (Clarke 2009, 28), in which international justice is produced through spectacular performances such as political trials.

Kamari Clarke has argued that, in the case of international criminal law in Africa, two conflicting "fictions of justice" compete: the "attention to individualized responsibility for guilt," which "draws on Western liberalist thought in its assignment of individualized guilt and its construction of self-reflective images of justice and freedom for all humanity," on the one hand, and the need for a "rethinking of the root causes at the core of violence in Sub-Saharan Africa or an interrogation of the political economy of state power of those under the jurisdiction of the Court (Uganda, DRC) versus the state powers outside its reach (the United States, China, Japan, India, and Pakistan, for example)" on the other (Clarke 2009, 55). Clarke clearly demonstrates that "international justice" and "African justice" are incompatible, even incommensurable normative frames (see Kelsall 2009 for a similar argument). These are the competing normative frames that structure the ICC debate in Africa.

In this chapter, I will examine some examples of micropractices of justice-in-the-making that deal with the perceived legitimacy of the International Criminal Court in Africa. It becomes visible in these performances how "African justice" and "Westernized international justice" clash. In the perspective I have developed here, these normative regimes can be treated as sentiments. The power to structure the grand debates on justice in Africa is the result of a politics of sentiment successfully engaging in the production of indignation regimes.

Such politics of sentiment include many of the processes and practices I have described in the preceding chapters of this book. I assert that numerous spectacular legal micropractices form a dialectical relationship with the macro practices of the formation of truth regimes, normative orders, and imaginaries of justice. If we are to take this seriously, we have to address the fact that all of these micropractices are determined by both the concrete affective arrangements in which the actors are embedded and the atmospheres created at these events. The curation of atmospheres I have described in Chapters 1 and 2 are hence of crucial importance. These micropractices are likewise determined by the learned and internalized emotion repertoires and feeling rules the actors carry with them – and the work actors do to produce, maintain, and transform such feeling rules as I have described in Chapter 5. The concrete practices of arranging and rearranging bodies are crucial in this respect. People mobilize bodies, objects, and subjects to create or destabilize performances of objectivity, as I have described in Chapter 4. They also engage in affective framing, the topic of Chapter 3. They evoke affective arrangements in which their versions of the past appear plausible to themselves and to their audiences. The affective discourse practices in these spectacular microsettings constantly feed back into the macro discourses of law and justice. They are aimed at the creation of sentiments and the establishment of indignation regimes.

IN THE TELEVISION STUDIO

It is March 12, 2016, in an Al Jazeera television studio (Figure 6.1). The news broadcaster presents the program *UpFront–Arena*. The topic of

Figure 6.1 The Al Jazeera television studio for the program *UpFront–Arena* on the topic "Is the ICC biased against African countries?" with former ICC Chief Prosecutor Luis Moreno Ocampo (left) and anthropology professor Mahmood Mamdani (center) from March 12, 2016. (A black and white version of this figure will appear in some formats. For the color version, please refer to the plate section.)

the day: "Is the ICC biased against African countries?"[6] It follows an adversarial talk show format: two guests with contrary views about a relevant political issue exchange arguments. A moderator structures the discussion. The debate lasts roughly twelve minutes.

Today, Luis Moreno Ocampo has been invited. The former chief prosecutor of the International Criminal Court had sought the indictment against Omar Al-Bashir, the sitting president of Sudan, in 2008 and provoked a serious crisis for the Court. Since that decision, the ICC has suffered a tangible crisis of legitimacy among African leaders. His counterpart is Mahmood Mamdani, an internationally known anthropology professor from Makerere University in Kampala, Uganda, and Columbia University in New York City. Mamdani, who is not physically present in the studio but is patched in via Skype, is an outspoken critic of the ICC's indictment of African heads of state and government.

The moderator begins questioning Ocampo. What does he think about the critique that the ICC is biased against African leaders? "It's hypocrisy, it's hypocrisy," he replies, already visibly agitated. "African bias was invented by President Bashir to cover up his genocide." In his view, the ICC investigates crimes in Africa for two reasons: first, because there are crimes under the jurisdiction of the ICC happening in Africa; second, African countries voluntarily subjected themselves to the Rome Statute, which compels the ICC to investigate these crimes. Additionally, it was the African governments themselves that had specifically asked the ICC to investigate these crimes in Uganda, the DRC, Mali, Côte d'Ivoire, and the Central African Republic (CAR). Ocampo is adamant about his arguments, outspoken and passionate. He speaks rapidly and forcefully, gesticulating often.

Mamdani, in contrast, strikes a very different pose. He is quieter and calmer. The more dominant Ocampo interrupts him frequently. The exchanges are tense, even hostile. At one point, Mamdani comes to the question of the ICC targeting heads of state of African countries:

MAMDANI: When you target a head of state, you are not just targeting an individual, an alleged perpetrator. You are also targeting the sovereignty of the country. . . . The ICC targets not only perpetrators, but Africa's sovereignty.

OCAMPO: Yes, head of states!

MAMDANI: That is not acceptable.

OCAMPO: I'm sorry, . . .
MAMDANI: . . . and should not be acceptable!
OCAMPO: But, Mahmood, they signed it!
MAMDANI: Nobody should be tried . . .
OCAMPO: They signed it! The treaty is very clear!
MAMDANI: I know, they signed it.
OCAMPO: They signed it, they read the Statute and they signed it, and in fact Mandela was the one pushing for it.[7]

Ocampo has brought a few maps with him, printed on sheets of paper. He holds them up to the camera. The maps show that most of the Rome Statute's signatory states are in Africa, while the Court has no jurisdiction in most Asian and Arab countries. By doing this, he is trying to justify his explanation of why African states are on the ICC's agenda – it is not because of any bias, but because they fall under the jurisdiction of the Court.

The moderator counters. If the ICC were only investigating those countries "that had voluntarily subjected themselves to the Rome Statute, what about the ICC's investigations in Sudan and Libya, which were not members of the ICC?" Ocampo counters that the UN Security Council had referred these cases to the Court, adding that when the Security Council decided to refer these cases, all five African members of the Security Council at that time – Nigeria, Benin, South Africa, Gabon, and Tanzania – had voted in favor. "So, the idea that the ICC jumped on Africa is wrong," he insists.

Mamdani interjects. The worst crimes in the world had not been committed in Africa, but in the Middle East, referring by implication to the wars in Iraq and Afghanistan as well as the ongoing civil wars in Syria and Yemen. The only thing preventing the ICC from investigating in those cases was bias in the UN Security Council:

MAMDANI: . . . a certain member of the Security Council will not allow them to be touched.
OCAMPO: Then blame the Security Council, not the ICC!
MAMDANI: No, but look. It says something about the ICC, not just blaming the Security Council, because the ICC promised us rule of law. And the test of rule of law . . .
OCAMPO: In the countries who signed it!
MAMDANI: . . . the test of rule of law is that it should apply to everybody . . .

OCAMPO: I agree.

MAMDANI: ... particularly the most powerful.

OCAMPO: I agree.

MAMDANI: When the rule of law does not apply to the most powerful, then it is not rule of law, it is warlordism. It is the rule of the powerful. Africa was taken for a ride. ...

MODERATOR: [asking Ocampo] ... All of the people over the last fourteen years have all been from the continent of Africa. That doesn't bother you at all?

OCAMPO: No! When you have crimes, you have victims and criminals. ...

MAMDANI: What was going on in Sudan was a civil war. ... In civil wars victims and perpetrators change sides. Violence is not a standalone event.

OCAMPO: So, for you, it's ok? The genocide in Darfur is ok for you?

MAMDANI: Just a minute, just a minute!

OCAMPO: It's ok what's happened in Darfur. That's what you're saying to me?

MAMDANI: Just a minute, just a minute! Violence is not a standalone event. There is a cycle of violence. Before the ICC got there, there was a UN commission of inquiry, and the UN commission of inquiry concluded that this was a civil war, where there were perpetrators on both sides. And any even-handed handling of that situation required the worst of the perpetrators on both sides be put on trial. The second thing the commission agreed was that there was no genocide. Genocide was a charge put up by the Save Darfur movement and the ICC together. Ok? And this was a political charge, it was a political charge.

OCAMPO: (looking at the moderator) Mahmood is saying I did not prosecute both sides in Sudan. It is wrong. In Sudan, I prosecuted militia rebels, I did it. So, he is telling me something wrong. And the fact is: political leaders in Africa and everywhere have to understand, crimes are not part of the political life. That's a limit, that's a limit they cannot cross. ...

MAMDANI:	I would acknowledge that political violence requires a political solution. Violence of civil wars is . . .
OCAMPO [laughs out loud]:	That is power to the powerful!
MAMDANI.	. . . is, listen, violence of civil wars is political violence.

The camera pans to Ocampo, who smiles and shakes his head to show his bafflement at Mamdani's argument.

In these few excerpts, the Argentinian lawyer Ocampo and the Ugandan anthropologist Mamdani display the whole array of typical clashing arguments when it comes to the legitimacy of the ICC in Africa and which have been formidably described in the work of Clarke (2009; 2019). They disagree in the way they construct who is victim and who is perpetrator. Ocampo insists on the stability of victim and perpetrator when he argues, "When you have crimes, you have victims and criminals." Mamdani challenges this clear dichotomy. He argues that "in civil wars, victims and perpetrators change sides." They disagree in the way they individualize or collectivize guilt. Ocampo argues that the ICC's African bias was invented by Omar Al-Bashir "to cover up *his* genocide." Mamdani insists that in the context of Sudan, "violence is not a standalone event"; he blames it on structural factors rather than on a single individual. When you blame it on an individual and when that individual is a head of state, according to Mamdani, "you are not just targeting an individual" but "you are also targeting the sovereignty of the country." They actively frame their dispute as law against politics. Mamdani emphasizes that "political violence requires a political solution." Ocampo sees agreeing to the primacy of politics over law as giving "power to the powerful."

But these clashing logics do not represent self-contained, standalone arguments. They are embedded in indignation regimes. These sentiments – law-over-politics versus politics-over-law, individual guilt versus collective guilt – depend on the relationality of bodies in the context of historical narratives. African countries signed on to the Rome Statute and subjected themselves to the ICC's oversight; they even voted for ICC referrals in the UN Security Council. Why should they be able to escape responsibility now? Africa was colonized by European countries, and African resistance cast off European colonialism. Why should they now again resubmit to a Western rule of law? These narratives are part of collective memory, and they are mobilized and contextualized via sentiments relating to victims, perpetrators, guilt, and the roots of violence.

The Al Jazeera television studio provides the affective arrangement for this process of clashing sentiments and the attempt to create, mobilize, challenge, and transform indignation regimes. The two speakers interrupt each other and exhibit passion in their performances; indeed, open displays of emotion are encouraged and even demanded by the television format. The exchange is dynamic. Both underline their historical narratives with specific bodily performances: shaking of the head in outrage; making exaggerated facial expressions to signal indignation, even contempt; laughing out loud to show disdain for the other's argument. The producers of the program have chosen to arrange the bodies in a specific way. For instance, the discussants confront each other antagonistically. But the participants try to do their own atmosphere work by bringing bodies into the affective arrangement, such as Ocampo with his printed maps. This is exactly the kind of spectacular micropractices that are aimed at shaping sentiments on a broad scale.

UNDER THE MANGO TREE

"Mamdani is losing it. Ehh . . . ." My conversation partner laughs out loud, shakes his head, throws his hands in the air and leans back in his chair. We are sitting under a large mango tree on a square behind the post office in Gulu. It's a sunny afternoon, although not too hot, and we have taken seats on plastic chairs in the shade. A low breeze blows through the leaves. We have been engaged in a stimulating conversation about the ICC in Uganda. My interlocutor is a retired rural development worker who has lived in Gulu his whole life, except for the time of his university studies in Kampala. He returned in 1986, the year of Museveni's ascension to power and the beginning of the rebellions in the north. Since then, he has worked in many NGOs and initiatives during and after the conflict, and he has his own views of critiques of the ICC like the one Mahmood Mamdani voiced above. "You see now … Has age caught up with him finally? Senility is catching up with the professor. The guy used to be a very rigorous analyst of issues."

My interlocutor is certainly no apologist for the ICC. In fact, he is highly critical of the inconsistencies that have emerged between the

ICC's investigation and the amnesty law. There should be a clear rule on how international criminal law and amnesty fit together. The resulting insecurities have disturbed the communities, he argues. But, at the same time, he has a healthy suspicion of the Museveni government and, more generally, the way many African heads of state and government put their interests before those of their constituencies: "Ehh … well, what is a president in the first place? What is a sitting president? It's just a person who has been elected to do certain things for a certain time and has been handed an office with certain instruments of power. That's a sitting president." He unequivocally rejects Mamdani's argument that indicting a sitting president means attacking a whole country: "I think Mamdani is losing it here. … The president is presidency. … Whether you are in it or you are out of it, you should be held accountable. I am shocked to hear Mamdani of all people taking that line. … I think he sees things in broader terms than that normally."

My interlocutor embeds this support for the ICC's indictment practice in narratives about African leaders' behavior. He talks about "tendencies of leaders to behave with impunity" and says to me: "If you ask me to describe an African leader, I would say, 'Who are they? Their mentality: I am the boss; I can do what I wish. Like a god.'" Like many other northerners critical of Museveni, he invokes a specific historical narrative on how he came to power:

> Museveni himself fought a sitting government and killed people until he got to power, okay. Fortunately, then the ICC was not there. But suppose it had been there – maybe the former government would have taken him to the ICC. Now, there are forms of getting into power. He's one of the most ostensible cases of fighting your way in. And other African leaders are not very different. But compared to other parts of the world, maybe people don't shoot their way into power just like that. … The way to get to power is seen in a different light in other parts of the world and I think the ICC is trying to universalize that perception of how to get into power. … Every leader should know that you are held liable for any action of yours, [whether that leader be] African or Chinese.

My interlocutor is indignant about the egregious violation of justice that "shooting your way into power" represents. To him it appears plausible and just that there should be universal standards for how you organize a change in government. When he studied social sciences in the 1980s, he was Mahmood Mamdani's student at Makerere

University. This personal biographical connection plays a major role for him. He feels somewhat betrayed because the anthropologist's views now differ so much from the views he professed earlier: "He taught me and he was the icon of clear thinking. Over time he got clouded with exhaustion from the pressure of mobilizing Makerere to retain its stature or restore its stature. I know that with age also you get tired. So, he begins to sing the songs of others. He's picking up a song, he's not starting a song." He starts laughing heartily and again lays back in his chair. "He's not starting a new song on this one."

IN THE COURTROOM

It is January 25, 2016, in Courtroom One of the International Criminal Court in The Hague. Paolina Massidda, the Principal Counsel of the Office of the Public Counsel for Victims at the ICC, is making a presentation in the case *The Prosecutor* v. *Dominic Ongwen* (Figure 6.2). She speaks on behalf of the victims of the former commander of the Lord's Resistance Army. Massidda's clients include civilians who lived in internally displaced persons camps at the time of the conflict. They or their relatives were injured, forced to haul looted goods (particularly foodstuffs), abducted – sometimes for short periods of time, sometimes for months or years – or even killed. Among

Figure 6.2 Paolina Massidda (left), Principal Counsel of the ICC's Office of the Public Counsel for Victims, in the courtroom. (A black and white version of this figure will appear in some formats. For the color version, please refer to the plate section.)

this group are men and boys who were abducted from their home villages and recruited into the LRA as child soldiers, many of whom have experienced great difficulties with reintegration (Amone-P'Olak 2007; Annan 2009; Pham 2009). But there is also a number of women and girls whom the LRA abducted in order to distribute them to LRA fighters (Allen 2006, 65; Annan et al. 2009). These "LRA wives" or "bush wives," as they are called, were held in the LRA as forced wives and sex slaves (Okello and Hovil 2007; Annan and Brier 2010).

She is adamant about pointing out Dominic Ongwen's responsibility for the crimes of sexual slavery and forced marriage. The crime of forced marriage is especially tricky, as the Court has not yet recognized forced marriage as a crime against humanity in its case law. There are precedents, however, from the International Criminal Tribunal for the Former Yugoslavia (ICTY) and the International Criminal Tribunal for Rwanda (ICTR). She cites this case law extensively to make her point; namely, that forced marriage and sexual slavery are not the same thing and that the former is not subsumed under the latter. In the victims' view, the act of forced marriage itself has an injurious scope beyond sexual slavery. Sexual slavery criminalizes the sexual intercourse that these women were forced to have with their "husbands" and the fact that they had to work to maintain their households, much like slaves. The crime of forced marriage, however, has a different scope. It criminalizes depriving the victims of their right to choose a husband. The forced marriage stigmatizes them, most likely for the rest of their lives, which often prevents them from marrying in the future. However, before Massidda engages in her legal argumentation in a narrower sense, she chooses to present a historical narrative:

> MS MASSIDDA: ... Allow me, your Honours, to quote from the History of Rome of Titus Livius, an expert which actually describes in similar terms what victims have described to us as the moment of their abduction.

I quote:

> ... Many people gather for the festival, especially those who live near. The Sabines, too, came with all their people, including their children and wives. ... When the time came for the show, and people's thoughts and eyes were busy with it, the preconcerted attack began. At a given signal the young Romans darted this way and that, to seize and carry off the maidens. In most cases these were taken by the men in whose path they were. Some, of exceptional beauty, had been marked out for the

> chief senators, and were carried off to their houses by plebeians to whom the office had been entrusted. . . . The sports broke up in a panic, and the parents of the maidens fled sorrowing . . . The stolen maidens were no more hopeful of their plight, nor less indignant.

End of quote.

> The episode is known as "The Rape of the Sabine Women" but, in fact, the English word "rape" is a conventional translation of the Latin "*raptio*," which in this context means "abduction," rather than its prevalent modern meaning in English language of sexual abuse. During the decades of armed conflict in northern Uganda the LRA systematically abducted girls for the purpose of forcibly marrying them to commanders and fighters. Abductions were normally perpetrated during the attacks. The majority of abducted girls forced into marriage were given to LRA commanders and higher-ranking fighters. Top commanders would describe the type of girl they wanted, including age, physical appearance and intelligence. If recent abductees matched these desired characteristics, then they were collected and distributed.[8]

After Massidda's presentation, the president of the Chamber comments on her performance:

PRESIDING JUDGE TARFUSSER: Thank you. Thank you very much, Mrs Massidda. May I have just one small point? Titus Livius should have been – could have been quoted in Latin, but that's something else. It was just . . .

MS MASSIDDA: I would have loved to, your Honours, but I was a little bit afraid of the translation.

PRESIDING JUDGE TARFUSSER: Okay. Okay. Accepted.[9]

Tarfusser and Massidda, who both smile during this exchange, are both Italians, undoubtedly well versed in the classics. Massidda's excursion into ancient Rome was addressed to a shared cultural repertoire, and the message found an eager recipient in the ICC judge. It is a moment in which the ICC appears very much like a European courtroom with European laws and European narratives, very much as postcolonial critics would characterize it.

Massidda's narrative is full of fear and panic, intended to trigger indignation. The rape of the Sabines is the crime of crimes against women and exemplifies the abuse of male power and of Rome's imperial power. The story itself is ancient, indicating to the counsel's listeners that this is the same old story: male power exerted over female innocence. It is also a story about the legitimacy of the ICC. If it had existed at the time, the Court would have been justified to try the Romans, and it is justified to try Dominic Ongwen in the here and now. The crime is as old as mankind, and mankind is as justified in condemning it today as it was then.

But Massidda's message about the universality of patriarchal crimes is not the only sentiment in the room. There are counternarratives, and Europe appears in them as well, albeit in a slightly shifted way.

On the same day, the defense begins its presentation. One important line of defense for Ongwen's representatives is to present him as a victim rather than as a perpetrator (see Chapter 3). Having been abducted himself as a child and constantly brainwashed and threatened with death in case of disobedience, so the defense's narrative goes, he was under constant duress and cannot be held criminally liable for his actions. Krispus Ayena Odongo, Dominic Ongwen's defense counsel, an experienced trial lawyer from northern Uganda who was also involved

Figure 6.3 Krispus Ayena Odongo (right), Dominic Ongwen's defense counsel, in the ICC courtroom. (A black and white version of this figure will appear in some formats. For the color version, please refer to the plate section.)

in the LRA peace talks in Juba from 2006 to 2008, also chooses to tell a story (Figure 6.3). It is not situated in Europe, however, but in Africa:

> MR ODONGO: . . . In the mind of Ongwen, your Honours, his indictment [is] tantamount to indicting the entire child soldier – I mean, soldiers in the world. As we speak now in this hall, your Honours, there are still multitudes of child soldiers waiting to hear from the international community represented by this Court what would happen to them if they risked to escape and come out. This Honourable Court should be reminded that it is a representative of that international community who yearns to protect the child soldier. The Defence hopes that this judicial institution of the international community will not behave like the Catholic convert who justified his actions by changing goalposts.
>
> Your Honours, the story is told that when the white man took his religion to Africa, he found a man who was called Aboku he had – he convinced him to convert to Catholicism, baptised him and called him John, and he told him, "John, in order to be a good Catholic there are two things you ought never to do. The first one is that a good Catholic never eats meat on a Friday. And the second one is that a good Catholic never tells a lie."
>
> Your Honours, finally the white priest went back to his home country on leave, but on the day when he came back he found John had had some problems, challenges in the family. He had gone out and killed a rabbit because there was famine, there was nothing to eat in the house. He went into the bush, killed a rabbit and here he was eating rabbit meat on a Friday.
>
> The priest said to John, "But John, how dare a good Catholic eat meat on a Friday?" And John said, "But father, what I'm eating is not meat, it is fish." The priest said, "But John, you have now committed two sins: first you are eating meat on a Friday and now you're telling me this is fish." And John said, "But father, I insist this is fish." He said, "How does it become fish?" John told father, "You know, father, when you came to Africa, me, I was called Aboku. You poured water on me and from Aboku I become John. So father, you know, when I cut this meat into pieces I sprinkled water on it and I said from meat you become fish. So I'm eating fish."
>
> The Defence hopes that this story will not come true in the representation of the international community by this Court. This Court, representing the international community, should make sure that the goalpost about protecting the child soldier is not shifted.

Odongo's story does not provoke a comment by the bench, which is not surprising, as this narrative is more challenging and multilayered. The convert in this story wants to change the rules of the game while it is still being played – or so it seems. He breaks the Catholic rules but, at the same time, he remains within a Catholic logic. He "christened" his rabbit to transform it into fish.

The humorous twist of this story is that John is not authorized to act in the way he does because he is not a priest. He is ignorant of the fact that only priests are allowed to perform the ritual – and to rename a thing or a person. The parable is a story about power relations, and the humorous element is that the convert does not understand his position in this field of power. It is also a story about colonialism and Europe's power to name and rename, and therefore to set the rules of the game. And it is a story about Eurocentrism, because the universal (Catholic) rules are not suited to African realities, not least of all economic realities. The convert goes out to catch the rabbit in the first place because he must feed his family. This eventuality is not foreseen in the logic of the rules the white priest had dictated. And finally, it is a story about pragmatism and law because it is about the attempt to bend the rules without breaking them, a way of acknowledging that they are generally right, but not applicable in all situations.

Odongo's narrative contains confusing humor and is intended to disrupt the feeling rules imposed by the Court that Massidda had tried to stabilize. It suggests a different normative logic, a logic in which the crime is not "the same old story," but "an always new story" interwoven in concrete relations of power, economic conditions, and the history of colonialism. The story of the rape of the Sabines is about universality: it was a crime 2,000 years ago, it is still a crime today. The story of the convert eating the rabbit is about relativism and the uneasy contradictions of law, power, and the uneven application of rules.

The two stories in the courtroom on January 25, 2016, represent two sentiments of justice, and they create two indignation regimes: one about the egregious abuse of male power over women, the other about the violent imposition of white rules on African realities. Two historical narratives affectively frame these regimes. The affective arrangements make it possible for both justice imaginaries to be plausible. A cheerful party disrupted by violent Roman soldiers who steal women as if they were property. A hungry man in need of food for his family, breaking rules that do not fit the everyday challenges he has to overcome.

IN THE NGO OFFICE

"The International Criminal Court . . . the major concern is let them really take on all cases equally. . . . Because all human beings are the same. There is no human being who is superior to the other or of higher quality than the other. We are all the same before the eyes of God." This is the reply to my question of selective justice before the ICC. My interlocutor is a Muslim cleric and a long-standing peace activist, and I am having my conversation with him in the office of the Acholi Religious Leaders' Peace Initiative (ARLPI) in Gulu in northern Uganda. The Muslim community in northern Uganda consists mainly of immigrants from Sudan, and he himself is also Sudanese by birth. Like many religious leaders, he was a staunch supporter of the 2000 Amnesty Act and still sees the ICC as endangering the processes of reconciliation in northern Uganda. In his view, the ICC is applying selective justice, and he provides me with ample historical precedents:

> President Bush, Tony Blair the prime minister of the United Kingdom, had their hands in the Iraq war. They pushed for that war and the international community justified that war, but there were no weapons of mass destruction. And after Iraq was destroyed completely, Saddam Hussein was killed, hanged. But what is Iraq now? . . . The garden between River Euphrates and Tigris, one of the seven world wonders, that beautiful garden, destroyed. One of the world's museums . . . lost! . . . The same if you follow the NATO invasion of Libya. Because of just one man. You cannot be patient to wait for him, at the right time just to pick him alone, but you destroy the whole nation. The US invasion of Afghanistan, to look for one man and you bomb with B52s the whole country. You want to bomb one man. What is the Court for? What is the ICC for? Why not use sanctions to get Osama Bin Laden and he faces justice . . . instead of destroying the whole country and causing a war that is going on and on. Where is the international community? Why aren't they seeing these? . . . These are the concerns. And if at times some of the African leaders are opening their eyes to that, it is just because there are some presidents and former presidents of bigger nations that are not prosecuted, and they are free. And they are even made an envoy to go and resolve conflicts in the Middle East.

My conversation partner contrasts these many historical references to war crimes that were not punished to the ICC's indictment of Omar Al-Bashir. "President Al-Bashir is still on the hook. Recently he visited Darfur. He was given a very, very warm and jubilant welcome in

Darfur." Why is it that Al-Bashir is targeted by the ICC, my interlocutor asks rhetorically. "Because he's an African president? Because he's a Muslim? Those are the questions we ask at times."

In the opinion of my conversation partner, other African presidents are far worse than Al-Bashir. He mentions the Kenyan President Uhuru Kenyatta, who was recently acquitted by the ICC after the prosecution had indicted him for inciting post-electoral violence: "You know people died in Kenya and the witnesses were killed. We know most of the witnesses perished. And out of fear, most of the witnesses were quiet about the crime when he was already in the International Criminal Court in The Hague. But Uhuru Kenyatta is a free man." My conversation partner goes on: "If I give you an example, just in Congo, Laurent Nkunda. Laurent Nkunda killed Eastern Congolese, many women raped, people slaughtered, young girls raped. But Laurent Nkunda was not convicted or indicted by the International Criminal Court. Why is it blind in some cases?"

My interlocutor's historical examples of selective justice by the ICC are full of affect-laden references and images – killings and rapes in Central Africa, museums in ruins and beautiful gardens destroyed in Iraq, warm and jubilant welcomes in Darfur – that can be analyzed as affective arrangements. They all merge into one indignation regime: selective justice and racial bias.

IN THE LECTURE HALL

It is June 20, 2016. I am entering the Senate Hall of Humboldt University in Berlin. I have arrived a little late and most of the seats have already been taken, so I choose a seat in the back. Chile Eboe-Osuji, the Nigerian judge at the International Criminal Court who would later become president of the Court, is giving a lecture titled "The Value of Criminal Jurisdiction for the African Court as an Instrument of Transnational Criminal Justice and Crime Prevention: Other Things Being Equal."

The event is organized by the South African–German Centre for Transnational Criminal Justice – a joint institution of Humboldt University in Berlin and the University of the Western Cape in Cape Town, South Africa. It is one of seven "Centres of African Excellence" funded by the German Academic Exchange Service (DAAD). The center offers an LLM (master of laws) and PhD program called "Transnational Criminal Justice and Crime

Prevention: An International and African Perspective." The room is roughly half full of students enrolled in this program, mostly from African countries. The other half comprises European academics, mostly Germans, interested in Eboe-Osuji's talk, including myself.

Eboe-Osuji begins by pointing out the potential of a criminal chamber within the African Court of Justice and Human Rights. The recent pan-Africanist pushback against the ICC had ignited discussions about coming up with an African alternative to the ICC. Eboe-Osuji summarizes the discussion in the African Union, noting that it is especially encouraging that the African Court would be able to try a number of crimes beyond the four core crimes the ICC is authorized to try, which are genocide, crimes against humanity, war crimes, and crimes of aggression. The Malabo Protocol, the African counterpart to the Rome Statute, enumerates ten additional criminal offenses that would be justiciable by the African Court: the crime of unconstitutional change of government (Art. 28E), piracy (Art. 28 F), terrorism (Art. 28 G), mercenarism (Art. 28 H), corruption (Art. 28I), money laundering (28I Bis), trafficking in persons (Art. 28 J), trafficking in drugs (Art. 28 K), trafficking in hazardous waste (Art. 28 L), and illicit exploitation of natural resources (Art. 28 L Bis).[10] Moreover, the new African Court would be authorized to find private corporations criminally liable for international crimes (Art. 46 C). The Rome Statute, which governs the proceedings of the ICC, does not explicitly mention such a mode of responsibility. As the ICC remains the court of last resort because of its principle of complementarity, Eboe-Osuji claims that there is nothing wrong with creating a criminal chamber in the African Court of Justice and Human Rights, "all things being equal."

But, as Eboe-Osuji further explains, all things are *not* equal regarding the new African Court, mainly because of Art. 46A Bis, the so-called immunity clause. The clause reads, "[N]o charges shall be commenced or continued before the Court against any serving AU Head of State or Government, or anybody acting or entitled to act in such capacity, or other senior state officials based on their functions, during their tenure of office." This immunity provision could serve as "an unwitting cover of severe crimes" and provides the "wrong incentive" for criminal heads of state or government (HoSG) "to remain in office as long as possible, even by committing further crimes" to avoid criminal prosecution. Additionally, according to Eboe-Osuji, certain paradoxes emerge as some of the crimes enumerated in the Statute can practically only be committed by HoSG, such as the crimes of unconstitutional change in government or aggression. They would then practically never be able to be tried by the African Court.

Eboe-Osuji refers to a decision of the African Union from October 2013, the time when the ICC trial against Uhuru Kenyatta, the president of the Republic of Kenya, began. This resolution, titled "Decision of Africa's Relationship with the International Criminal Court (ICC),"[11] asserts "that this is the first time that a sitting Head of State and his deputy are being tried in an international court." The AU member states stressed "the gravity of this situation, which could undermine the sovereignty, stability, and peace in that country and in other Member States as well as reconciliation and reconstruction and the normal functioning of constitutional institutions."

The resolution entails a legal argument with its reference to "the principles deriving from national laws and international customary law by which sitting Heads of State and other senior state officials are granted immunities during their tenure of office." Eboe-Osuji argues that this resolution effectively accuses the ICC and, with it, the international legal community dominated by the West of deliberately deviating from a settled principle of international law – the immunity from prosecution of heads of state or government – in order to prosecute African leaders.

Eboe-Osuji's main goal in Berlin this day is to produce a counternarrative against this argument. According to him, the AU's entire argument is based on a false premise, namely, that the immunity of HoSG for international crimes was ever a principle of international law. Eboe-Osuji concedes that it is true that states and their higher officials usually enjoy immunity before national courts. This principle is called "sovereign immunity" and is derived from the more general principle of the "sovereign equality of states," which is accentuated in the UN Charter (Kelsen 1944).[12] Just a few years before, the principle of sovereign immunity was reiterated by the International Court of Justice in its famous judgment *Germany* v. *Italy*.[13] But what Eboe-Osuji highlights is that from its inception, international criminal law has always explicitly denied any form of immunity for HoSG.

To underscore this contention, Eboe-Osuji embarks on a legal historical narrative. The Treaty of Versailles, which ended the First World War, already contained provisions for an international criminal tribunal to try the German emperor (although this never came to pass). At the time only the US representative to the Versailles negotiations objected to these provisions on the basis of sovereign immunity but was voted down by the overwhelming majority of state parties. After the Second World War, the Nuremberg and Tokyo tribunals also explicitly denied any immunity for higher state officials, which was affirmed by the United Nations General Assembly in its first session in 1946.[14] Denying heads of state and government immunity for international crimes was therefore not "Western imperialism" directed against African politicians. On the contrary, Eboe-Osuji emphasizes, the first heads of government ever found guilty in international tribunals were a German president and a Japanese prime minister.[15] He concludes with the observation that "the Nuremberg Principles had nothing to do with prosecuting Africans, but with prosecuting the most powerful Europeans at the time."

There is not much tension in the air on that day in Humboldt University's lecture hall. All participants, mostly African and European lawyers, have more or less the same opinion on the issue. They see an immunity clause shielding African heads of state and government from being prosecuted for the worst crimes imaginable as irreconcilable with universal principles of justice and, therefore, as thoroughly illegitimate. It would be difficult to identify any passionate displays of emotions in most of Eboe-Osuji's performance, especially if we compare it to the dynamic exchange in the Al Jazeera television program I reported on earlier in the chapter.

But Eboe-Osuji's argumentation is no less intended to create and maintain an indignation regime. In countering the accusation of "race hunting" through the instrument of the ICC levied against "European colonialists," Eboe-Osuji evokes yet another affective arrangement: the Nazi criminal on trial in Nuremberg. Both historical narratives are fraught with sentiments. One's evaluation of the legitimacy of the ICC depends on which of these indignation regimes one taps into. The one who stands in line with the history of the noble anti-colonial freedom fighter and hence opposes the ICC's neocolonial intervention is part of a moral community and follows a just cause. The one who stands in line with the history of the noble liberator bringing Nazi criminals to justice is in equally good company. Both indignation regimes invite the audience to join the moral community they imply. Affectively grounded historical narratives give plausibility to them. Even a thoroughly constructed legal history argument, presented in an academic setting without emotional tension in the room, cannot be made without engaging in a politics of sentiment.

***

At the beginning of this chapter, I brought up the question of the relationship between law and politics. I wondered if it might be possible to conceive of law and politics as anything other than divided by the degree to which they are affective: politics as governed by heated passions, law as governed by cold rationality.

My argument is that it is a mistake to see law and politics as occupying opposing ends of a spectrum with *ratio* at one extreme and *emotio* at the other. My plea is to pay close attention to the role of sentiment in both law and politics. The concept of sentiment crosscuts the *ratio–emotio* divide by acknowledging that affective processes are always at work when people make judgments, be they political or legal.

The debate on the legitimacy of the ICC in Africa is one important example of a debate that seems to be about the primacy of law over politics or of politics over law, but can be much more clearly described as the competition between different sentiments and people vying to create indignation regimes to stabilize and mobilize them. In the course of this book, I have presented many instances of people being able to switch between different normative orders and imaginaries of justice. They can do so because a politics of sentiment allows for a variety of ways to make them plausible (Chapter 3), objective (Chapter 4), and just (Chapter 5).

In the ICC in Africa debate, different indignation regimes are at work: the anti-colonial struggle, the fight against impunity after the Holocaust, resistance against selective justice, the refusal to accept violent regime change against democratic rules, condemnation of violence against women, opposition to racism, the pushback against the intrusion of colonial rules of the game. All of these indignation regimes stabilize sentiments – more or less fixed ways to feel what is right and what is wrong – and imply moral communities that one can align oneself with. No legal and no political judgment can be understood in their subjective dimension without taking them into account.

7

WE HAVE NEVER BEEN RATIONAL

On the Emotions of Liberal Legalism and the Affective Politics of Modernity

Commen vouloir les lumières sans la modernité?[1]

Bruno Latour, *Nous n'avons jamais été moderne* (1991, 22)

On March 5, 2012, a video of about thirty minutes titled *Kony 2012* was posted online by a US NGO called Invisible Children. The video is about the personal journey of a handsome young white man from the United States who worked as a humanitarian aid worker in Uganda and his adorably cute blond-haired son. The film opens with images of the son's birth. We learn of Jacob, a former child soldier from northern Uganda who had been abducted by the LRA and who breaks down in tears when he talks about the loss of his brother in the military conflict. The viewers are asked to become active by wearing *Kony 2012* bracelets and hanging *Kony 2012* posters to create awareness of Joseph Kony, the leader of the LRA, and his crimes. The video is a call to find and arrest Kony by the end of the year 2012. As we know, this did not happen. In the hope of helping to locate Kony, the video's stated goal is to "make Joseph Kony a household name." That, it did achieve. One month after its release the video had been watched more than 100 million times by people all over the world (Brown et al. 2012, 3).[2]

The emotion-laden video's agenda is a staggeringly stereotypical depiction of violent conflicts in Africa. Focusing only on the individual Joseph Kony, it fails to provide any historical context to the war in northern Uganda, which – at the time of the video – had been, for all intents and purposes, over for several years. According to the video, Kony does not follow any rational agenda. "He is not fighting for any cause, but only to maintain his power." The video cannot imagine any measure to end the practices of the LRA other than to deploy US troops to help the Ugandan army capture him. The video is full of young activists, none of them local to Uganda. The colonial vision of "helping" Africa through Western intervention is celebrated. Toward the end of the video, the adorable blond-haired son declares: "I'm going to be like you, dad, when I grow up. I'm going with you to Africa."

It is not surprising that this campaign video provoked heavy criticism from Ugandan civil society and large parts of the academic community, particularly those in anthropology and African studies (Brown et al. 2012; Clarke 2012; Finnström 2012; Sangokoya 2012; Finnegan 2013; Levin 2013; Gould 2014). Although some agree that it created awareness of and interest in African politics, most denounce the film for its many stereotypical depictions of Africa. Most importantly, by failing to provide any social, political, cultural, or economic context to Joseph Kony and the LRA, as well as by ignoring possible explanations for their actions, the video feeds into preconceptions of Africa as a space of irrationality and savagery. In other words, modernity's other.

It is exactly this question of rational modernity and its other that underlies this whole book and which I aim to tackle head-on in this concluding chapter. Modernity, rationality, and the law are deeply entangled, and they depend on exorcising their antitheses – the non-modern, the nonrational, and the nonlegal – to establish and maintain both their conceptual and normative validity. It has been one of anthropology's most legitimate instincts to question these concepts and their production processes (for Africa, see Geschiere, Meyer, and Pels 2008). In this chapter, I will tap into these anthropological critiques and focus on affect and emotion to further them. Emotion is, in its traditional conceptions, all three: non-modern, nonrational, and nonlegal. Shattering this assumption opens up new perspectives to think about this whole array of basic concepts of the contemporary world.

MODERNITY, RATIONALITY, AND THE LAW

European modernity has been imagined as the consistent and systematic penetration of rationality into the social, cultural, and economic order. Rationality is the key imaginary of the two dominant theoretical streams of modernity: liberalism and Marxism. Both European theories of the social and the cultural are, at their core, based on an evolutionary progression from savagery to civilization. And it is the law that facilitates this evolution.

In liberalism, the idea of the social contract constitutes the key step in the evolution from savagery to civilization. The contractualists of the seventeenth and eighteenth centuries, Thomas Hobbes (1651), Jean-Jacques Rousseau (1762), and John Locke (1764), argued that before civilized society there was the state of nature when rationality did not yet govern society. To end this savage existence, people developed modern law. They entered into a social contract to organize society along with the criteria rationality dictates. This prevalence of rationality was, and still is, reminiscent of ancient and medieval European ideas of natural law. The world, so this idea goes, is organized according to ordering principles – given by God or, in its more secular variant, by the universe. One can discover these ordering principles through rational investigation and thereby arrive at universal natural law. Contemporary international law, particularly the human rights idea, is still based on such natural law conceptions (Pagden 2003; Bens 2020).

Marxist thought is similarly based on the development from savagery to civilization. As Friedrich Engels (1884) explained in explicit reference to nineteenth-century evolutionist anthropology, humans made the step from savagery to civilization through the development of a legal system recognizing private property. Rationality is likewise the guiding force of this development. Marx is very much a Hegelian in following the notion that the universe develops according to its own rules. The difference is that in Hegel's (1807) view these are the rules of the development of the human spirit, whereas in Marx's (1859) view these are the rules of the development of the relations of production – and property law was a key component of the mode of production.

There is a key difference between the two main theories of modernity – Marxism and liberalism – when it comes to the law. While liberal theorists see the juridification of human relations as a desirable development that helps to guarantee people's freedom, Marxist thinkers see the development of liberal legalism as an undesirable, though inevitable, development on the road to capitalism, and that it lays the groundwork for the exploitation of people. While liberals see modern statehood and liberal legalism as an ideal form of human society, Marxists see them as a necessary intermediary step toward something yet to come: a communist society in which much of the liberal law is no longer needed. In any case, both agree that modernity is the manifestation of rationality in society and that the law is the facilitator of this rationalization.

This relationship of modernity, rationality, and law is nowhere more clearly expressed than in the work of Max Weber. The theorist of modernity sees law as the prime device for the rationalization of society. For Weber, premodern "primitive legality" is characterized by "magical formalism and prophetic irrationality." Only in a development "toward a more and more disciplinary, juridical, therefore logical, rationality and systematization" can there come into being a modern, "rational legal technique" (Weber 1921, 503–504). This conceptualization of law and modernity in Europe as rational necessitates ascribing irrationality and emotionality to the non-modern Rest.

Postcolonial theory has been very sensitive to these ascriptions of irrational emotion to the non-West. In *Orientalism* (1978), one of the founding works of postcolonial theory, Edward Said has shown how European discourse practices have constructed the non-European Orient by way of feminization, sexualization, and emotionalization. In anthropology, the work of Ann Stoler (1995, 2002) has shown how European empires deployed strategies of affective governance in which the ascription of emotions to the non-European world served as a basis to further their colonial projects.

PROVINCIALIZING MODERNITY AND LIBERALISM

It is one of anthropology's most prevalent instincts to be skeptical of such conceptions of modernity and pre-modernity. In the early years of the discipline, the founding figures of twentieth-century anthropology were already arguing not so much against how modernity theorists conceptualized the development of European societies but against how they described non-European societies as irrational and emotion-driven. Franz Boas, one of the founders of US anthropology, made it his life's work to argue against the racial devaluation inherent in this description of the non-European other and made a forceful plea for cultural relativism in order to investigate non-European cultures on their own terms instead only in relation to European modernity (1911, 1928, 1940). Bronislaw Malinowski (1922), one of the founders of British anthropology, devoted his ethnographic work to showing that the Trobriand Islanders he investigated in what is now Papua New Guinea were no less rational actors than Europeans.

Legal anthropology was always at the forefront of this project. Malinowski (1926) himself argued that, far from being a feature exclusive to modern statehood, a conception of law as a set of guidelines for the rational decisions of actors was a prevalent feature of non-Western societies. In what has become a classic of legal anthropology in Africa, Max Gluckman (1955) argued that one of the guiding principles of the Barotse legal system in southern Africa was concerned with the idea of the "reasonable man."

Anthropological research on the war in northern Uganda has followed a similar course. Many observers of the conflict, particularly those in the international mass media, depicted the practice of child recruitment as evidence of the savage, uncivilized, and irrational character of the LRA. The *Kony 2012* video I introduced at the beginning of this chapter is a prime example of this discourse. Such a view of the LRA has been criticized by some academics, who argue against these more stereotyping views and promote instead an image of the LRA as a violent but ultimately rational actor with a political agenda (Allen 2006, 62–64; Dolan 2009, 74–75). This line of thought argues that there is "cold rationality" behind the abduction of children in that it is a way of exploiting the only natural resource available to the LRA, which is the Acholi population (Bevan 2007). Such arguments are intended to make clear that actors in northern Uganda are no less "reasonable" – to pick up on Gluckman's term – than Europeans.

It is noteworthy that during the time when Gluckman made his "reasonable man" argument, it provoked a critique that came to define legal anthropology for decades. In a legal ethnography of the Tiv in West Africa, Paul Bohannan (1957) criticized Gluckman for imposing English common-law legal terminology on Barotse legal thought. Instead of using the Barotse terms to discuss the legal concepts he was analyzing, Gluckman resorted to English-language equivalents, terms that were already theoretically grounded in European legal thinking. Conversely, Bohannan insisted on using Tiv terms to describe and discuss Tiv law. The resulting Bohannan–Gluckman debate, which circled around the question of the limits of cross-cultural comparison and can be seen as a precursor in legal anthropology to the emic/etic distinction (Harris 1976) that would later become a commonplace in anthropology, had good arguments on both sides. What I would like to focus on here is Bohannan's suspicion that Gluckman's method was somehow an epistemological imposition on the African legal order he was investigating, a suspicion that I would agree with.

As much as anthropology sees itself as an advocate for non-European rationality, demonstrating through ethnographic studies that the rational is no less prevalent outside of Europe than it is inside Europe, it nevertheless remains largely within the dominant frame of modernity theory. The triad of modernity, rationality, and law is taken for granted; it is merely universalized and projected onto the whole of mankind. Even sociologist Shmuel Eisenstadt's (2000) oft-cited concept of "multiple modernity" is not terribly helpful in overcoming this predilection. It takes the idea of modernity with rational legalization at its core intact and argues that it has not only developed in Europe, but also elsewhere, and that it has even been globalized and could encompass the whole world in the form of a global modern capitalism (Wallerstein 1983). I am not, however, arguing that there is no global capitalist society. I contend, rather, that anthropologists would be well advised to question the standard *characterization* of global capitalism and ask whether global capitalism has ever been "modern" in the sense European modernity theory would have it – with the exorcising of emotion at its center.

Studies of colonialism have placed a strong emphasis on the dialectical workings of colonialism. The colonial endeavor did not bring the pre-modern, non-European space under the control of modern Europe. Colonialism created modern Europe in the first place. European modernity was made in a dialectical relationship with the colonies (Stoler and Cooper 1997; Veer 2001), particularly through the global expansion of the capitalist economy (Wolf 1982; Mintz 1985). Achille Mbembe (2013) has shown that modern statehood and liberal legalism were not only constituted under the conditions of slavery and colonial exploitation but that they are constitutively inscribed into rational modernity. Civilized modernity entails the savagery of the plantation.

If we take seriously this dialectical relationship, anthropologists should engage in a critique of modernity that is much more fundamental than merely being more generous in its acknowledgment of the existence of rationality outside of Europe. As an anthropology of modernity, it should ask, with Bruno Latour (1991), if Europe has ever been modern. That means, of course, to investigate distinctively modern settings such as the laboratory and the courtroom, as Latour has done (Latour and Woolgar 1979; Latour 2002). But the most crucial aspect is something quite different: it is to question, on a very basic level, if conceptions of modernity as they have come out of European thought since the seventeenth century accurately describe the world we live in, and that means taking full account of the dialectical character of modernity. It will not suffice to limit such an inquiry to Europe; it must be approached through a comparative lens that includes contexts outside of Europe. This might lead us to the insight that modernity has never been rational – at least not in the sense of a rationality that is antithetical to emotion and affect.

MODERN AFFECT AND LIBERAL EMOTION

I make a plea to criticize the triad of modernity, rationality, and law insofar as it depends on the exclusion of affect and emotion. I propose to rethink all three terms, as well as their relationship, by suggesting that they are grounded in affect. In this book, I have attempted to show that legal proceedings, even if they follow their internal logic of the cold, rational application of rules, depend on affective and emotional dynamics. To the degree that the law is performed in particular spaces, be it the courtroom or beyond, it is embedded in atmospheres. Key legal terms such as plausibility, objectivity, and justice cannot come into existence without sentiment. Conflicts over law and politics must be understood as embroiled in a politics of atmosphere and sentiment. This suggests that cold rationality itself must be seen as an affective register. It is as much a feeling as heated passion is. Modernity is, as much as its premodern other, something that must be felt by people.

Why does it not appear like this? Why is it that modernity is so thoroughly conceptualized as free of emotion? I believe it is because, as I have argued elsewhere in the context of the affective embeddedness of democratic deliberation (Bens et al. 2019), emotions are only recognized as such when they are the emotions of the others. This means that one's own learned and socialized emotion repertoires, the internalized indignation regimes and sentiments, generally do not feel particularly emotional. It is mostly in moments of tension when people disagree about what the right way to feel about things is that emotions are made a topic of negotiation. When participants in a courtroom infringe on the feeling rules liberal legalism has set up, these infringements are felt as emotional outbreaks. But the degree to which established courtroom feeling rules such as sitting quietly and assuming a somber demeanor are also affective practices remains unacknowledged.

In German sociology, there has been a surge of interest in investigating "late modernity" in terms of affect (Rosa 2016; Reckwitz 2018). The "late" remains quite squarely in modernity's evolutionary paradigm – not unlike the idea of "late liberalism" gaining popularity in anthropology (Povinelli 2006, 2011, 2016). The "late" also indicates that the stereotypes of modernity and liberalism might not apply anymore. As Reckwitz (2018) has argued, late modernity is far too obviously governed by affect to be classically modern, and he proposes the term *Affektgesellschaft* ("society of affect") to describe it. This "new" affectivity in the modern West is seen by many contemporary theorists of modernity as a sign of a political and cultural crisis (Nussbaum 2018; Mouffe 2018; Reckwitz 2019).

The arguments I have put forth in this book suggest a reframing of the question. Is there actually a "new" affectivity in modern society, or is it that we have never been rational? Instead of conceiving of affect as a crisis of modernity and liberal legalism, it is crucial to investigate modern affect and liberal emotion. The affective life of the law is a crucial starting point for this endeavor. It opens up a field of inquiry in which assessing the role of affect and emotion in (post)modern life becomes an integral element in assessing the past, present, and future of the relationship between the Global North and the Global South. This entails in a crucial respect decolonizing modernity not only by realizing that the West is no more rational than the Rest, but also by questioning whether rationality, at its core, is really any more independent of subjective feeling than emotion.

EPILOGUE

Affect and Colonialism

On February 4, 2021, as I was preparing this book for publication, the judges of the ICC found Dominic Ongwen guilty of war crimes and crimes against humanity.[1] Two weeks earlier, Yoweri Kaguta Museveni had won the general election and, despite allegations of election fraud and violent suppression of the political opposition, entered his sixth term as president of Uganda.[2] Ongwen's conviction, which carries a prison sentence of twenty-five years,[3] most likely marks the end of the ICC's criminal prosecution in northern Uganda. Of the other four commanders of the Lord's Resistance Army against whom warrants are outstanding, only Joseph Kony is rumored to still be alive. But as of now, it does not appear likely that he will ever be captured and tried in The Hague. Cases against other actors in the conflict, particularly from the side of the government, are not on the horizon.

The judgment was presented by the presiding judge, Bertram Schmitt, from Germany. He made his remarks slowly and carefully, his face showing a solemn expression. The years-long trial and the severity of the occasion seemed to weigh on him. Toward the beginning of the hearing, he made a few preliminary remarks on how he intended to summarize the judgment. Among those remarks, he put this statement to the audience:

> Let me emphasise that it was difficult for the Chamber to ascertain the names of every victim of the several crimes. Yet, in many cases the Chamber was able to do so. These victims have a right not to be forgotten. They have the right to be mentioned explicitly today, as

> they are in the judgment as well. Please bear with me if I pronounce names incorrectly.[4]

This brief scene profoundly affected me, but in several quite ambivalent ways. It triggered an intense awareness of the colonial structure of our contemporary world. What struck me immediately, and maybe this was just on the surface of the arrangement, was the constellation of bodies: a white European man sitting in judgment over a black African, deciding his fate. This encapsulates the colonial constellation in a nutshell. Second, Schmitt evokes the African victims of violence to legitimize this constellation of bodies in which he speaks. He presents himself and his colleagues at the bench as people who take the side of the victims and do not want them to be forgotten. The "specter of the victim" as a prevalent trope of colonialism at the center of international criminal justice has been formidably and critically analyzed by Kamari Clarke in *Fictions of Justice* (2009). Colonialism can mean many different things, but at its core, it means intervening in the sphere of others and deriving the legitimation for this intervention from one's own system of rules. Schmitt is aware that he is meddling in the affairs of others whose names he has difficulty pronouncing. He is doomed to let this awareness show in his awkward apology to the audience. This small scene brings the colonial constellation to life in an uncanny way – it is a colonial awkwardness that feels all too familiar.

During his presentation, Schmitt went through long lists of names of people who have lost their lives. Some of them he pronounced well, others he did not get quite right. While listening to him, I detected the same inflections coming out of my own mouth when speaking English and similar mispronunciations when I try to say Luo names and terms. In many ways, Schmitt and I are similar people. Although he is twenty-five years older than me, we both grew up and had our professional socialization in postwar, post-reunification Germany. We both went to law school, although he went on to practice law as a judge, while I became an anthropologist teaching at a university. Having both been educated in similar institutions, we have learned of "Nuremberg" not only as a trope in discourses of international criminal justice but as a turning point in German history, the beginning of the postwar democratic order – something deeply ingrained in German national identity today. In recent years we have both been concerned with international criminal justice: he from the inside as a practitioner, I from the outside as an analyst. Listening to Schmitt deliver his judgment, not being able to avoid his German accent, I realize that in some respects, I could also not avoid writing this book with a German accent.

As I write this, I have just finished reading *Neither Settler Nor Native* (2020), the most recent book by Ugandan anthropologist and theorist of colonialism Mahmood Mamdani. In this book, Mamdani heavily criticizes "the Nuremberg model" as the wrong template for bringing justice in the aftermath of violence. Dividing a society into victims and perpetrators and punishing individuals according to Western notions of criminal justice only universalizes the German experience of the horrors of Nazi rule and the Holocaust but also reproduces the European nation-state model and the ethnic divisionism that comes with it. In Mamdani's analysis, the Nuremberg tribunals did not even work in Germany in the late 1940s. In his book, Mamdani proposes something else: instead of constructing victims and perpetrators after violent conflict, a society should come together as survivors of violence – the prime example being South Africa, where this aspiration, Mamdani contends, has been realized better than elsewhere.

I agree with Mamdani's analysis, which is shared by most of the anthropologists who write about transitional justice, that the system of international criminal justice cannot be separated from the colonial structures governing the global capitalist order in which it was conceived and in which it operates. But I cannot deny that I find Mamdani's suggestion that "Nuremberg" was a mistake, that it was the wrong thing to do, thoroughly repellent. It feels inconceivable to me that Jewish Germans who survived the death camps and former Nazi officials could ever somehow come together as "survivors of the Third Reich." These are not only my sentiments. The proposition that it would have been better to avoid a criminal justice approach to Nazi perpetrators would probably only find support on the very extreme right in Germany.

I come from a family of practicing lawyers. Both my mother and my father began to study law in 1968, a time of global upheaval and a formative time for postwar West Germany. A generation of young intellectuals born after the Second World War realized how imperial powers wanted to protect what remained of formal colonialism and Euro-American dominance through devastating wars, and they wanted change. But the German case was also particular. The popular motto *Trau keinem über dreißig!* ("Don't trust anyone over thirty!"), which Herbert Lewis (2014) analyzes as also having had a transformative effect on anthropological thinking, was, for my parents' generation, more than a mere expression of youthful defiance. It meant that everybody over thirty years old – their teachers, their professors, even their own parents – could all have been perpetrators of unimaginable atrocities. They were outraged when they realized that they had been born into a country that had systematically hidden the truth of their fathers' and mothers' guilt from them. They felt betrayed. If you were to ask my parents what problems they see with the Nuremberg tribunals, they would answer that an all too small number of Nazi perpetrators has been punished; that too many got off scot-free.

This socialization created a certain empathy in me for the sentiment of punishment. I felt it in many people in northern Uganda – particularly in those groups who fight for reparations for the damage done to lives and livelihoods during the military conflict. Among those who advocate for reconciliation inside northern Uganda, between LRA fighters and civilians, there are many who nevertheless wish for government troops to be punished. This wish for punishment resonates with my own socialization as a German and as an anti-fascist. I realize, however, that these are uncomfortable sentiments for critics of criminal justice and proponents of a politics of reconciliation.

Is this German accent with which I have approached this research my way of apologizing for the colonialism inherent in international criminal justice in the name of an emotional urge for punishment? Does taking affect seriously have the effect of taming more radical critiques of colonialism? Certainly not. As Kamari Clarke has shown in *Affective Justice* (2019), a focus on affect can be a powerful tool to make visible the workings of colonialism. I would argue that a critique of colonialism that does not take into account the politics of sentiment at play might still be able to come up with valid and carefully considered analyses of the works of the kind of organized inequality that our contemporary world produces on a daily basis. But it might be less able to shed light on the often messy ambivalences that colonialism creates in the feeling lives of the people who are affected by it in the myriad of subject positions it imposes. As a result, critiques of colonialism might miss opportunities to map out and navigate sentiment in order to affect change in the often partial and tactical manner that characterizes struggles for change.

I sympathize with the indignation my parents and their contemporaries must have felt when, as students in their early twenties, they began to learn of the atrocities that their parents had kept from them. I believe

I see a similar indignation in the eyes of my students when they, emgerging anthropologists in their early twenties, begin to learn of the atrocities of German colonialism, which they have usually not heard anything about in their school education, and when they realize the degree to which colonialism remains a formative structure of our contemporary world order. In some of them, this indignation provokes an activism, not unlike that of my parents' generation, which is gaining traction in Germany and elsewhere in Europe (Ivanov and Bens 2021; Benker 2021). It feels like German society has a lot of work ahead of it to realize the extent to which colonialism still shapes its systems of economy, knowledge production, and governance. Without indignation, however, this will never come to pass.

This whole book begs the question of what is to be gained by underscoring the affective life of international criminal justice and the proposition of a critique of colonialism through affect. In a way, including affect in our analyses of the world makes everything more complicated, for better and for worse. It makes visible the fact that all systems of power govern and are governed by conflicting sentiments that bind people together and draw them apart, often at the same time. Colonialism is such an omnipresent structure that shapes the sentiments of people. One cannot but navigate and partly reproduce these sentiments. When people are in a position to reproduce colonial sentiment, when they feel compelled by forces larger than themselves and try to do the right thing nevertheless, then the kind of colonial awkwardness emerges that one can feel in Judge Schmitt's apology. Even those who see themselves as fighters against colonial injustice will not be able to avoid feeling such colonial awkwardness. The question is: Do we perceive these affective dynamics of colonialism merely as a mechanism of subjugation, or as an unavoidable starting point for resistance against a world that produces and reproduces enormous inequality every day? The fact that colonialism has an affective life with all its ambivalences and contradictions can also be seen as a sign of hope. It means that not only do the workings of colonialism shape people's sentiments but that people's sentiments also shape colonialism. This opens up a space for imagining what a truly postcolonial world could look like, a world in which colonialism is *actually* over.

NOTES

INTRODUCTION

1. "The formal properties of the law develop out of a combination of magical formalism and prophetic irrationality in primitive legality ... toward a more and more disciplinary juridical, therefore logical rationality and systematization, and – at least as it appears outwardly – more and more toward logical sublimation and strict deductionism in law, hence more and more toward a rational legal technique" (Weber 1921, 503–504, translation by the author).
2. The German original is *stahlhartes Gehäuse*, which means a "casing" or a "shell" as hard as steel. When Talcott Parsons translated Weber's *The Protestant Ethic and the Spirit of Capitalism* into English in 1930, he used the term "iron cage." Baehr (2001) makes a lot of these differences in translation and contends that it has led to misunderstandings of Weber's theory. I like Parsons's translation, though, because it already hints at a certain critique of modernity that also reverberates through a lot of the law-and-emotion research, namely, that modernity somehow imprisons the human being by repressing feeling. It is this conception of emotionless modernity that I would like to question on a quite basic level in this book.
3. In the original, *Polarnacht von eisiger Finsternis und Härte*.
4. The term *dispositif* is central to Michel Foucault's thinking on processes of subjectivation in institutions. He defines the term in an interview as "a thoroughly heterogeneous ensemble consisting of discourses, institutions, architectural forms, regulatory decisions, laws, administrative measures, scientific statements, philosophical, moral and philanthropic propositions – in short, the said as much as the unsaid. Such are the elements of the apparatus. The apparatus itself is the system of relations that can be established between these elements. ... What I am trying to identify in this apparatus is precisely the nature of the connection that can exist between these heterogeneous elements. ... Between these elements, whether discursive or non-discursive, there is a sort of interplay of shifts of position and modifications of function which can also vary very widely. ... I understand by the term 'apparatus' a ... formation which has as its major function at a given historical moment that of responding to an urgent need. The apparatus thus has a dominant strategic function" (1972, 194–195).

5. The most extensive theorization on how to understand affect as embedded in Michel Foucault's theory of power has been achieved by Rainer Mühlhoff in his monograph *Immersive Macht: Affekttheorie nach Foucault und Spinoza* (2018).
6. Article 5(1) of the Rome Statute.
7. A strict rule of complementarity governs the workings of the ICC. The Court only has jurisdiction to take on cases that national courts are not able or willing to entertain (El Zeidy 2008; Kleffner 2008). This rule of complementarity plays a major role in the debates around the ICC's prosecution strategy, which is seen as intrusive by many African heads of state and government officials. For a thorough analysis of this problem, see Nouwen (2013).
8. At the time of writing this book, the ICC had initiated proceedings in twenty-seven cases since it began its operations in 2002. All of these had been against perpetrators from Africa (see www.icc-cpi.int/Pages/cases.aspx, accessed April 3, 2020). Thirteen situations were currently under investigation by the Office of the Prosecutor, all but three (Georgia, Afghanistan, and Bangladesh/Myanmar) concerning situations in African countries (see www.icc-cpi.int/pages/situation.aspx, accessed April 3, 2020).
9. African Union General Assembly resolutions criticizing the ICC include: Assembly/AU/Dec.296 (XV); Assembly/AU/Dec.221 (XII); Assembly/AU/Dec.245 (XIII); Assembly/AU/Dec.366 (XVII); and Assembly/AU/Dec.482 (XXI).
10. The relativistic outlook of the anthropology of emotion is a direct consequence of anthropology's rejection of the contention that emotions are primarily biological phenomena. Those who see emotions merely as somatic reactions to physical disturbances tend to argue that emotions are basically the same across cultures (Ekman 1999). The anthropological view, which takes seriously the cultural construction of emotion(s), tends to argue the opposite, namely that emotions are very different across cultures, and that this has important implications for ethnographic methodology, cross-cultural comparison, and theories of human development (Beatty 2005). When taken to its logical extreme, this difference has profound methodological implications. The use of empathy to investigate the emotions of others, for instance, can appear suspect and naïve, as doing so might take for granted the universality of emotions (Solomon 1984). Still, there are anthropologists who argue for empathy and "resonance" to understand what people feel beyond words (Wikan 1994). Ultimately, doing ethnography of emotions is walking a fine line: trying to decipher the emotions of others (in part by developing an emotional relationship with one's interlocutors that goes beyond words) without all too hastily assuming that one can feel the same as somebody else. This paradoxical art is difficult to say the least, but is still probably the most rewarding approach to understanding emotion.
11. Other anthropologists who approach culture and society in a way similar to that which I have outlined have decided to use descriptive language

other than emotion. Some of these kindred concepts are "embodiment" (Csordas 1990, 1995; Desjarlais 1992), "subjectivity" (Biehl, Good, and Kleinman 2007), and "experience" (Luhrmann 2012). There are also those who argue for an "anthropology of the senses" (Stoller 1989; Classen 1997). Some anthropologists tend to avoid the term "emotion," as they want to avoid being construed as referring exclusively to physio-biological states. Some suggest replacing the word "emotion" either with "sentiment" (Abu-Lughod 1986) or with "affect" (Besnier 1990; Navaro-Yashin 2012). I also use these terms in this book, carefully distinguished and specifically defined for analytical purposes, as I see the whole array of terms, including emotion, with all their different implications, as a valuable resource when used judiciously.

12. I have elaborated in detail what I mean by "sentiments" in earlier publications coauthored with Olaf Zenker (Bens and Zenker 2017a, 2019).

1 COURTROOM ATMOSPHERES

1. Antoine Garapon's work (1997) is formative for understanding the ritual dimension of courtroom performances. Based on his analysis, and connecting it with Erving Goffman's (1967) broader notion of "interaction ritual" as well as Katherine Fischer Taylor's (1993) work on the theatrical aspects of courtroom architecture, David Tait (2001) has proposed an ethnographic approach to investigating courtroom performances within their spatial and symbolic environment and focused particularly on how they represent different styles and expressions of state sovereignty. In many ways, this chapter is in conversation with these approaches by drawing out the affective dimension of such courtroom rituals. In a certain respect, this also means taking seriously Emile Durkheim's (1912) famous observations on the emotional dimension of ritual. On this, see also Chapter 2.
2. I have developed a perspective on ethnographic legal studies elsewhere (Bens and Vetters 2018).
3. There are a number of fascinating studies based on the idea that the courtroom systematically suppresses emotion while showing convincingly how the courtroom setting regularly fails to limit the emergence of emotions, sometimes as the result of subversive acts by courtroom actors (see, e.g., Dahlberg 2009; Emde 2014; Brooks 2019).
4. In 2006, the LRA entered into peace talks with the Museveni government that were carried out in Juba, the capital of South Sudan. The so-called Juba Peace Talks failed to result in an accord because the rebel leader, Joseph Kony, eventually decided not to sign the negotiated settlement (Schomerus 2012). Since that time, the LRA has not been able to operate in northern Uganda. There are reports that it is still active in the Democratic Republic of Congo (DRC), the Central African Republic (CAR), and maybe even South Sudan. At the time of this writing, a webpage of the NGO Invisible Children, the *LRA Crisis Tracker*, was

still publishing reports of LRA activities in these regions (see https://crisistracker.org, accessed April 2020).

5. International Criminal Court, *The Prosecutor* v. *Dominic Ongwen*, Pre-Trial Chamber II, Decision on the Confirmation of Charges against Dominic Ongwen, March 23, 2016, ICC-02/04–01/15–422-Red.
6. Séléka (Sango for "alliance") is a coalition of several Muslim rebel groups in the CAR (see Käihkö and Utas 2014).
7. BBC, "LRA Rebel Dominic Ongwen Surrenders to US Forces in CAR" (January 7, 2015), www.bbc.com/news/world-africa-30705649, accessed April 2020.
8. A confirmation of charges hearing is a pretrial proceeding at the ICC in which it is determined whether there is sufficient evidence that the accused has committed the crimes with which he is charged (see Art. 61(7) Rome Statute).
9. The quotes from Jeremy Elderfield are from the transcript of the confirmation of charges hearing, January 21, 2016, ICC-02/04–01/15-T-20-Red-ENG.
10. On law's overlapping temporalities, see also Benda-Beckmann (2014).
11. The philosopher of language J. L. Austin (1962) has most prominently expressed the argument that speaking is a practice with consequences, that one can *do* something with words. Central to his theory is his famous distinction between constative and performative utterances. Austin argues that speech acts often not only describe reality (the constative utterance) but also produce and transform it (the performative utterance). Austin sees legal language as a prototypical example of the performative dimension of language, a perspective that plays a central role in the legal theory of poststructuralist philosophy (Derrida 1989; Butler 1997a, 1997b). What is said and done in the courtroom not only *represents* the world outside of it but is also a powerful actor in *creating* the structures of meaning through which it is represented.
12. In this respect Silverstein's work connects to Benjamin Lee Whorf's (1952) work on metalinguistics in American Indian languages.
13. While an intensive investigation into people's subjective emotional experiences is largely absent from the courtroom ethnography literature, Susan Hirsch has shown in her pathbreaking ethnography *In the Moment of Greatest Calamity* (2006) how a thick description of one's own emotional and affective experiences can benefit ethnographic writing. In this exceptional ethnography of the trial of the murderers of her own husband, she masterfully writes her own emotions into the narrative.
14. On the role of interpretations of Spinoza for post-Marxist thought more generally, see Diefenbach (2018).
15. For an extensive study on the body in affect theory, see Blackman (2012). For the consequences in social theory, see Seyfert (2012).
16. Anthropologists who have explicitly referred to affect theory in their ethnographic works include Yael Navaro-Yashin (2012) and Kathleen Stewart (2007).
17. Lutz (2017, 188) remarks that "the recent literature on affect rehearses work done in the 1980s," by which she is referring to the classic texts of the

anthropology of emotion (Briggs 1970; Rosaldo 1980; Lutz 1988; Abu-Lughod and Lutz 1990). A more recent line of the anthropological research on emotion is the Berlin school of psychological anthropology (Röttger-Rössler 2004; Stodulka 2016; Reynaud 2017; Sakti 2017; Scheidecker 2017).

18. More recent courtroom ethnography has gone in this direction with what is termed a "multimodal approach" (Mondada 2016). Video and sound recordings from courtroom proceedings are analyzed to show how courtroom participants use their bodies in relation to the material environment for the creation of meaning (Matoesian 2018). McElhinny (2010, 310) has criticized the newer approaches to affect for ignoring recent work on multimodality in linguistic anthropology. While I would agree with this assessment, I would still argue that a certain amount of eclecticism in perspectives might help and even strengthen ethnographic analysis. The multimodal approach in linguistic anthropology still remains within the paradigm of analytic logocentrism – albeit with a significantly broadened understanding of what counts as language. Consequently, it conceptualizes the affective dimension of court proceedings as derived from the linguistic or paralinguistic utterances made by human bodies. Approaches from affect studies refrain from this analytical positioning and insist on a relational paradigm that is even more radical. An atmosphere, then, becomes an affective occurrence in its own right.
19. There are some strands of affect theory, however, that challenge traditional legal anthropology at a very basic level. In these approaches, affect has come to stand for all that is "*not* semiosis, *not* meaning, *not* structure, *not* apparatus, but the felt visceral, immediate, sensed, embodied, excessive" (Brinkema 2014, xii–xiii, emphasis in original). Moreover, "the 'turn to affect' has been framed as a response to the problems of cultural inscription and discourse determinism which have been argued to show up the limits of work on text, language and discourse across the humanities. Discursive approaches are seen to have sidelined the body, emotion, affect and sensation in understanding communication processes" (Blackman 2012, xviii). Legal anthropology, if it wishes to make meaningful contributions to understanding the law, will be unable to uncritically join in the missionary zeal that accompanies many anti-logocentric and anti-structural polemics in affect theory (Massumi 2002). But it is my claim that affect theory can be read as pointing to the ethnographic endeavor more generally – as a research practice that has "being there" at its core. Thinking about affect can be a helpful reminder that courtroom ethnography must pay close attention to the relational dynamics that unfold between co-present bodies in space and the overall atmospheric feel that emerges as the result of these dynamics.
20. Although atmospheres can be seen as an always-present undercurrent in ethnographic work and are discussed in personal field notes, academic texts, and sometimes even as a topic of anthropological theorizing (Ingold 2016), there is little systematic methodological exploration of how to come to terms with atmosphere in ethnography (Schroer and Schmitt

2018). The topic of atmosphere is not new to anthropology, but has traditionally been described in different terms. Emile Durkheim's (1912) concept of *effervescence* in his studies on religion, Marcel Mauss's (1925) concept of *mana* in his studies on the economy, and the way Clifford Geertz (1973) writes about the role of *moods* for ethnography all bear a certain resemblance to the idea of atmosphere. For a review of the literature, see Schroer and Schmitt (2018).

21. As Michael Richardson has shown in his work on testimonies of torture, images "not only show but also produce intensities and provoke bodies" and "call the viewing body into relation to them through the capacity to affect" (2016, 75). No wonder, then, that the investigation of images plays a major role in affect and emotion research (Schankweiler and Wüschner 2019). I have elaborated elsewhere on the affective dimension of images in the political trial (Bens 2019a).
22. Anthropologists have long argued that sound and voice are key to emotional expression and impact (Feld 1982), and that sound can shape and generate emotions (Bretèque 2012). Ethnomusicologists have recently argued for closely linking sound and atmosphere (Riedel 2015, 111). With reference to the phenomenon of voice, the philosopher Mladen Dolar (2006) has argued that, while it may emerge from speaking bodies, it is neither fully defined by nor fully independent of the speaker – an idea that fits well into the concept of atmosphere (Lawy 2017).
23. It has to be added that the term "event" in (international) law is a complex concept, and that at least two interrelated layers have to be differentiated: On the one hand, the court proceeding itself is an event, the political trial even more publicly so (Christodoulidis 2011). On the other hand, historical events are the "raw material" for international law because court proceedings are ostensibly about them. "But these historical events cannot be totally and finally reduced to international law's own ends . . . . No conditioning, contextualizing and reduction can totally neutralize the disruptive potential of events. They remain open to new modes of appropriation, new interpretations" (Johns, Joyce, and Pahuja 2011, 7–8).
24. This idea is quite traditional, echoing the famous call for "extended case studies" by the members of the Manchester School of anthropology (Gluckman 1973). Conducting such an extended case study basically means trying to observe a "trouble case" from its inception through to its resolution and even its aftermath by engaging in long-term ethnographic fieldwork. For legal anthropology, Gluckman defines an extended case study as the attempt to trace "the origins of a breach or disagreement backwards in time to see how it emerged, and then pursuing forwards in time the development of social relationships among the persons involved, possibly after adjudication or settlement or ritual reconciliation" (1973, 612). It is undoubtedly important to strive for this ideal. In my ethnography of the Dominic Ongwen case before the ICC, I divided my fieldwork time – a total of 12 months over a period of about two and a half years – into four phases, starting in The Hague, then traveling to northern

Uganda, then again conducting fieldwork in The Hague, and finally conducting research back in northern Uganda again. Nevertheless, I was not able to cover all of the court proceedings that took place in the time of the research project, let alone completely fulfill the aspirations of an extended case study in its most ideal sense. No matter how much one tries to observe cases over an extended period of time, a profound methodological problem remains: How can one account for process *inside* the event; in other words, how does one find process and structure in the observation data (Bens 2018)?

25. Thomas Scheffer has made this point by arguing for a "trans-sequential analysis" which focuses on an "object-in-becoming" (*Objekt-im-Werden*) that reappears in several events in a sequence (Scheffer 2015). This object also gives material form to both the past and the future. His proposition includes an approach to investigating "cases-in-becoming," which he has illustrated with his own ethnography of court cases (Scheffer 2010).

2 TRANSITIONAL JUSTICE ATMOSPHERES

1. On the legal concept of crimes against humanity, see Robertson (2006). Philosophically, the concept of crimes against humanity comes from natural law ideas in Europe (Graven 1950). The ICC is sometimes criticized for overstretching the notion of crimes against humanity so that it also encompasses crimes by minor actors below the level of mass atrocities, and hence tends to trivialize the concept (May 2005).
2. Projects of transitional justice in the context of post-conflict reconstruction are often connected to "state building," which entails interventions into administrative policies (Vetters 2014, 2019) and even constitution-making (Seidel 2015; Seidel and Sureau 2015).
3. On the "peace versus justice" debate, there are basically three positions. Some argue that criminal justice measures negatively impact peace negotiations and that the international community should refrain from imposing them so as not to endanger peace talks (see, e. g., Anonymous 1996). Some have argued against this view, asserting that ICC involvement does not negatively impact peace negotiations and can even promote them (see, e. g., Akhavan 2009; Gissel 2015). Yet others have argued that international justice measures should be taken even if they negatively impact peace negotiations so as not to sacrifice accountability for peace (see Bassiouni 2003).
4. Much of the transitional justice debate is structured by an analysis that sees the legal and political aspects of transitional justice at odds with each other (see Vinjamuri and Snyder 2015).
5. Branch (2004), for example, criticizes the international criminal justice approach to northern Uganda for neglecting local demands. There are, however, also a number of voices in the literature that question whether local transitional justice alternatives are actually always fairer or more effective than their international counterparts (see, e.g., Thomson 2011; McAuliffe 2013).

6. The breadth of what has come to be called the "translational turn" in the anthropology of international law is well represented in an edited volume by Merry and Goodale (2007).
7. It is in this second, broader metaphorical way that translation has become a widely used concept for cultural analysis in the "translational turn" in the social sciences and the humanities (Bachmann-Medick 2006). In social science approaches to international law, one can surely see the prevalence of the translation metaphor (Bachmann-Medick 2012).
8. There exists an International Crimes Division (ICD) at the High Court of Uganda. This special chamber of the High Court was created as a result of the Juba Peace Talks. Because of the Amnesty Act of 2000 and the warrants for the "top 5" commanders by the ICC, the scope of the ICD is quite narrow. To date, the ICD has only tried one case – against former LRA commander Thomas Kwoyelo – which is still ongoing (see McNamara 2013; Macdonald and Porter 2016).
9. On competing dispute resolution forums, see Benda-Beckmann (1981).
10. For analytic purposes, in this text I have made a clear distinction between Acholi law and religious ethics of forgiveness. In practice, however, these two normative systems frequently interact. Traditional leaders employ religious rhetoric and religious leaders talk about Acholi tradition. The two systems have become discursively more and more compatible with each other (see Ward 2001).
11. Whether reparations are actually connected to formal participation in the trial and of what nature such reparations might be in the future is seen very differently by different actors. While the ICC personnel seem to aspire to collective reparations in the form of development projects, many villagers in northern Uganda believe that they can expect individual reparations and that they need to "get on the list" if they wish to be eligible for them.
12. Moore (2010, 83) defines "retributivism" as the theory of punishment that underlies the idea that "the justification for punishing a criminal is simply that the criminal deserves to be punished."
13. Menkel-Meadow (2007, 162) defines "restorative justice" as "a variety of different practices, including apologies, restitution, and acknowledgments of harm and injury, as well as other efforts to provide healing and reintegration of offenders into their communities, with or without additional punishment. . . . In its most idealized form, there are four Rs of restorative justice: repair, restore, reconcile, and reintegrate the offenders and victims to each other and to their shared community."
14. Infrastructure itself can be the object of ethnographic research (see Star 1999; Larkin 2013). For an excellent example of such research in the anthropology of Africa, see Calkins (2016).

3 THE SENTIMENT OF PLAUSIBILITY

1. For an insightful ethnomethodological study on the practice of truth, see Dupret (2011).

2. Most of the quantitative data regarding the numbers of abducted fighters rely on the registration data gathered at the reception centers that were put up in the course of the Amnesty Act (Pham, Vinck, and Stover 2008). Qualitative, interview-based studies conducted at reception centers give insights into the experiences of child soldiers in the LRA (Allen and Schomerus 2006; Vindevogel et al. 2011). When I interviewed the officer responsible for the Gulu amnesty reception center in 2017, the reception center was still open, but only a few fighters registered there every year.
3. Child Soldiers International, *Child Soldiers Global Report 2001 – Uganda*, 2001, www.refworld.org/docid/498805c32d.html, accessed September 2, 2019.
4. Human Rights Watch, *Stolen Children: Abduction and Recruitment in Northern Uganda*, March 28, 2003, www.hrw.org/report/2003/03/28/stolen-children/abduction-and-recruitment-northern-uganda#251d1c, accessed September 2, 2019).
5. In this respect, the LRA stands in the tradition of other rebel militias in Africa that are led by spirits. The most relevant precursor of the LRA is the Holy Spirit Movement, led by spirit medium Alice Auma (also known as Lakwena). For an ethnographic account, see Behrend (1993). On the role of spirit possession and political violence in Uganda, see Cline (2003); for modern Africa in general, see Behrend and Luig (1999).
6. Human Rights Watch, *The Scars of Death: Children Abducted by the Lord's Resistance Army in Uganda*, September 1, 1997, 1–56432–221–1, www.refworld.org/docid/3ae6a8410.html, accessed September 2, 2019).
7. ICC-02/04–01/15-T-22-ENG ET WT 25–01–2016 52/72 SZ PT, pp. 52–53.
8. ICC-02/04–01/15-T-22-ENG ET WT 25–01–2016 52/72 SZ PT, p. 57.
9. ICC-02/04–01/15-T-23-Red-ENG WT 26–01–2016 63/67 SZ PT, p. 63.
10. In the theory of evidence in law, the argument has been made that the term "plausibility" is better suited to understanding evidentiary practices than the commonly used concept of "probability" (Pardo and Allen 2008). Some have even proclaimed a paradigm shift in Anglo-American law from probability to plausibility (Allen and Pardo 2019). Without engaging too deeply in that debate, I tend to agree that from an ethnographic perspective the term "plausibility" seems to be able to encompass the workings of social relations, including their affective dimension, governing the process of coming to terms with the question of "what actually happened?" better than the term "probability," which suggests a mathematical operation independent of the people who conduct it.
11. Sigurd D'hondt (2020) has made a similar argument on stance taking in his analysis of the Dutch "Black Pete" debate. In his view, taking a stance regularly includes the production of we-ness. Speakers who are able to refer to hegemonic understandings of how the public realm is constituted, who "speak from within," have to do less metapragmatic work to make plausible their stance. Those speakers, usually minorities, who claim inclusion into hegemonic conceptions of we-ness have more work to do to make their stance plausible.

4 THE SENTIMENT OF OBJECTIVITY

1. "For the colonized, objectivity is always directed against them" (translation by the author).
2. That is not to say that human action is always characterized by judgments. Acting and deciding are by no means synonymous. On the contrary, most actions are done without conscious decision. As Pierre Bourdieu has convincingly argued, the main problem with the concept of the *homo oeconomicus* in mainstream economic theory is that it overestimates the degree to which people make conscious decisions (Bourdieu 1994, 147–167). The question of how people make judgments about justice is the topic of Chapter 5.
3. In his classic study on Lozi courts in southern Africa, for example, Max Gluckman describes evidential hearings going on for days (1955, 44). Similar observations have been presented in much of the anthropological literature on dispute resolution in societies all over the world (Llewellyn and Hoebel 1941; Bohannan 1957; Nader and Todd 1978; Comaroff and Roberts 1981; Benda-Beckmann 1984; Hirsch 1998; Richland 2008).
4. ICC-02/04–01/15-T-21-Red-ENG WT 22–01–2016 1/86 SZ PT, p. 13.
5. ICC-02/04–01/15-T-21-Red-ENG WT 22–01–2016 1/86 SZ PT, p. 13.
6. Feeling rules govern what people are allowed to feel in certain situations and how they are allowed to display emotions. On the role of feeling rules in the courtroom, see Bens (2018b).
7. ICC-02/04–01/15-T-28-ENG ET WT 16–01–2017 5/105 SZ T, pp. 4–5.
8. Gerhard Anders (2014b) has provided an insightful ethnographic perspective on anthropological expert witnessing in the Special Court for Sierra Leone.
9. Maquet provides a critique of mechanical objectivity on the most general level. Taking photography as the prototype of objectivity in the natural sciences, he engages in a dialogue with Daston and Galison *avant la lettre*: "The same camera, fixed in front of the same object illuminated by a constant light, focused at the same distance, with time and aperture remaining the same, will give identical pictures even when operated by different photographers, but only if each exposure is made on emulsions having the same characteristics (such as color sensitivity, speed, graininess, contrast). The pictures will be different if the film sheets used are ortho or panchromatic, color or infrared. Although perceived by an impersonal instrument, the object will produce different images. All of them are 'objective' in the sense that they are partly determined by the object but not in the sense that the participation of the subject is eliminated" (Maquet 1964, 53).
10. The defense lawyer used the phrase three times during his cross examination; see ICC-02/04–01/15-T-29-Red2-ENG WT 17–01–2017 22/112 SZ T, pp. 31, 38, 44.
11. ICC-02/04–01/15-T-29-Red2-ENG WT 17–01–2017 22/112 SZ T, p. 45.
12. Human Rights Watch, *The Scars of Death: Children Abducted by the Lord's Resistance Army in Uganda*, September 1, 1997, 1–56432–221–1, www.refworld.org/docid/3ae6a8410.html, accessed September 2, 2019.

13. In fact, the power over religious cleansing rituals has played a key role in the history of spirit militias in northern Uganda. For many young men who have fought in the Ugandan civil war in the 1980s, the idea of attaching themselves to one of the rebel groups, particularly the Holy Spirit Movement of Alice Auma (Lakwena), was appealing because their leaders could perform cleansing rituals. Having gained independence from their kin groups during their military careers, they were often not willing to subject themselves again to the authority of their clan elders, who were traditionally responsible for these cleansing rituals (Branch 2010).
14. In Chapter 3, I highlighted an excerpt from the transcript of the William Kennedy Smith rape trial. In this short excerpt, the defense attorney manages the witness's account during cross examination by asking yes/no questions. When the witness tried to assert her subjectivity by narrating freely, the lawyer cut her off, saying, "That's not my question Miss Mercer."

5 THE SENTIMENT OF JUSTICE

1. For insightful critiques of the legal pluralism approach, see Tamanaha (1993) and Dupret (2007).
2. Assembly/AU/Dec.296 (XV), Assembly/AU/Dec.221 (XII), Assembly/AU/Dec.245 (XIII), Assembly/AU/Dec.366 (XVII), Assembly/AU/Dc.482 (XXI).
3. "ICC a Bunch of Useless People," *New Vision Newspaper*, May 12, 2016, www.newvision.co.ug/new_vision/news/1424384/icc-bunch-useless-people-museveni, accessed April 7, 2020.
4. Electoral Commission, Election Results, www.ec.or.ug/2016-general-elections, accessed April 16, 2020.
5. During the 1990s, the LRA was dependent on military and logistical support from Sudan. At that time, the Khartoum government under Omar Al-Bashir (who was in 2016 again in Museveni's good graces during his inauguration) supported the LRA in order to keep the South Sudanese separatist movement in check. The deal was that the LRA would receive arms and training in their fight against Museveni, and in return had to fight against the South Sudanese rebels – especially the Sudan People's Liberation Army (SPLA). This arrangement broke down in 2005. In that year, the SPLA and the Sudanese government came to a peace agreement and the Al-Bashir government lost interest in the LRA. The military support from Khartoum dried up. It was mainly this development that forced the LRA into peace negotiations with the Ugandan government, which took place from 2006 to 2008 in Juba, the capital of South Sudan (Atkinson 2010; Schomerus 2012).
6. Paragraph 23 of the "Annexure to the Agreement on Accountability and Reconciliation" says: "Subject to clause 4.1 of the Principal Agreement, the Government shall ensure that serious crimes committed during the conflict are addressed by the special Division of the High Court;

traditional justice mechanisms; and any other alternative justice mechanism established under the Principal Agreement, but not the military courts."

7. In the international law debate, the principle of complementarity is controversial. Some see complementarity as going too far by intruding into national jurisdiction in those cases where states have a legitimate interest in not prosecuting certain crimes (Morris 2000). Others point out that the complementarity principle provides a good mechanism for facilitating compromise between national and international criminal law (Kleffner 2008). For a legal view on the intricacies of complementarity in the case of Uganda, see Greenawalt (2009).
8. For a description of Acholi traditional kinship structure, see Girling (1960).
9. For a detailed description and analysis of these rituals, see Harlacher et al. (2006) and Lenhart (2012).
10. On the anthropology of retaliation more broadly, see Turner (2017).
11. The investigation of customary law in Africa has been a key interest of anthropologists for more than a hundred years and still remains a fruitful field of study. For outstanding monographs in this field, see Schapera (1938), Gluckman (1955), Bohannan (1957), Moore (1986), Griffiths (1997), and Johnson (2018). Reviews of the field of the anthropology of customary law in Africa include Merry (1991), Zenker and Höhne (2018), and Johnson (2019).
12. See also Tim Allen (2010) on the "invention of traditional justice" in northern Uganda. These arguments connect to a debate in 1980s historiography about the degree of "authenticity" of those cultural features termed "traditional" in East African societies (Ranger 1983; 1993; see also the more general argument in Anderson 1983). This line of thinking also inspired studies in legal anthropology about the colonial invention of customary law in Africa (Chanock 1985; Moore 1986) and studies on the "invention" of African tribes (Vail 1989; Lentz 1995). Regarding the more specific case at the core of this book, some argue that Acholi identity itself was "invented" by technologies of colonial governance of indirect rule and as an imagined community (Behrend 1993; Allen 2006; Amone and Muura 2014; Amone 2015).

    This concern about the degree to which African communities and their law really are "traditional" still structures the debates on these topics – and for good reason. First, these views challenge popular stereotypes, particularly in Europe, about African societies as "backward" and stuck in an unchanging past. Second, they highlight the enormous impact colonial power relations have had and continue to have on African social and political structures. But the idea of the "invention of tradition" also tends to obscure other important aspects. An all-too-strict insistence on the invention of tradition can unintentionally give succor to yet another colonial stereotype, namely that of the "people without history" (Wolf 1982). As Atkinson (1994, 2) remarks in his study of Acholi precolonial history, "the colonial and post-colonial representations of ethnic identities in Uganda, however distorted or manipulative, have not been plucked from the air or created out of nothingness." British colonialism in particular was dependent on utilizing existing social structures to administer the colonized in the mode of indirect rule (Iliffe 1979). When referring to the cultural constructed-ness of tradition and ethnicity inside colonial power relations, it is important not to underestimate East Africans' agency in actively engaging in the process of this construction before, during, and after formal colonialism (Cohen and Odihambo 1989; Spear and Waller 1993; Schoenbrun 1998; Ivanov 2000; Mamdani 2001; Glassmann 2011; Lynch 2011).

As important as this debate is for historians, an ethnographic perspective – particularly one that is largely focused on subjective experience (as is the one I am advocating in this book) – reveals that the question of how authentic certain normative systems are from a historical perspective is often of little importance for actors on the ground. There are two main reasons for this. First, it might be good to remember that "scholars trained in the Western tradition cannot really expect to find others solving the metaphysical problems of Western thought" (Strathern 1988, 3). The question of how authentic African ethnic categories really are is in itself more a reflection of the analysts' concern with questions of ethnohistorical coherence in the European nation-state than it is a reflection of their concern with African societies. The idea of "one people, one nation" still preoccupies Western theories of the nation-state (Hobsbawm 1990; Smith 1996). Proponents of the invention of tradition hope to disprove this theory with reference to the workings of African societies. They often do so successfully, but that does not mean that they are working on a question that actors in African societies see as most relevant. A second reason refers simply to the very basic social science insight that if people "define situations as real, they are real in their consequences" (Thomas and Thomas 1928, 572). For most people in northern Uganda, traditional legal mechanisms are real, albeit not unproblematic, options for pursuing claims for justice, and that is what matters to them (Harlacher et al. 2006; Lenhart 2012).

13. The ARLPI's critical stance against the ICC may have been tempered a bit since the Ongwen trial began. Leading figures of the ARLPI were part of a delegation to The Hague during the opening of the ICC's trial against Ongwen. In an accompanying statement the delegation stated, "This trial is at its beginning and we hope to see it continue smoothly and be beneficial to the victims of Northern Uganda." This may be the beginning of a more conciliatory rhetoric toward the ICC. See "Acholi Leaders Issue Statement on Ongwen Trial," *Northern News Wire*, www.facebook.com/northernewswire/posts/1295776023816488:0, accessed April 7, 2020.
14. Most of the *rwodi* are members of an organization called *Ker Kwaro Acholi*. This organization also elects an Acholi paramount chief, who is responsible for representing the Acholi clan leaders who are members of the organization. In the interpretation of religious leaders, forgiveness is a central value in both Christianity and Islam, as well as in the

community-oriented Acholi legal system. They base this claim on the fact that in interclan conflicts, individual offenders are often not punished, but reparations are negotiated. As Ward (2001) has shown, political actors during the conflict have attempted, often successfully, to fuse religious ethics and traditional Acholi legal ideas into a common discourse on "the local view," which favors a politics of forgiveness.

15. Quite illuminating in this respect is a newspaper article in *The New Vision Newspaper* (November 20, 2007) reporting on the Juba peace talks, written by Norbert Mao, a prominent politician from northern Uganda who was involved in the negotiations. In this article it is reported that an LRA delegation arrived in Banyoro and a cleansing ritual, *nyono tongg-weno*, was performed before the talks could begin. This ritual must be performed by strangers or those who have been away for some time in order to cleanse them of bad influences that they might have been subjected to during their travels – not least of all *cen*, the evil spirits of dead people (see Chapter 4). As is customary in the course of this ritual, the LRA delegation members were asked to step over an *opobo* twig, which symbolizes cleansing, and to step on an egg, a symbol of innocence (see Harlacher et al. 2006, 68). The newspaper article notes, however: "One of them said, he was a born-again Christian and so he should be excused. He insisted even when we explained to him that this ceremony was not a form of witchcraft but a part of our timeless traditions" (Mao 2007). On the ground, tensions remain between Christian and Muslim ethics and "heathen" practices originating in precolonial times. Traditional leaders and religious leaders do not always have the same agenda. (I am particularly indebted to Leonie Benker (2020), who found this article in the course of her master's research on the history of the LRA conflict.)
16. *A Statement on the Position of ARLPI on Ongwen Dominic, Former LRA Commander, January 20, 2015*, https://drive.google.com/file/d/0BwyHGIEA97AyQVBydUNndVhvbmM/view, accessed April 7, 2020.
17. The degree to which that is successful is another question. Johnson rightly contends that the "more recent literature focusing on what has been called 'transitional justice' has returned justice to the title line of legal anthropological studies, but rarely has it been 'justice' that scholars in this field have come to theorize" (2019, 91).
18. That becomes evident in those cases when people mobilize the law against the state (Eckert et al. 2012); on the intricate, though complex, relationship between law and justice in particular, see Eckert (2012).
19. For an insightful study on "de-judicialization," see Zenker (2015).
20. In some respects, this argument is based on the idea that morality is bound to the social group, a basic assumption particularly relevant in kinship-based societies, as Sahlins has argued in his theory of reciprocity (1972, 196–203).
21. For a psychiatric perspective on the mental health dimension of forgiveness, see Cerci and Colucci (2017).
22. The distinction between etic and emic is the simple but nonetheless incisive proposition that the way in which research subjects frame and

communicate actions and events, hence produce their perceptions, is a level of analysis distinct from the perception, terminology, and framing of the researcher. Emic and etic descriptions frequently diverge. People perceive things differently than analytical narratives about them suggest. That emic and etic descriptions and categories diverge is the main reason why ethnographic research is done: to come to a grounded analysis of what is going on by balancing emic and etic descriptions in a thick ethnography of culture. I make my point here by invoking the emic/etic distinction, although I am aware that, strictly speaking, etic conceptions are just as "emic" as the conceptions of the research subjects; it's just that they are the emic conceptions of the academic community. As Sahlins argues, "[I]n anthropology, it's emic all the way down" (2017, 158). But even granted this perfectly valid point, the argument against procedural justice is just as forceful, and perhaps even more so.

23. This relates to a much broader debate on politics and emotions, namely the question of whether there are particular kinds of emotions that should be encouraged in political processes and others that should be avoided. Political philosopher Martha Nussbaum (2013), for instance, argues that certain kinds of love should be promoted in democratic societies, while hatred should be avoided. I have argued elsewhere that the still prevalent debate on "good" political emotions and "bad" political emotions, in other words, those emotions that further productive democratic politics and those that hinder it, is ultimately futile (Bens et al. 2019, 47–82).
24. One can identify similar motivations underpinning religious leaders' efforts to assert the relevance of religious ethics vis-à-vis other political moralities in the public sphere.

6 THE POLITICS OF ATMOSPHERE AND SENTIMENT

1. "War against the conditions in Germany! . . . In the fight against them, *critique* is not the passion of the head, but the head of the passions. . . . It is no longer *a means in itself*; it is *a means to an end.* Its main pathos is *indignation*, its main work is *denunciation*" (Marx 1844, 380, translation by the author, emphasis in the original).
2. For an anthropological perspective on indignation as a form of political anger, see Scheidecker (2019).
3. Assembly/AU/Dec.296 (XV), Assembly/AU/Dec.221 (XII), Assembly/AU/Dec.245 (XIII), Assembly/AU/Dec.366 (XVII), Assembly/AU/Dc.482 (XXI).
4. "African leaders accuse ICC of 'race hunt.'" *Al Jazeera*, May 28, 2013, www.aljazeera.com/news/africa/2013/05/201352722331270466.html, accessed April 16, 2020.
5. See also *Malabo Protocol: Legal and Institutional Implications of the Merged and Expanded African Court* (London: Amnesty International, 2016).

6. The program is available online at www.youtube.com/watch?v=1XHyJYOYZDk, accessed April 12, 2020.
7. Ocampo is referring to the late Nelson Mandela, the first black president of South Africa.
8. ICC-02/04–01/15-T-22-ENG ET WT 25–01–2016 10/72 SZ PT, pp. 9–10.
9. ICC-02/04–01/15-T-22-ENG ET WT 25–01–2016 10/72 SZ PT, p. 19.
10. The relevant legal documents are contained in the Malabo Protocol (see n. 4).
11. Ext/Assembly/AU/Dec.1 (October 2013).
12. Art. 2 (1) of the Charter of the United Nations reads: "The Organization is based on the principle of the sovereign equality of all its members." The principle of sovereign equality entails the principle of sovereign immunity, which declares that, consequently, no state shall sit in judgment of another state.
13. *Jurisdictional Immunities of the State* (*Germany* v. *Italy: Greece intervening*), Judgment, I.C.J. Reports 2012, p. 99. In this case Italian and Greek courts decided in favor of claims by their citizens demanding reparations from the Federal Republic of Germany for war crimes committed during the Second World War. The International Court of Justice found that the principle of sovereign immunity barred any lawsuits against Germany before the courts of another country.
14. G.A. Res 95/1, U.N. Doc. A/Res/1/95 (December 11, 1946). Article 3 of the Nuremberg Principles, which the International Law Commission compiled on the basis of this General Assembly resolution, reads: "The fact that a person who committed an act which constitutes a crime under international law acted as Head of State or responsible government official does not relieve him from responsibility under international law."
15. In 1946, the Nuremberg tribunal found Karl Dönitz, after Hitler's death the last president of the German Reich, guilty of crimes of aggression and war crimes and sentenced him to ten years' confinement. The Tokyo tribunal found the Japanese prime minister Tōjō Hideki guilty of war crimes and sentenced him to death in 1948.

7 WE HAVE NEVER BEEN RATIONAL

1. "Can we aspire to Enlightenment without modernity?" (translation by the author).
2. This campaign video shares some aesthetic characteristics with many other audiovisual accounts of witnessing that have come to be known as "image testimonies" (Schankweiler, Straub, and Wendl 2018). Kerstin Schankweiler has thoroughly theorized image testimonies both in their particular affectivity (2018) and in relation to the role they play in contemporary political protest (2019).

EPILOGUE

1. A transcript of the judgment hearing (record ICC-02/04–01/15-T-259-ENG ET WT 04–02–2021 1/42 SZ T) can be found at www.icc-cpi.int/Transcripts/CR2021_01038.PDF. The judgment itself is more than 1,000 pages long (record ICC-02/04–01/15–1762-Red 04–02–2021 1/1077 NM T) and can be found at www.icc-cpi.int/CourtRecords/CR2021_01026.PDF.
2. Aljazeera, "Museveni declared winner of disputed Uganda presidential election," January 17, 2021, www.aljazeera.com/news/2021/1/16/ugandas-museveni-declared-winner-of-presidential-election.
3. See the sentence from May 6, 2021, ICC-02/04–01/15.
4. See transcript of judgment hearing (note 1), p. 7.

BIBLIOGRAPHY

Abrams, Kathryn, and Hila Keren. 2009. "Who Is Afraid of Law and the Emotions?" *Minnesota Law Review* 94 (6): 1997–2074.

Abu-Lughod, Lila. 1986. *Veiled Sentiments: Honor and Poetry in a Bedouin Society*. Berkeley: University of California Press.

Abu-Lughod, Lila. 1991. "Writing against Culture." In *Recapturing Anthropology: Working in the Present*, edited by Richard Gabriel Fox, 137–162. Santa Fe: School of American Research Press.

Abu-Lughod, Lila, and Catherine A. Lutz, eds. 1990. *Language and the Politics of Emotion*. Cambridge: Cambridge University Press.

Ahmed, Sara. 2004a. "Affective Economies." *Social Text* 22 (2): 117–139.

Ahmed, Sara. 2004b. *The Cultural Politics of Emotion*. Edinburgh: Edinburgh University Press.

Ahmed, Sara. 2007. "A Phenomenology of Whiteness." *Feminist Theory* 8 (2): 149–168.

Akhavan, Payam. 2005. "The Lord's Resistance Army Case: Uganda's Submission of the First State Referral to the International Criminal Court." *The American Journal of International Law* 99 (2): 403–421. doi: 10.2307/1562505.

Akhavan, Payam. 2009. "Are International Criminal Tribunals a Disincentive to Peace? Reconciling Judicial Romanticism with Political Realism." *Human Rights Quarterly* 31 (3): 624–654.

Allen, Ronald J., and Michael S. Pardo. 2019. "Relative Plausibility and Its Critics." *The International Journal of Evidence and Proof* 23 (1–2):5–59. doi: 10.1177/1365712718813781.

Allen, Tim. 2006. *Trial Justice: The International Criminal Court and the Lord's Resistance Army*. London: Zed Books.

Allen, Tim. 2007. "The International Criminal Court and the Invention of Traditional Justice in Northern Uganda." *Politique Africaine* 107 (3): 147–166.

Allen, Tim. 2010. "Bitter Roots: The Invention of Acholi Traditional Justice." In *The Lord's Resistance Army: Myth and Reality*, edited by Tim Allen and Koen Vlassenroot, 242–261. London: Zed Books.

Allen, Tim, and Mareike Schomerus. 2006. *A Hard Homecoming: Lessons Learned from the Reception Center Process in Northern Uganda: An*

Independent Study. Washington, DC: US Agency for International Development and United Nations Children's Fund.

Allen, Tim, and Koen Vlassenroot. 2010a. "Introduction." In *The Lord's Resistance Army: Myth and Reality*, edited by Tim Allen and Koen Vlassenroot, 1–24. London: Zed Books.

Allen, Tim, and Koen Vlassenroot, eds. 2010b. *The Lord's Resistance Army: Myth and Reality*. London: Zed Books.

Althusser, Louis. 1970. "Idéologie et appareils idéologiques d'état: Notes pour une recherche." *La Pensée* 150 (5): 67–125.

Amone, Charles. 2015. "Constructivism, Instrumentalism and the Rise of Acholi Ethnicity in Northern Uganda." *African Identities* 13 (2): 129–143.

Amone, Charles, and Okullu Muura. 2014. "British Colonialism and the Creation of Acholi Ethnic Identity in Uganda, 1894 to 1962." *The Journal of Imperial and Commonwealth History* 42 (2): 239–257.

Amone-P'Olak, Kennedy. 2007. "Coping with Life in Rebel Captivity and the Challenge of Reintegrating Formerly Abducted Boys in Northern Uganda." *Journal of Refugee Studies* 20 (4): 641–661.

Anders, Gerhard. 2009. "The New Global Legal Order as Local Phenomenon: The Special Court for Sierra Leone." In *Spatializing Law: An Anthropological Geography of Law in Society*, edited by Franz von Benda-Beckmann and Keebet von Benda-Beckmann, 137–156. London: Routledge.

Anders, Gerhard. 2014a. "Transitional Justice, States of Emergency and Business as Usual in Sierra Leone." *Development and Change* 45 (3): 524–542. doi: 10.1111/dech.12095.

Anders, Gerhard. 2014b. "Contesting Expertise: Anthropologists at the Special Court for Sierra Leone." *Journal of the Royal Anthropological Institute* 20:426–444. doi: 10.1111/1467-9655.12118.

Anders, Gerhard, and Olaf Zenker. 2014a. "Transition and Justice: An Introduction." *Development and Change* 45 (3): 395–414. doi: 10.1111/dech.12096.

Anders, Gerhard, and Olaf Zenker, eds. 2014b. *Transition and Justice: Negotiating the Terms of New Beginnings in Africa*. Hoboken: Wiley-Blackwell.

Anderson, Ben. 2009. "Affective Atmospheres." *Emotion, Space and Society* 2 (2): 77–81. doi: 10.1016/j.emospa.2009.08.005.

Anderson, Benedict. 1983. *Imagined Communities: Reflections on the Origin and Spread of Nationalism*. London: Verso.

Annan, Jeannie, and Moriah Brier. 2010. "The Risk of Return: Intimate Partner Violence in Northern Uganda's Armed Conflict." *Social Science & Medicine* 70 (1): 152–159.

Annan, Jeannie, Moriah Brier, and Filder Aryemo. 2009. "From 'Rebel' to 'Returnee': Daily Life and Reintegration for Young Soldiers in Northern Uganda." *Journal of Adolescent Research* 24 (6): 639–667.

Annan, Jeannie, Christopher Blattman, Dyan Mazurana, and Khristopher Carlson. 2009. "Women and Girls at War: 'Wives', Mothers, and Fighters in the Lord's Resistance Army." Households in Conflict Network (HiCN) Working Papers: 63.

Anonymous. 1996. "Human Rights in Peace Negotiations." *Human Rights Quarterly* 18 (2): 249–258.

Anyeko, Ketty, Erin Baines, Emon Komakech, Boniface Ojok, Lino Owor Ogora, and Letha Victor. 2012. "'The Cooling of Hearts': Community Truth-Telling in Northern Uganda." *Human Rights Review* 13 (1): 107–124. doi: 10.1007/s12142-011-0202-2.

Appadurai, Arjun. 1990. "Disjuncture and Difference in the Global Cultural Economy." *Theory, Culture & Society* 7 (2–3): 295–310. doi: 10.1177/026327690007002017.

Apuuli, Kasaija Phillip. 2011. "Peace over Justice: The Acholi Religious Leaders Peace Initiative (ARLPI) vs. the International Criminal Court (ICC) in Northern Uganda." *Studies in Ethnicity and Nationalism* 11 (1): 116–129.

Arendt, Hannah. 1963. *Eichmann in Jerusalem: A Report on the Banality of Evil.* New York: Viking Press.

Argenti, Nicholas. 2007. *The Intestines of the State: Youth, Violence, and Belated Histories in the Cameroon Grassfields.* Chicago: University of Chicago Press.

Aristotle. 2018. *The Art of Rhetoric.* Oxford: Oxford University Press.

Armstrong, Kimberley. 2014. "Justice without Peace? International Justice and Conflict Resolution in Northern Uganda." *Development and Change* 45 (3): 589–607. doi: 10.1111/dech.12090.

Assier-Andrieu, Louis. 2015. "Dificultad y necesidad de la antropología del derecho." *Revista de Antropología Social* 24: 35–52.

Assmann, Jan. 1995. "Erinnern, um dazuzugehören: Kulturelles Gedächtnis, Zugehörigkeitsstruktur und normative Vergangenheit." In *Generation und Gedächtnis: Erinnerungen und kollektive Identitäten*, edited by Kristin Platt and Mihran Dabag, 51–75. Opladen: Springer.

Atkinson, Ronald R. 1994. *The Roots of Ethnicity: The Origins of the Acholi of Uganda before 1800*, Ethnohistory Series. Philadelphia: University of Pennsylvania Press.

Atkinson, Ronald R. 2010. "'The Realists in Juba'? An Analysis of the Juba Peace Talks." In *The Lord's Resistance Army: Myth and Reality*, edited by Tim Allen and Koen Vlassenroot, 205–222. London: Zed Books.

Austin, John Langshaw. 1962. *How To Do Things with Words: The William James Lectures Delivered at Harvard University in 1955.* New York: Oxford University Press.

Bachmann-Medick, Doris. 2006. *Cultural Turns: Neuorientierungen in den Kulturwissenschaften.* Reinbek: Rowohlt.

Bachmann-Medick, Doris. 2012. "Menschenrechte als Übersetzungsproblem." *Geschichte und Gesellschaft* 38: 331–359.

Baehr, Peter. 2001. "The 'Iron Cage' and the 'Shell as Hard as Steel': Parsons, Weber, and the Stahlhartes Gehäuse Metaphor in the Protestant Ethic and the Spirit of Capitalism." *History and Theory* 40 (2): 153–169.

Baines, Erin K. 2007. "The Haunting of Alice: Local Approaches to Justice and Reconciliation in Northern Uganda." *International Journal of Transitional Justice* 1 (1): 91–114. doi: 10.1093/ijtj/ijm007.

Baines, Erin K. 2009. "Complex Political Perpetrators: Reflections on Dominic Ongwen." *Journal of Modern African Studies* 47 (2): 163–191. doi: 10.1017/S0022278X09003796.

Baines, Erin K. 2010. "Spirits and Social Reconstruction After Mass Violence: Rethinking Transitional Justice." *African Affairs* 109: 409–430. doi: 10.1093/afraf/adq023.

Bandes, Susan A., ed. 2001. *The Passions of Law*. New York: New York University Press.

Bandes, Susan A., and Jeremy A. Blumenthal. 2012. "Emotion and the Law." *Annual Review of Law and Social Science* 8: 161–181. doi: 10.1146/annurev-lawsocsci-102811-173825.

Bassiouni, M. Cherif. 2003. "Justice and Peace: The Importance of Choosing Accountability over Realpolitik." *Case Western Reserve Law Journal* 35 (2): 191–204.

Bateson, Gregory. 1972. *Steps to an Ecology of Mind: Collected Essays in Anthropology, Psychiatry, Evolution, and Epistemology*. Chicago: University of Chicago Press.

Bauman, Richard. 1977. *Verbal Art as Performance*. Rowley: Newbury House.

Bauman, Richard, and Charles L. Briggs. 1990. "Poetics and Performance as Critical Perspectives on Language and Social Life." *Annual Review of Anthropology* 19: 59–88.

Beard, Madeline. 2011. "The Children of Northern Ugadan: The Effects of Civil War." *Global Majority E-Journal* 2 (1): 4–18.

Beatty, Andrew. 2005. "Emotions in the Field: What Are We Talking About?" *Journal of the Royal Anthropological Institute* 11 (1): 17–37. doi: 10.1111/j.1467-9655.2005.00224.x.

Behrend, Heike. 1993. *Alice und die Geister: Krieg im Norden Ugandas*. München: Trickster.

Behrend, Heike. 1999. "Power to Heal, Power to Kill: Spirit Possession & War in Northern Uganda (1986–1994)." In *Spirit Possession: Modernity & Power in Africa*, edited by Heike Behrend and Ute Luig, 20–33. Oxford: Currey.

Benda-Beckmann, Franz von. 2002. "Who's Afraid of Legal Pluralism?" *The Journal of Legal Pluralism and Unofficial Law* 47 (1): 37–82.

Benda-Beckmann, Franz von, Keebet von Benda-Beckmann, and Anne Griffiths. 2009. "Space and Legal Pluralism: An Introduction." In

Spatializing Law: An Anthropological Geography of Law in Society, edited by Franz von Benda-Beckmann and Keebet von Benda-Beckmann, 1–29. London: Routledge.

Benda-Beckmann, Keebet. 1981. "Forum Shopping and Shopping Forums: Dispute Settlement in a Minangkabau Village in West Sumatra." *Journal of Legal Pluralism* 13 (1): 117–159.

Benda-Beckmann, Keebet. 1984. *The Broken Stairways to Consensus: Village Justice and State Courts in Minankabau*. Dordrecht: ICG.

Benda-Beckmann, Keebet von. 2014. "Trust and the Temporalities of Law." *The Journal of Legal Pluralism and Unofficial Law* 46 (1): 1–17. doi: 10.1080/07329113.2014.894743.

Benda-Beckmann, Keebet von, and Bertram Turner. 2018. "Legal Pluralism, Social Theory, and the State." *Journal of Legal Pluralism and Unofficial Law* 50 (3): 255–274.

Benedict, Ruth F. 1946. *The Chrysanthemum and the Sword: Patterns of Japanese Culture*. Boston: Houghton Mifflin.

Benei, Veronique. 2008. *Schooling Passions: Nation, History, and Language in Contemporary Western India*. Stanford: Stanford University Press.

Benker, Leonie. 2020. "'Not enough has yet been told about this war': Competing Narratives About the Armed Conflict in Northern Uganda." Master's Thesis, Department of History, Freie Universität Berlin.

Benker, Leonie. 2021. "Koloniales Erbe und deutsche Erinnerungskultur: Die Debatte um Restitution und ihre Fortläufer in deutschen Medien (2018–2020)." *Baessler Archiv* 86 (1): 51–65.

Bens, Jonas. 2016. "Anthropology and the Law: Historicising the Epistemological Divide." *International Journal of Law in Context* 12 (3): 235–252.

Bens, Jonas. 2018a. "The Courtroom as an Affective Arrangement: Analysing Atmospheres in Courtroom Ethnography." *Journal of Legal Pluralism and Unofficial Law* 50 (3): 336–355. doi: 10.1080/07329113.2018.1550313.

Bens, Jonas. 2018b. "Sentimentalising Persons and Things: Creating Normative Arrangements of Bodies through Courtroom Talk." *Journal of Legal Anthropology* 2 (1): 72–91. doi: 10.3167/jla.2018.020105.

Bens, Jonas. 2019a. "Affective Images and the Political Trial." In *Image Testimonies: Witnessing in Times of Social Media*, edited by Kerstin Schankweiler, Verena Straub and Tobias Wendl, 30–44. London: Routledge.

Bens, Jonas. 2019b. "The Ethnography of Affect in Discourse Practice: Performing Sentiment in the Time Machine." In *Analyzing Affective Societies: Methods and Methodologies*, edited by Antje Kahl, 199–213. London: Routledge.

Bens, Jonas. 2019c. "Wie ansteckend ist Hassrede? Normative Kausalität bei der Strafbarkeit affektiven Sprechens." In *Hass/Literatur: Literatur- und kulturwissenschaftliche Beiträge zu einer Theorie- und Diskursgeschichte*, edited by Jürgen Brokhoff and Robert Walter-Jochum, 193–207. Bielefeld: Transcript.

Bens, Jonas. 2020. *The Indigenous Paradox: Sovereignty, Culture, and Rights in the Americas*. Philadelphia: University of Pennsylvania Press.

Bens, Jonas, and Larissa Vetters. 2018. "Ethnographic Legal Studies: Reconecting Anthropological and Sociological Traditions." *Journal of Legal Pluralism and Unofficial Law* 50 (3): 239–254.

Bens, Jonas, and Olaf Zenker. 2017a. "Gerechtigkeitsgefühle: Eine Einführung." In *Gerechtigkeitsgefühle: Zur affektiven und emotionalen Legitimität von Normen*, edited by Jonas Bens and Olaf Zenker, 11–36. Bielefeld: Transcript.

Bens, Jonas, and Olaf Zenker, eds. 2017b. *Gerechtigkeitsgefühle: Zur affektiven und emotionalen Legitimität von Normen*. Bielefeld: Transcript.

Bens, Jonas, and Olaf Zenker. 2019. "Sentiment." In *Affective Societies: Key Concepts*, edited by Jan Slaby and Christian von Scheve, 96–106. New York: Routledge.

Bens, Jonas, Aletta Diefenbach, Thomas John, Antje Kahl, Hauke Lehmann, Matthias Lüthjohann, Friederike Oberkrome, Hans Roth, Gabriel Scheidecker, Gerhard Thonhauser, Nur-Yasemin Ural, Dina Wahba, Robert Walter-Jochum, and M. Ragıp Zık. 2019. *The Politics of Affective Societies: An Interdisciplinary Essay*. Bielefeld: Transcript.

Berg, Ulla D., and Ana Y. Ramos-Zayas. 2015. "Racializing Affect." *Current Anthropology* 56 (5): 654–677. doi: 10.1086/683053.

Berliner, David. 2005. "An 'Im possible' Transmission: Youth Religious Memories in Guinea-Conakry." *American Ethnologist* 32 (4): 576–592.

Berthomé, François, and Michael Houseman. 2010. "Ritual and Emotions: Moving Relations, Patterned Effusions." *Religion and Society* 1 (1): 57–75.

Besnier, Niko. 1990. "Language and Affect." *Annual Review of Anthropology* 19: 419–451. doi: 10.1146/annurev.an.19.100190.002223.

Besnier, Niko. 1994. "Involvement in Linguistic Practice: An Ethnographic Appraisal." *Journal of Pragmatics* 22 (1994): 279–299.

Bevan, James. 2007. "The Myth of Madness: Cold Rationality and 'Resource' Plunder by the Lord's Resistance Army." *Civil Wars* 9 (4): 343–358.

Biehl, João Guilherme, Byron Good, and Arthur Kleinman, eds. 2007. *Subjectivity: Ethnographic Investigations, Ethnographic Studies in Subjectivity*. Berkeley: University of California Press.

Blackman, Lisa. 2012. *Immaterial Bodies: Affect, Embodiment, Mediation*. Los Angeles: Sage.

Blix, Stina Bergmann, and Åsa Wettergren. 2018. *Professional Emotions in Court: A Sociological Perspective*. London: Routledge.

Boas, Franz. 1911. *The Mind of Primitive Man*. New York: Macmillan.

Boas, Franz. 1928. *Anthropology and Modern Life*. New York: W. W. Norton.

Boas, Franz. 1940. *Race, Language and Culture*. New York: Macmillan.

Bohannan, Paul. 1957. *Justice and Judgment Among the Tiv*. Oxford: Oxford University Press.

Bonhomme, Julien. 2008. "Des pleurs ou des coups: Affects et relations dans l'initiation au Bwete Misoko (Gabon)." *Systèmes de Pensée en Afrique Noire* 18: 133–163.

Bornstein, Brian H., and Richard L. Wiener, eds. 2010. *Emotion and the Law: Psychological Perspectives*. New York: Springer.

Bourdieu, Pierre. 1972. *Esquisse d'une théorie de la pratique, prencédé de trois études d'ethnologie kabyle*. Genève: Librairie Droz.

Bourdieu, Pierre. 1994. *Raisons practiques: Sur la théorie de l'action*. Paris: Editions du Seuil.

Branch, Adam. 2004. "International Justice, Local Injustice." *Dissent* (Summer 2014) 51 (3): 22–26.

Branch, Adam. 2005. "Neither Peace nor Justice: Political Violence and the Peasantry in Northern Uganda, 1986–1998." *African Studies Quarterly* 8 (2): 1–31.

Branch, Adam. 2007. "Uganda's Civil War and the Politics of ICC Intervention." *Ethics and International Affairs* 21 (2): 179–198.

Branch, Adam. 2010. "Exploring the Roots of LRA Violence: Political Crisis and Ethnic Politics in Acholiland." In *The Lord's Resistance Army: Myth and Reality*, edited by Tim Allen and Koen Vlassenroot, 25–44. London: Zed Books.

Branch, Adam. 2011. *Displacing Human Rights: War and Intervention in Northern Uganda*. Cambridge: Cambridge University Press.

Branch, Adam. 2014. "The Violence of Peace: Ethnojustice in Northern Uganda." *Development and Change* 45 (3): 608–630.

Branch, Adam. 2017. "Dominic Ongwen on Trial: The ICC's African Dilemmas." *International Journal of Transitional Justice* 11 (1): 30–49. doi: 10.1093/ijtj/ijw027.

Briggs, Jane L. 1970. *Never in Anger: Portrait of an Eskimo Family*. Cambridge: Harvard University Press.

Brinkema, Eugenie. 2014. *The Forms of Affect*. Durham: Duke University Press.

Brooks, Victoria. 2019. "Interrupting the Courtroom Organism: Screaming Bodies, Material Affects and the Theatre of Cruelty." *Law, Culture and the Humanities* 15 (2): 332–351.

Brown, Barbara B., John D. Metzler, Christine Root, and Patrick Vinck. 2010. "React and Respond: The Phenomenon of Kony 2012." East Lansing: Association of Concerned Africa Scholars.

Brudholm, Thomas, and Johannes Lang. 2018. *Emotions and Mass Atrocity: Philosophical and Theoretical Explorations*. New York: Cambridge University Press.

Brunegger, Sandra, and Karen Faulk, eds. 2016. *A Sense of Justice: Legal Knowledge and Lived Experience in Latin America*. Stanford: Stanford University Press.

Buckley-Zistel, Susanne, Teresa Koloma Beck, Christian Braun, and Friederike Mieth, eds. 2013. *Transitional Justice Theories*. New York: Taylor and Francis.

Burke-White, William W. 2003. "Regionalization of International Criminal Law Enforcement: A Preliminary Exploration." *Texas International Law Journal* 38: 729–761.

Burkitt, Ian. 2014. *Emotions and Social Relations*. London: Sage.

Butler, Judith. 1997a. *Excitable Speech: A Politics of the Performative*. New York: Routledge.

Butler, Judith. 1997b. *The Psychic Life of Power: Theories in Subjection*. Stanford: Stanford University Press.

Calkins, Sandra. 2016. "How 'Clean Gold' Came to Matter: Metal Detectors, Infrastructure, and Valuation." *HAU: Journal of Ethnographic Theory* 6 (2): 173–195.

Capps, Lisa, and Elinor Ochs. 1995. *Constructing Panic: The Discourse of Agoraphobia*. Cambridge: Harvard University Press.

Carayon, Gaelle, and Jonathan O'Donohue. 2017. "The International Criminal Court's Strategies in Relation to Victims." *Journal of International Criminal Justice* 15 (3): 567–591. doi: 10.1093/jicj/mqx023.

Carsten, Janet, ed. 2007. *Ghosts of Memory: Essays on Relatedness and Remembering*. Malden: Blackwell.

Cassese, Antonio. 2012. "The Legitimacy of International Criminal Tribunals and the Current Prospects of International Criminal Justice." *Leiden Journal of International Law* 25 (2): 491–501. doi: 10.1017/S0922156512000167.

Cattell, Maria G., and Jacob J. Climo. 2002. "Introduction: Meaning in Social Memory and History." In *Social Memory and History: Anthropological Perspectives*, edited by Jacob J. Climo and Maria G. Cattell, 1–39. New York: Altamira.

Celermajer, Daniel, Millicent Churcher, Moira Gatens, and Anna Hush. 2019. "Institutional Transformations: Imagination, Embodiment, and Affect." *Angelaki: Journal of the Theoretical Humanities* 24 (4): 3–21.

Cerci, Deniz, and Erminia Colucci. 2017. "Forgiveness in PTSD after Man-Made Traumatic Events: A Systematic Review." *Traumatology* 27(1): 47–54.

Chanock, Martin. 1985. *Law, Custom, and Social Order: The Colonial Experience in Malawai and Zambia*. Cambridge: Cambridge University Press.

Chomsky, Noam. 1965. *Aspects of the Theory of Syntax*. Cambridge: MIT Press.

Christodoulidis, Emilios. 2011. "Political Trials as Events." In *Events: The Force of International Law*, edited by Fleur Johns, Richard Joyce and Sundhya Pahuja, 130–144. London: Routledge.

Clark, Janine Natalya. 2008. "The Three Rs: Retributive Justice, Restorative Justice, and Reconciliation." *Contemporary Justice Review* 11 (4): 331–350. doi: 10.1080/10282580802482603.

Clark, Janine Natalaya. 2010. "The ICC, Uganda and the LRA: Framing the Debate." *African Studies* 69: 141–160. doi: 10.1080/00020181003647256.

Clarke, Kamari Maxine. 2012. "Kony 2012, the ICC, and the Problem with the Peace-and-Justice-Divide." *Proceedings of the Annual Meeting (American Society of International Law)* 106: 309–313.

Clarke, Kamari Maxine. 2009. *Fictions of Justice: The International Criminal Court and the Challenge of Legal Pluralism in Sub-Sahara Africa*. Cambridge: Cambridge University Press.

Clarke, Kamari Maxine. 2019. *Affective Justice: The International Criminal Court and the Pan-Africanist Pushback*. Durham: Duke University Press.

Clarke, Kamari Maxine, and Mark Goodale, eds. 2010. *Mirrors of Justice: Law and Power in the Post-Cold War Era*. Cambridge: Cambridge University Press.

Clarke, Kamari Maxine, Abel S. Knotterus, and Eefje de Volder, eds. 2016. *Africa and the ICC: Perceptions of Justice*. Cambridge: Cambridge University Press.

Classen, Constance. 1997. "Foundations for an Anthropology of the Senses." *International Social Science* 49 (152): 401–412.

Clifford, James. 1988. *The Predicament of Culture: Twentieth-Century Ethnography, Literature, and Art*. Cambridge: Harvard University Press.

Cline, Lawrence. 2003. "Spirits and the Cross: Religiously Based Violence in Uganda." *Small Wars & Insurgencies* 14 (2): 113–130.

Clough, Patricia Ticineto, and Jean Halley, eds. 2007. *The Affective Turn: Theorizing the Social*. Durham: Duke University Press.

Cohen, David William, and E. S. Atieno Odhiambo. 1989. *Siaya: The Historical Anthropology of an African Landscape*. London: James Currey.

Cole, Catherine M. 2009. *Performing South Africa's Truth Commission: Stages of Transition*. Bloomington: Indiana University Press.

Cole, Rowland J. V. 2013. "Africa's Relationship with the International Criminal Court: More Political Than Legal." *Melbourne Journal of International Law* 14 (2): 1–29.

Coleman, Stephen. 2013. *How Voters Feel*. Cambridge: Cambridge University Press.

Comaroff, Jean, and John Comaroff. 2006. *Law and Disorder in the Postcolony*. Chicago: University of Chicago Press.

Comaroff, Jean, and John Comaroff. 2007. "Law and Disorder in the Postcolony." *Social Anthropology* 15: 133–152. doi: 10.1111/j.0964-0282.2007.00010.x.

Comaroff, John L., and Simon Roberts. 1981. *Rules and Processes: The Cultural Logic of Dispute in an African Context*. Chicago: University Of Chicago Press.

Conley, John M., and William M. O'Barr. 1990. *Rules versus Relationships: The Ethnography of Legal Discourse*. Chicago: Chicago University Press.

Conley, John M., and William M. O'Barr. 2019. *Just Words: Law, Language, and Power*. 3 ed. Chicago: Chicago University Press.

Conti, Joseph A. 2016. "Legitimacy Chains: Legitimation of Compliance with International Courts across Social Fields." *Law & Society Review* 50: 154–188. doi: 10.1111/lasr.12181.

Csordas, Thomas J. 1990. "Embodiment as a Paradigm for Anthropology." *Ethos* 18 (1): 5–47.

Csordas, Thomas J., ed. 1995. *Embodiment and Experience: The Existential Grounds of Culture and Self*. Cambridge: Cambridge University Press.

Csordas, Thomas J. 1997. *Language, Charisma, and Creativity: Ritual Life in the Catholic Charismatic Renewal*. New York: Palgrave Macmillan.

D'hondt, Sigurd. 2009. "Good Cops, Bad Cops: Intertextuality, Agency, and Structure in Criminal Trial Discourse." *Research on Language & Social Interaction* 42 (3): 249–275. doi: 10.1080/08351810903089183.

D'hondt, Sigurd. 2019. "Humanity and Its Beneficiaries: Footing and Stance-Taking in an International Criminal Trial." *Signs and Society* 7 (3): 427–453. doi: 10.1086/705279.

D'hondt, Sigurd. 2020. "Confronting Blackface: Stancetaking in the Dutch Black Pete Debate." *Pragmatics*. doi: 10.1075/prag.18039.dho

D'hondt, Sigurd. 2021. "Why Being There Mattered: Staged Transparency (and How to Study it) at the International Criminal Court." *Journal of Pragmatics* 182 (October 2021): 168–178.

D'hondt, Sigurd, and Fleur van der Houwen. 2014. "Quoting from the Case File: How Intertextual Practices Shape Discourse at Various Stages in the Legal Trajectory." *Language and Communication* 36: 1–6. doi: 10.1016/j.langcom.2013.12.008.

Dahlberg, Leif. 2009. "Emotional Tropes in the Courtroom: On Representation of Affect and Emotion in Legal Court Proceedings." *Law and Humanities* 3 (2): 175–205.

Daston, Lorraine, and Peter Galison. 2007. *Objectivity*. New York: Zone Books.

De Castro, Eduardo Viveiros. 1998. "Cosmological Deixis and Amerindian Perspectivism." *The Journal of the Royal Anthropological Institute* 4: 469. doi: 10.2307/3034157.

De La Bretèque, Estelle Amy. 2012. "Voices of Sorrow: Melodized Speech, Laments, and Heroic Narratives Among the Yezidis of Armenia." *Yearbook for Traditional Music* 44: 129–148. doi: 10.5921/yeartradmusi.44.0129.

Deleuze, Gilles. 1968. *Spinoza et le problème de l'expression*. Paris: Les Editions de Minuit.

Deleuze, Gilles. 1970. *Spinoza: Philosophie practique*. Paris: Presses Universitaires de France.

Derrida, Jacques. 1989. "Force de loi: Le fondement mystique de l'autorite / Force of Law: The Mystical Foundations of Authority." *Cardozo Law Review* 11 (3): 920–1045.

Dersso, Solomon A. 2016. "The ICC's Africa Problem: A Spotlight on the Politics and Limits of International Criminal Justice." In *Africa and the ICC: Perceptions of Justice*, edited by Kamari Maxine Clarke, Abel S. Knotterus and Eefje de Volder, 61–77. Cambridge: Cambridge University Press.

Descola, Philippe. 2005. *Par-delà nature et culture*. Paris: Gallimard.

Desjarlais, Robert R. 1992. *Body and Emotion: The Aesthetics of Illness and Healing in the Nepal Himalayas*. Philadelphia: University of Pennsylvania Press.

Desjarlais, Robert, and Jason C. Throop. 2011. "Phenomenological Approaches in Anthropology." *Annual Review of Anthropology* 40: 87–102. doi: 10.1146/annurev-anthro-092010-153345.

Dickinson, Laura. 2003. "The Promise of Hybrid Courts." *American Journal of International Law* 97 (2): 295–310.

Diefenbach, Katja. 2018. *Spekulativer Materialismus: Spinoza in der postmarxistischen Philosophie*. Wien: Turia und Kant.

Diehl, Paula, Henning Grundwald, Thomas Scheffer, and Christoph Wulf, eds. 2006. *Performanz des Rechts: Inszenierung und Diskurs*. Vol. 15, *Paragrana: Internationale Zeitschrift für historische Anthropologie*. Berlin: Akademie-Verlag.

Dilger, Hansjörg, Dominik Mattes, and Omar Kasmani. 2018. "Spatialities of Belonging: Affective Place-Making Among Diasporic Neo-Pentecostal and Sufi Groups in Berlin's Cityscape." In *Affect in Relation: Essays on Affectivity and Subject Formation in the 21st Century*, edited by Birgitt Röttger-Rössler and Jan Slaby, 93–114. London: Routledge.

Dilger, Hansjörg, Marian Burchardt, Wilhelm-Solomon Matthew, and Astrid Bochow. 2020. "Affective Trajectories in Religious African Cityscapes." In *Affective Trajectories: Religion and Emotion in African City-Scapes*, edited by Hansjörg Dilger, Astrid Bochow, Marian Burchardt and Wilhelm-Solomon Matthew, 1–28. Durham: Duke University Press.

Dolan, Chris. 2009. *Social Torture: The Case of Northern Uganda, 1986–2006*. New York: Berghahn.

Dolar, Mladen. 2006. *A Voice and Nothing More*. Cambridge: MIT Press.

Doughty, Kristin C. 2010. *Remediation in Rwanda: Grassroots Legal Forums*. Philadelphia: Pennsylvania University Press.

Dubber, Markus Dirk. 2005. "Making Sense of the Sense of Justice." *Buffalo Law Reveiw* 53 (3): 815–858.

Dupret, Baudouin. 2007. "Legal Pluralism, Plurality of Laws, and Legal Practices: Theories, Critiques, and Praxeological Re-Specification." *European Journal of Legal Studies* 1 (1): 296–318.

Dupret, Baudouin. 2011. *Practices of Truth: An Ethnomethodological Inquiry Into Arab Contexts*. Amsterdam: John Benjaminis.

Duranti, Alessandro. 2006. "Narrating the Political Self in a Campaign for US Congress." *Language in Society* 35 (4): 467–497.

Durkheim, Emile. 1912. *Les formes élémentaires de la vie religieuse*. Paris: Félix Alcan.

Durkheim, Emile. 1915. *The Elementary Forms of Religious Life*. London: George Allen & Unwin.

Eades, Diana. 2008. *Courtroom Talk and Neocolonial Control*. Berlin: De Gruyter.

Eckert, Julia. 2012. "Rumors of Rights." In *Law against the State: Ethnographic Forays into Law's Transformations*, edited by Julia Eckert, Brian Donahoe, Christian Strümpell and Zerrin Özlem Biner, 147–170. Cambridge: Cambridge University Press.

Eckert, Julia, Brian Donahoe, Christian Strümpell, and Zerrin Özlem Biner, eds. 2012. *Law against the State: Ethnographic Forays into Law's Transformations*. Cambridge: Cambridge University Press.

Edmond, Gary. 2004. "Thick Decisions: Expertise, Advocacy and Reasonableness in the Federal Court of Australia." *Oceania* 74 (3): 190–230.

Edmondson, Laura. 2018. *Performing Trauma in Central Africa: Shadows of Empire*. Bloomington: Indiana University Press.

Ehrenreich, Rosa. 1998. "The Stories We Must Tell: Ugandan Children and the Atrocities of the Lord's Resistance Army." *Africa Today* 45 (1): 79–102.

Ehrlich, Susan. 2001. *Representing Rape: Language and Sexual Consent*. London: Routledge.

Ehrlich, Susan. 2012. "Text Trajectories, Legal Discourse and Gendered Inequalities." *Applied Linguistics Review* 3 (1): 47–73. doi: 10.1515/applirev-2012-0003.

Eichstaedt, Peter. 2009. *First Kill Your Family: Child Soldiers of Uganda and the Lord's Resistance Army*. Chicago: Lawrence Hill Books.

Eisenstadt, S. N. 2000. "Multiple Modernities." *Daedalus* 129 (1): 1–29.

Ekman, Paul. 1999. "Basic Emotions." In *Handbook of Cognition and Emotion*, edited by T. Dalgleish and M. Power, 45–60. Sussex: Wiley.

El Zeidy, Mohammed M. 2008. *The Principle of Complementarity in International Criminal Law: Origin, Development and Practice*. The Hague: Brill.

Eltringham, Nigel. 2004. *Accounting for Horror: Post-Genocide Debates in Rwanda*. London: Pluto.

Eltringham, Nigel. 2012. "Spectators to the Spectacle of Law: The Formation of a 'Validating Public' at the International Criminal Tribunal for Rwanda." *Ethnos* 77 (3): 425–445. doi: 10.1080/00141844.2011.620131.

Emde, Sina. 2014. "Please Compose Yourself: Testimony, Remembering, and Emotion at the Extraordinary Chambers in the Courts of Cambodia." In *Trauma, Memory, and Transformation: Southeast Asian Experiences*, edited by

Sharon A. Bong, 53–73. Petaling Jaya, Selangor, Malaysia: Strategic Information and Research Development Centre.
Engels, Friedrich. 1884. *Der Usprung der Familie, des Privateigenthums und des Staats: Im Anschluss an Lewis H. Morgan's Forschungen*. Hottingen-Zürich: Verlag der Schweizerischen Volksbuchhandlung.
Englund, Harri. 2006. *Prisoners of Freedom: Human Rights and the African Poor, California Series in Public Anthropology*. Berkeley: University of California Press.
Englund, Harri. 2012. "Human Rights and Village Headmen in Malawi: Translation Beyond Vernaculatization." In *Law Against the State: Ethnographic Forays into Law's Transformations*, edited by Julia Maria Eckert, Brian Donahoe, Christian Strümpell and Zerrin Özlem Biner, 70–93. Cambridge: Cambridge University Press.
Entman, Robert M. 1993. "Framing: Toward Clarification of a Fractured Paradigm." *Journal of Communication* 43 (4): 51–58.
Ertür, Başak. 2015. "Spectacles and Spectres: Political Trials, Performativity and Scences of Sovereignty." PhD, School of Law, Birkbeck, University of London.
Fanon, Frantz. 1961. *Les damnés de la terre*. Paris: François Maspero Éditeur.
Fassin, Didier. 2012. *Humanitarian Reason: A Moral History of the Present*. Berkeley: University of California Press.
Feld, Steven. 1982. *Sound and Sentiment: Birds, Weeping, Poetics, and Song in Kaluli Expression*. Philadelphia: University of Pennsylvania Press.
Finnegan, Amy C. 2013. "Beneath Kony 2012: Americans Aligning with Arms and Aiding Others." *Africa Today* 59: 136–162.
Finnström, Sverker. 2008. *Living With Bad Surroundings: War, History, and Everyday Moments in Northern Uganda*. Durham: Duke University Press.
Finnström, Sverker. 2012. "KONY 2012, Military Humanitarianism, and the Magic of Occult Economies." *Africa Spectrum* 47: 127–135.
Flower, Lisa. 2014. "The (Un)Emotional Law Student." *International Journal of Work Organisation and Emotion* 6 (3): 295–309.
Ford, Stuart. 2012. "A Social Psychology Model of the Perceived Legitimacy of International Criminal Courts: Implications for the Success of Transitional Justice Mechanisms." *Vanderbilt Journal of Transnational Law* 45 (2): 405–476.
Foucault, Michel. 1972. *Power / Knowledge: Selected Interviews and Other Writings*. New York: Pantheon Books.
Franck, Georg. 1998. *Ökonomie der Aufmerksamkeit: Ein Entwurf*. München: Hanser.
Freeland, Valerie. 2015. "Rebranding the State: Uganda's Strategic Use of the International Criminal Court." *Development and Change* 46 (2): 293–319. doi: 10.1111/dech.12147.
Freire de Andrade Neves, Marcos. 2018. "States of Uncertainty: Plural Laws and Affective Governance in the Context of Assisted Suicide in Germany."

Journal of Legal Pluralism and Unofficial Law 50 (3): 317–329. doi: 10.1080/07329113.2018.1550706.

Garapon, Antoine. 1997. *Bien juger: Essai sur le rituel judiciare*. Paris: Odile Jacob.

Geertz, Clifford. 1973. *The Interpretation of Cultures: Selected Essays*. New York: Basic Books.

Geertz, Clifford. 1983. "Local Knowlegde: Fact and Law in Comparative Perspective." In *Local Knowledge: Further Essays in Interpretive Anthropology*, edited by Geertz, Clifford, 167–234. New York: Basic Books.

Geschiere, Peter, Birgitt Meyer, and Peter Pels, eds. 2008. *Readings in Modernity in Africa*. Bloomington: Indiana University Press.

Girling, F. K. 1960. *The Acholi of Uganda. Vol. 30, Colonical Research Studies / Colonial Office*. London: Her Majesty's Stationery Office.

Gissel, Line Engbo. 2015. "Justice Tides: How and When Levels of ICC Involvement Affect Peace Processes." *International Journal of Transitional Justice* 9: 428–448. doi: 10.1093/ijtj/ijv021.

Glassman, Jonathon. 2011. *War of Words, War of Stones: Racial Thought and Violence in Colonial Zanzibar*. Bloomington: Indiana University Press.

Gluckman, Max. 1955. *The Judicial Process among the Barotse of Northern Rhodesia*. Manchester: Manchester University Press.

Gluckman, Max. 1973. "Limitations of the Case-Method in the Study of Tribal Law." *Law and Society Review* 7 (4): 611–641.

Goffman, Erving. 1956. *The Presentation of Self in Everyday Life*. Edinburgh: University of Edinburgh Social Science Research Centre.

Goffman, Erving. 1967. *Interaction Ritual: Essays on Face-to-Face Behavior*. Middlesex: Penguin.

Goffman, Erving. 1974. *Frame Analysis: An Essay on the Organization of Experience*. Boston: Northeastern University Press.

Good, Anthony. 2004. "'Undoubtedly an Expert'? Anthropologists in British Asylum Courts." *The Journal of the Royal Anthropological Institute* 10: 113–133.

Goodale, Mark. 2009. *Dilemmas of Modernity: Bolivian Encounters with Law and Liberalism*. Stanford: Stanford University Press.

Goodale, Mark, and Sally Engle Merry. 2007. *The Practice of Human Rights: Tracking Law between the Global and the Local*. Cambridge: Cambridge University Press.

Goodale, Mark, and Kamari Maxine Clarke. 2010. "Introduction: Understanding the Multiplicity of Justice." In *Mirrors of Justice: Law and Power in the Post-Cold War Era*, edited by Kamari Maxine Clarke and Mark Goodale, 1–27. Cambridge: Cambridge University Press.

Goodwin, Jeff, James M. Jasper, and Francesca Polletta, eds. 2001. *Passionate Politics: Emotions and Social Movements*. Chicago: University of Chicago Press.

Gould, Deborah. 2009. *Moving Politics: Emotion and ACT UP's Fight Against AIDS*. Chicago: University of Chicago Press.
Gould, Lauren M. 2014. "The Politics of Portrayal in Violent Conflict: The Case of the Kony 2012 Campaign." *Alternatives: Global, Local, Political* 39 (4): 207–230.
Graven, Jean. 1950. "Les crimes contre l'humanité." *Recueil des cours* 76: 433–605.
Greenawalt, Alexander K. A. 2009. "Complementarity in Crisis: Uganda, Alternative Justice, and the International Criminal Court." *Virginia Journal of International Law* 50 (1): 115–162.
Gregg, Melissa, and Gregory J. Seigworth, eds. 2010. *The Affect Theory Reader*. Durham: Duke University Press.
Griffero, Tonino. 2014. "Atmospheres and Lived Space." *Studia Phenomenologica* 14: 29–51.
Griffiths, Anne M. O. 1997. *In the Shadow of Marriage: Gender and Justice in an African Community*. Chicago: University of Chicago Press.
Griffiths, John. 1986. "What is Legal Pluralism?" *Journal of Legal Pluralism and Unofficial Law* 24: 1–55.
Habermas, Jürgen. 1992. *Faktizität und Geltung: Beiträge zur Diskurstheorie des Rechts und des demokratischen Rechtsstaats*. Frankfurt am Main: Suhrkamp.
Habermas, Jürgen. 1996. *Between Facts and Norms: Contributions to a Discourse Theory of Law and Democracy*. Cambridge: MIT Press.
Halpern, Jodi, and Harvey M. Weinstein. 2004. "Rehumanizing the Other: Empathy and Reconciliation." *Human Rights Quarterly* 26 (3): 561–583.
Harlacher, Thomas, Francis Xavier, Okot Caroline, Aloyo Obonyo, Mychelle Balthazard, and Ronald R. Atkinson. 2006. *Traditional Ways of Coping in Acholi: Cultural Provisions for Reconciliation and Healing From War*. Gulu: Caritas Gulu Archdiocese.
Harris, Marvin. 1976. "History and Significance of the Emic/Etic Distinction." *Annual Review of Anthropology* 5: 329–350.
Hegel, Georg Wilhelm Friedrich. 1807. *Phänomenologie des Geistes*. Bamberg: Joseph Anton Geobhardt.
Henham, Ralph. 2007. "Theorising Law and Legitimacy in International Criminal Justice." *International Journal of Law in Context* 3 (3): 257–274. doi: 10.1017/S1744552307003047.
Higonnet, Etelle R. 2006. "Restructuring Hybrid Courts: Local Empowerment and National Criminal Justice Reform." *Arizona Journal of International and Comparative Law* 23 (2): 347–435.
Hinton, Alexander L. 2010a. "Introduction: Toward an Anthropology of Transitional Justice." In *Transitional Justice: Global Mechanisms and Local Realities after Genocide and Mass Violence*, edited by Hinton, Alexander L., 1–22. New Brunswick: Rutgers University Press.

Hinton, Alexander L., ed. 2010b. *Transitional Justice: Global Mechanisms and Local Realities after Genocide and Mass Violence*. New Brunswick: Rutgers University Press.

Hirsch, Susan F. 2006. *In the Moment of Greatest Calamity: Terrorism, Grief, and a Victim's Quest for Justice*. Princeton: Princeton University Press.

Hirsch, Susan F. 1998. *Pronouncing and Persevering: Gender and the Discourses of Disputing in an African Islamic Court*. Chicago: University of Chicago Press.

Hobbes, Thomas. 1651. *Leviathan or The Matter, Forme and Power of a Common-Wealth Ecclesiasticall and Civil*. London: Andrew Crooke.

Hobsbawm, Eric. 1990. *Nations and Nationalism Since 1780*. Cambridge: Cambridge University Press.

Hochschild, Arlie Russell. 1979. "Emotion Work, Feeling Rules, and Social Structure." *American Journal of Sociology* 85: 551–575.

Hochschild, Arlie Russell. 1983. *The Managed Heart: Commerzialization of Human Feeling*. Berkeley: University of California Press.

Höhne, Markus. 2016. "The Strategic Use of Epistemological Positions in a Power-Laden Arena: Anthropological Expertise in Asylum Cases in the UK." *International Journal of Law in Context* 12 (3): 253–271.

Hume, David. 1751. *An Enquiry Concerning the Principles of Morals*. London: A. Millar.

Humphreys, Stephen. 2010. *Theatre of the Rule of Law: Transnational Legal Intervention in Theory and Practice*. Cambridge: Cambridge University Press.

Iliffe, John. 1979. *A Modern History of Tanganyika*. Cambridge: Cambridge University Press.

Ingold, Tim. 2016. "On Place and the Atmosphere." *PAN: Philosophy, Activism, Nature* 12: 11–12.

Ivanov, Paola. 2000. *Vorkoloniale Geschichte und Expansion der Avungara-Azande: Eine quellenkritische Untersuchung*. Köln: Köppe.

Ivanov, Paola, and Jonas Bens. 2021. "Koloniale Diversität: Die Affektiven Regierungsmodi Des Liberalismus Am Beispiel Des Humboldt Forums." In *Umkämpfte Vielfalt: Affektive Dynamiken Institutioneller Diversifizierung*, edited by Hansjörg Dilger and Matthias Warstatt, 164–185. Frankfurt: Campus.

Jackson, Michael. 2012. *Lifeworlds: Essays in Existential Anthropology*. Chicago: University of Chicago Press.

Jalloh, Charles Chernor, Dapo Akande, and Max du Plessis. 2011. "Assessing the African Union Concerns about Article 16 of the Rome Statute of the International Criminal Court." *African Journal of Legal Studies* 4: 5–50.

Johns, Fleur, Richard Joyce, and Sundhya Pahuja, eds. 2011. *Events: The Force of International Law*. London: Routledge.

Johnson, Jessica. 2018. *In Search of Gender Justice: Rights and Relationships in Matrilineal Malawi*. Cambridge: Cambridge University Press.

Johnson, Jessica. 2019. "Law, Dispute Resolution, and Justice." In *A Compantion to the Anthropology of Africa*, edited by Roy R. Grinker, Stephen C. Lubkemann, Christopher B. Steiner, and Euclides Gonçalves, 81–95. Malden: Wiley.

Johnson, Jessica, and George Hamandishe Karekwaivanane. 2018a. "Introduction: Re-centering Justice in African Studies." In *Pursuing Justice in Africa: Competing Imaginaries and Contested Practices*, edited by Jessica Johnson and George Hamandishe Karekwaivanane, 1–30. Athens: Ohio University Press.

Johnson, Jessica, and George Hamandishe Karekwaivanane, eds. 2018b. *Pursuing Justice in Africa: Competing Imaginaries and Contested Practices.* Athens: Ohio University Press.

Käihkö, Ilmari, and Mats Utas. 2014. "The Crisis in CAR: Navigating Myths and Interests." *Africa Spectrum* 49 (1): 69–77.

Kapferer, Bruce. 1979. "Emotion and Feeling in Sinhalese Healing Rites." *Social Analysis* 1: 153–176.

Kaufman, Stuart J. 2006. "Escaping the Symbolic Politics Trap: Reconciliation Initiatives and Conflict Resolution in Ethnic Wars." *Journal of Peace Research* 43 (2): 201–218.

Kelsall, Tim. 2009. *Culture Under Cross-Examination: International Justice and the Special Court for Sierra Leone.* Cambridge: Cambridge University Press.

Kelsen, Hans. 1944. "The Principle of Sovereign Equality of States as a Basis for International Organization." *The Yale Law Journal* 53: 207. doi: 10.2307/792798.

Kieran, McEvoy. 2007. "Beyond Legalism: Towards a Thicker Understanding of Transitional Justice." *Journal of Law and Society* 34 (4): 411–440.

Kirchheimer, Otto. 1961. *Political Justice: The Use of Legal Procedure for Political Ends.* Princeton: Princeton University Press.

Kleffner, Jann. 2008. *Complementarity in the Rome Statute and National Criminal Jurisdictions.* Oxford: Oxford University Press.

Kulick, Don, and Charles H. Klein. 2003. "Scandalous Acts: The Politics of Shame Among Brazilian Travesti Prostitutes." In *Recognition Struggles and Social Movements: Contested Identities*, edited by Barbara Hobson, 215–238. Cambridge: Cambridge University Press.

Lanni, Adriaan. 2006. *Law and Justice in the Courts of Classical Athens.* Cambridge University Press.

Larkin, Brian. 2013. "The Politics and Poetics of Infrastructure." *Annual Review of Anthropology* 42 (1): 327–343. doi: 10.1146/annurev-anthro-092412-155522.

Laszczkowski, Mateusz, and Madeleine Reeves, eds. 2017. *Affective States: Entanglements, Suspensions, Suspicions.* New York: Berghahn.

Latour, Bruno. 1991. *Nous n'avons jamais été modernes: Essai d'anthropologie symétrique.* Paris: Éditions Le Découverte.

Latour, Bruno. 2005. *Reassembling the Social: An Introduction to Actor-Network-Theory*. Oxford: Oxford University Press.

Latour, Bruno. 2002. *La fabrique du droit: Une ethnographie du Conseil d'État*. Paris: Editions La Découverte.

Latour, Bruno, and Steve Woolgar. 1979. *Laboratory Life: The Construction of Scientific Facts*. Princeton: Princeton University Press.

Lawy, Jenny R. 2017. "Theorizing Voice: Performativity, Politics and Listening." *Anthropological Theory* 17 (2): 192–215. doi: 10.1177/1463499617713138.

Leavitt, John. 1996. "Meaning and Feeling in the Anthropology of Emotions." *American Ethnologist* 23 (3): 514–539.

Lehmann, Hauke, Hans Roth, and Kerstin Schankweiler. 2019. "Affective Economy." In *Affective Societies: Key Concepts*, edited by Jan Slaby and Christian von Scheve, 140–151. London: Routledge.

Lenhart, Lioba. 2006. "Der Krieg im Norden Ugandas: Konfliktdimensionen und Friedenspotenziale." *Journal für Entwicklungspolitik* 12 (3): 84–113.

Lenhart, Lioba. 2012. "Negotiating Justice for Northern Uganda." In *Conflict and Peace Studies in Africa*, edited by E. Ovuga, E. Opiyo, J. A. Obika and K. Olido, 90–114. Gulu: Gulu University.

Lentz, Carola. 1995. "'Tribalism' and Ethnicity in Africa: A Review of Four Decades of Anglophone Research." *Cahiers des sciences humaines* 31 (2): 303–328.

Levin, Anthony. 2013. "Making the Invisible Visible: Photographic Trials in Neil Abramson's Soldier Child." *Research in African Literatures* 44 (2): 105–124. doi: 10.2979/reseafrilite.44.2.105.

Levitt, Peggy, and Sally Engle Merry. 2009. "Vernacularization on the Ground: Local Uses of Global Women's Rights in Peru, China, India and the United States." *Global Networks* 9 (4): 441–461.

Levy, Robert I. 1973. *Tahitians: Mind and Experience in the Society Islands*. Chicago: University of Chicago Press.

Llewellyn, Karl N., and Edward Adamson Hoebel. 1941. *The Cheyenne Way: Conflict and Case Law in Primitive Jurisprudence*. Norman: University of Oklahoma Press.

Locke, John. 1764. *Two Treatises of Government*. 5 ed. London: printed MDCLXXXVIIII reprinted the seventh time by J. Whiston, W. Strahan, J. and F. Rivington, L. Davis, W. Owen [and 18 others in London], 1772.

Löw, Martina. 2008. "The Constitution of Space: The Structuration of Spaces through the Simultaneity of Effect and Perception." *European Journal of Social Theory* 11: 25–49. doi: 10.1177/1368431007085286.

Luhrmann, Tanya M. 2012. *When God Talks Back: Understanding the American Evangelical Relationship with God*. New York: Alfred E. Knopf.

Lünenborg, Margreth. 2019. "Affective Publics." In *Affective Societies: Key Concepts*, edited by Jan Slaby and Christian von Scheve, 319–329. London: Routledge.

Lutz, Catherine. 1988. *Unnatural Emotions: Everyday Sentiments on a Micronesian Atoll and Their Challenge to Western Theory*. Chicago: University of Chicago Press.

Lutz, Catherine. 2017. "What Matters." *Cultural Anthropology* 32 (2): 181–191. doi: 10.14506/ca32.2.02.

Lynch, Gabrielle. 2011. *I Say to You: Ethnic Politics and the Kalenjin in Kenya*. Chicago: University of Chicago Press.

Lyon, Margot L. 1995. "Missing Emotions: The Limitations of Cultural Constructionism in the Study of Emotion." *Cultural Anthropology* 10 (2): 244–263.

Macdonald, Anna. 2017. "Justice in Transition? Transitional Justice and Political Economies of Survival in Post-Conflict Northern Uganda." *Development & Change* 48 (2): 286–311.

Macdonald, Anna, and Holly Porter. 2016. "The Trial of Thomas Kwoyelo: Opportunity or Spectre? Reflections from the Ground on the First Lra Prosecution." *Africa* 86 (4): 698–722. doi: 10.1017/s000197201600053x.

Mahmood, Saba. 2001. "Rehearsed Spontaneity and the Conventionality of Ritual: Disciplines of 'Salāt'." *American Ethnologist* 28 (4): 827–853.

Malinowski, Bronislaw. 1922. *Argonauts of the Western Pacific: An Account of Native Enterprise and Adventure in the Archipelagoes of Melanesian New Guinea*. London: Routledge.

Malinowski, Bronislaw. 1926. *Crime and Custom in Savage Society*. London: Kegan Paul.

Malinowski, Bronislaw. 1927. *Sex and Repression in Savage Society*. London: Kegan Paul.

Mamdani, Mahmood. 1996. *Citizen and Subject: Contemporary Africa and the Legacy of Late Colonialism*. Princeton: Princeton University Press.

Mamdani, Mahmoud. 2001. *When Victims Become Killers: Colonialism, Nativism, and the Genocide in Rwanda*. Oxford: James Currey.

Mamdani, Mahmood. 2009. *Saviors and Survivors: Darfur, Politics, and the War on Terror*. New York: Pantheon.

Mamdani, Mahmood. 2020. *Neither Settler nor Native: The Making and Unmaking of Permanent Minorities*. Cambridge: Harvard University Press.

Mao, Norbert. 2007. "The Delegation Was Met By Wailing And Mourning in Barlonyo: The LRA Victims Want to Be Part of the Peace Process." The New Vision Newspaper, November 20, 2007.

Maquet, Jacques J. 1964. "Objectivity in Anthropology." *Current Anthropology* 5 (1): 47–55.

Marcus, George E. 1991. "On Ideologies of Reflexivity in Contemporary Efforst to Remake the Human Sciences." *Poetics Today* 15 (3): 383–404.

Marcus, George E. 1995. "Ethnography in/of the World System: The Emergence of Multi-Sited Ethnography." *Annual Review of Anthropology* 24: 95–117. doi: 10.1146/annurev.an.24.100195.000523.

Marcus, George E. 2002. *The Sentimental Citizen: Emotion in Democratic Politics*. University Park: Pennsylvania State University Press.

Maroney, Terry A. 2006. "Law and Emotion: A Proposed Taxonomy of an Emerging Field." *Law and Human Behavior* 30 (1): 119–142. doi: 10.1007/s10979-006-9029-9.

Marx, Karl. 1859. *Zur Kritik der politischen Ökonomie: Erstes Heft*. Berlin: Franz Duncker.

Maryns, Katrijn. 2014. "The Interdiscursive Construction of Irresponsibility as a Defence Strategy in the Belgian Assize Court." *Language & Communication* 36: 25–36. doi: 10.1016/j.langcom.2013.12.009.

Massumi, Brian. 1995. "The Autonomy of Affect." *Cultural Critique* 31 (1): 83–109.

Massumi, Brian. 2002. *Parables for the Virtual: Movement, Affect, Sensation*. Edited by Stanley Fish and Fredric Jameson. Durham: Duke University Press.

Massumi, Brian. 2014. *The Power at the End of the Economy*. Durham: Duke Unversity Press.

Matasi, Martin, and Jürgen Bröhmer. 2012. "The Proposed International Criminal Chamber Section of the African Court of Justice and Human Rights: A Legal Analysis." *South African Yearbook of International Law* 37 (1): 248–268.

Matoesian, Gregory. 1998. "Discursive Hegemony in the Kennedy Smith Rape Trial." *Pragmatics* 8 (1): 3–19. doi: 10.1075/prag.8.1.01mat.

Matoesian, Gregory. 1999. "Intertextuality, Affect, and Ideology in Legal Discourse." *Text* 19 (1): 73–110.

Matoesian, Gregory M. 2001. *Law and the Language of Identity: Discourse in the William Kennedy Smith Rape Trial*. Chicago: University of Chicago Press.

Matoesian, Gregory. 2018. "This Is Not a Course in Trial Practice: Multimodal Participation in Objections." *Journal of Pragmatics* 129: 199–219. doi: 10.1016/j.pragma.2018.03.022.

Mattes, Dominik, Omar Kasmani, Marion Acker, and Edda Heyken. 2019. "Belonging." In *Affective Societies: Key Concepts*, edited by Jan Slaby and Christian von Scheve, 300–309. London: Routledge.

Mauss, Marcel. 1925. *Essai sur le don: Forme et raison de l'échange dans les sociétés archaïques*. Paris: Alcan.

May, Larry. 2005. *Crimes against Humanity: A Normative Account*. Cambridge: Cambridge University Press.

Mbembe, Achille. 2013. *Critique de la raison nègre*. Paris: Éditions la Découverte.

McAuliffe, Padraig. 2013. "Romanticization versus Integration: Indigenous Justice in Rule of Law Reconstruction and Transitional Justice Discourse." *Goettingen Journal of International Law* 5 (1): 41–86.

McElhinny, Bonnie. 2010. "The Audacity of Affect: Gender, Race, and History in Linguistic Accounts of Legitimacy and Belonging." *Annual Review of Anthropology* 39: 309–328. doi: 10.1146/annurev-anthro-091908-164358.

McNamara, Kirsty. 2013. "Seeking Justice in Ugandan Courts: Amnesty and the Case of Thomas Kwoyelo." *Washington University Global Studies Law Review* 12 (3): 653–671.

Meier, Barbara. 2013. "'Death does not rot': Transitional Justice and Local 'Truths' in the Aftermath of the War in Northern Uganda." *Africa Spectrum* 48 (2): 25–50.

Menkel-Meadow, Carrie. 2007. "Restorative Justice: What Is It and Does It Work?" *Annual Review of Law and Social Science* 3: 161–187. doi: 10.1146/annurev.lawsocsci.2.081805.110005.

Merry, Sally Engle. 1988. "Legal Pluralism." *Law & Society Review* 22 (5): 869–896.

Merry, Sally Engle. 1990. *Getting Justice and Getting Even: Legal Consciousness Among Working Class Americans*. Chicago: University of Chicago Press.

Merry, Sally Engle. 1991. "Law and Colonialism." *Law and Society Review* 25 (4): 889–922.

Merry, Sally Engle. 2006a. "Anthropology and International Law." *Annual Review of Anthropology* 35: 99–116.

Merry, Sally Engle. 2006b. *Human Rights and Gender Violence: Translating International Law into Local Justice, Chicago Series in Law and Society*. Chicago: University of Chicago Press.

Merry, Sally Engle. 2006c. "Transnational Human Rights and Local Activism: Mapping the Middle." *American Anthropologist* 108: 38–51. doi: 10.1525/aa.2006.108.1.38.

Mertz, Elizabeth. 2007a. *The Language of Law School: Learning to "Think Like a Lawyer."* Oxford: Oxford University Press.

Mertz, Elizabeth. 2007b. "Semiotic Anthropology." *Annual Review of Anthropology* 36 (1): 337–353. doi: 10.1146/annurev.anthro.36.081406.094417.

Mihai, Mihaela. 2016. *Negative Emotions and Transitional Justice*. Now York: University of Columbia Press.

Minow, Martha. 1998. *Vengeance and Forgiveness: Facing History after Genocide and Mass Violence*. Boston: Beacon.

Mintz, Sidney Wilfred. 1985. *Sweetness and Power: The Place of Sugar in Modern History*. New York: Viking.

Mondada, Lorenza. 2016. "Challenges of Multimodality: Langauge and the Body in Social Interaction." *Journal of Sociolinguistics* 20 (3): 336–366.

Moore, Michael S. 2010. *Placing Blame: A Theory of the Criminal Law*. Oxford: Oxford University Press.

Moore, Sally Falk. 1978. *Law as Process: An Anthropological Approach*. 2nd ed. London: Routledge.

Moore, Sally Falk. 1986. *Social Facts and Fabrications: Customary Law on Kilimanjaro, 1880–1980*. Cambridge: Cambridge University Press.

Morris, Madeleine. 2000. "Complementarity and Conflict: States, Victims, and the ICC." In *The United States and the International Criminal Court: National Security and International Law*, edited by Sarah B. Sewall and Carl Kaysen, 195–210. Lanham: Rowman and Littlefield.

Mouffe, Chantal. 2013. *Agonistics: Thinking the World Politically*. London: Verso.

Mouffe, Chantal. 2018. *For a Left Populism*. London: Verso.

Mühlhoff, Rainer. 2018. *Immersive Macht: Affekttheorie nach Foucault und Spinoza*. Frankfurt: Campus.

Müller-Mall, Sabine. 2013. *Legal Spaces*. Berlin: Springer.

Nader, Laura, and Harry F. Todd. 1978. *The Disputing Process: Law in Ten Societies*. New York: Columbia University Press.

Navaro-Yashin, Yael. 2009. "Affective Spaces, Melancholic Objects: Ruination and the Production of Anthropological Knowledge." *Journal of the Royal Anthropological Institute* 15 (1): 1–18.

Navaro-Yashin, Yael. 2012. *The Make-Believe Space: Affective Geography in a Postwar Polity*. Durham: Duke University Press.

Nouwen, Sarah M. H. 2013. *Complementarity in the Line of Fire: The Catalysing Effect of The International Criminal Court in Uganda and Sudan*. Cambridge: Cambridge University Press.

Novak, Andrew. 2015. *The International Criminal Court: An Introduction*. Cham: Springer.

Nussbaum, Martha C. 2013. *Political Emotions: Why Love Matters for Justice*. Cambridge: Harvard University Press.

Nussbaum, Martha C. 2018. *The Monarchy of Fear: A Philosopher Looks at Our Political Crisis*. New York: Simon and Schuster.

Ochs, Elinor. 2012. "Experiencing Language." *Anthropological Theory* 12 (2): 142–160.

Ochs, Elinor, and Bambi B. Schieffelin. 1989. "Language Has a Heart." *Text* 9 (1): 7–25.

Okafor, Obiora Chinedu, and Uchechukwu Ngwaba. 2014. "The International Criminal Court as a 'Transitional Justice' Mechanism in Africa: Some Critical Reflections." *International Journal of Transitional Justice* 9 (1): 90–108. doi: 10.1093/ijtj/iju025.

Okello, Moses Chrispus, and Luci Hovil. 2007. "Confronting the Reality of Gender-Based Violence in Northern Uganda." *International Journal of Transitional Justice* 1 (3): 433–443.

Oloya, Opiyo. 2018. *Child to Soldier: Stories from Joseph Kony's Lord's Resistance Army*. Toronto: University of Toronto Press.

Pagden, Anthony. 2003. "Human Rights, Natural Rights, and Europe's Imperial Legacy." *Political Theory* 31 (2): 171–199.

Papoulias, Constantina, and Felicity Callard. 2010. "Biology's Gift: Interrogating the Turn to Affect." *Body & Society* 16 (1): 29–56.

Pardo, Michael S., and Ronald J. Allen. 2008. "Juridical Proof and the Best Explanation." *Law and Philosophy* 27 (3): 223–268.

Paschukanis, Jewgeni Bronislawowitsch. 1929. *Allgemeine Rechtslehre und Marxismus: Versuch einer Kritik der juristischen Grundbegriffe*. Wien: Verlag für Literatur und Politik.

P'Bitek, Okot. 2011 [1971]. *Decolonizing African Religions: A Short History of African Religions in Western Scholarship*. New Revised Edition. New York: Diasporic African Press.

Peskin, Victor. 2009. "Caution and Confrontation in the International Criminal Court's Pursuit of Accountability in Uganda and Sudan." *Human Rights Quarterly* 31: 655–691.

Pham, Phuong, Patrick Vinck, and Eric Stover. 2008. "The Lord's Resistance Army and Forced Conscription in Northern Uganda." *Human Rights Quarterly* 30 (2): 404–411.

Pham, Phuong N., Patrick Vinck, and Eric Stover. 2009. "Returning Home: Forced Conscription, Reintegration, and Mental Health Status of Former Abductees of the Lord's Resistance Army in Northern Uganda." *BMC Psychiatry* 9 (1): 23–36.

Philippopoulos-Mihalopoulos, Andreas. 2015. *Spatial Justice: Body, Lawscape, Atmosphere, Space, Materiality, and the Normative*. Abingdon: Routledge.

Pottage, Alain, and Martha Mundy. 2004. *Law, Anthropology, and the Constitution of the Social: Making Persons and Things, Cambridge Studies in Law and Society*. Cambridge: Cambridge University Press.

Povinelli, Elizabeth A. 2006. *The Empire of Love: Toward a Theory of Intimacy, Genealogy, and Carnality*. Durham: Duke University Press.

Povinelli, Elizabeth A. 2011. *Economies of Abandonment: Social Belonging and Endurance in Late Liberalism*. Durham: Duke University Press.

Povinelli, Elizabeth A. 2016. *Geontologies: A Requiem to Late Liberalism*. Durham: Duke University Press.

Preston, Justin M. 2015. "'If They Abduct You, You Don't Come Back': Understanding Ugandan Former Child Soldiers in the Context of their Life." *Peace and Conflict: Journal of Peace Psychology* 21 (3): 432–444. doi: 10.1037/pac0000120.

Pupavac, Vanessa. 2004. "War on the Couch: The Emotionology of the New International Security Paradigm." *European Journal of Social Theory* 7 (4): 149–170.

Quinn, Naomi. 2005. "Universals of Child Rearing." *Anthropological Theory* 5 (4): 477–516. doi: 10.1177/1463499605059233.

Quinn, Naomi, and Holly F. Mathews. 2016. "Emotional Arousal in the Making of Cultural Selves." *Anthropological Theory* 16 (4): 359–389. doi: 10.1177/1463499616684051.

Ramaswamy, Sumathi. 1997. *Passions of the Tongue: Language Devotion in Tamil India, 1891–1970*. Berkeley: University of California Press.

Ramji-Nogales, Jaya. 2010. "Designing Bespoke Transitional Justice: A Pluralist Process Approach." *Michigan Journal of International Law* 32 (1): 1–72.

Ranger, Terence. 1983. "The Invention of Tradition in Colonial Africa." In *The Invention of Tradition*, edited by Eric Hobsbawm and Terence Ranger, 211–262. Cambridge: Cambridge University Press.

Ranger, Terence. 1993. "The Invention of Tradition Revisited: The Case of Africa." In *Legitimacy and the State in Twentieth Century Africa*, edited by Terence Ranger and Olufemi Vaughan, 62–111. Basingstoke: Macmillan.

Rawls, John. 1971. *A Theory of Justice*. Oxford: Oxford University Press.

Reckwitz, Andreas. 2018. *Die Gesellschaft der Singularitäten: Zum Strukturwandel der Moderne*. Frankfurt: Suhrkamp.

Reckwitz, Andreas. 2019. *Das Ende der Illusionen: Politik, Ökonomie und Kultur in der Spätmoderne*. Berlin: Suhrkamp.

Reinelt, Janelle. 2006. "Toward a Poetics of Theatre and Public Events: In the Case of Stephen Lawrence." *The Drama Review* 50 (3): 69–87.

Reynaud, Anne-Marie. 2017. *Emotions, Remembering and Feeling Better: Dealing with the Indian Residential Schools Settlement Agreement in Canada*. Bielefeld: Transcript.

Richardson, Michael. 2016. *Gestures of Testimony Torture, Trauma, and Affect in Literature*. London: Bloomsbury Academic.

Richland, Justin B. 2008. *Arguing with Tradition: The Language of Law in Hopi Tribal Court*. Chicago: University of Chicago Press.

Riedel, Friedlind. 2015. "Music as Atmosphere: Lines of Becoming in Congregational Worship." *Lebenswelt* 6: 80–111.

Riedel, Friedlind. 2019. "Atmosphere." In *Affective Societies: Key Concepts*, edited by Jan Slaby and Christian von Scheve, 85–95. London: Routledge.

Rigby, Peter, and Peter Sevareid. 1992. "Lawyers, Anthropologists, and the Knowledge of Facts." *NAPA Bulletin* 11: 5–21.

Riles, Annelise. 2001. *The Network Inside Out*. Ann Arbor: University of Michigan Press.

Riles, Annelise. 2004. "Property as Legal Knowledge: Means and Ends." *Journal of the Royal Anthropological Institute* 10: 775–795.

Robertson, Geoffrey. 2006. *Crimes against Humanity: The Struggle for Global Justice*. 3 ed. New York: The New Press.
Rosa, Hartmut. 2016. *Resonanz: Eine Soziologie der Weltbeziehung*. Berlin: Suhrkamp.
Rosaldo, Michelle Z. 1980. *Knowledge and Passion: Ilongot Notions of Self and Social Life*. Cambridge: Cambridge University Press.
Rosaldo, Michelle Z. 1984. "Toward and Anthropology of Self and Feeling." In *Culture Theory: Essays on Mind, Self, and Emotion*, edited by Richard A. Shweder and Robert A. LeVine, 137–149. Cambridge: Cambridge University Press.
Rosenberg, Daniel V. 1990. "Language in the Discourse of the Emotions." In *Language and the Politics of Emotion*, edited by Lila Abu-Lughod and Catherine Lutz, 162–185. Cambridge: Cambridge University Press.
Ross, Fiona C. 2003. *Bearing Witness: Women and the Truth and Reconciliation Commission in South Africa*. London: Pluto.
Röttger-Rössler, Birgitt. 2002. "Emotion und Kultur: Einige Grundfragen." *Zeitschrift für Ethnologie* 127 (2): 147–162.
Röttger-Rössler, Birgitt. 2004. *Die kulturelle Modellierung des Gefühls: Ein Beitrag zur Theorie und Methodik ethnologischer Emotionsforschung anhand indonesischer Fallstudien*. Münster: Lit-Verlag.
Röttger-Rössler, Birgitt. 2012. "The Emotional Meaning of Ritual." In *Emotions in Rituals and Performances*, edited by Axel Michaels and Christoph Wulf, 41–54. London: Routledge.
Röttger-Rössler, Birgitt, and Hans Jürgen Markowitsch, eds. 2009. *Emotions as Bio-Cultural Processes*. New York: Springer.
Röttger-Rössler, Birgitt, Gabriel Scheidecker, and Leberecht Funk. 2015. "Learning (by) Feeling: A Cross-Cultural Comparison of the Socialization and Development of Emotions." *Ethos* 43 (3): 187–220.
Rousseau, Jean-Jacques. 1762. *Du contrat social ou principes du droit politique*. Amsterdam: Marc Michel Rey.
Rutherford, Danilyn. 2016. "Affect Theory and the Empirical." *Annual Review of Anthropology* 45 (1): 285–300. doi: 10.1146/annurev-anthro-102215-095843.
Sahlins, Marshall. 2017. "In Anthropology, It's Emic All The Way Down." *HAU: Journal of Ethnographic Theory* 7 (2): 91–128.
Sahlins, Marshall David. 1972. *Stone Age Economics, Stone Age Economics*. New York: Aldine de Gruyter.
Said, Edward W. 1978. *Orientalism*. New York: Pantheon Books.
Sakti, Victoria Kumala. 2017. "Im/mobile Subjects: Identity, Conflict and Emotion Work among East Timorese Meto Diaspora." *Social Identities* 23 (4): 462–477. doi: 10.1080/13504630.2017.1281469.
Sangokoya, David. 2012. "Selling Old Newspapers Shouldn't Be Profitable: Invisible Children and Kony 2012." *Traveling While Black: In Search of the*

Intersection between Dignity and Development. https://davidsangokoya.wordpress.com/2012/03/07/selling-old-newspapers-shouldnt-be-profitable-invisible-children-and-kony-2012/.

Sarkin, Jeremy. 2012. "Enhancing the Legitimacy, Status, and Role of the International Criminal Court Globally by Using Transitional Justice and Restorative Justice Strategies." *Interdisciplinary Journal of Human Rights Law* 6 (1): 83–101.

Schankweiler, Kerstin. 2019. *Bildproteste*. Berlin: Wagenbach.

Schankweiler, Kerstin. 2018. "'Moroccan Lives Matter': Practices and Politics of Affecting." In *Image Testimonies: Witnessing in Times of Social Media*, edited by Kerstin Schankweiler, Verena Straub and Tobias Wendl, 59–71. London: Routledge.

Schankweiler, Kerstin, Verena Straub, and Tobias Wendl, eds. 2018. *Image Testimonies: Witnessing in Times of Social Media*. London: Routledge.

Schankweiler, Kerstin, and Philipp Wüschner. 2019. "Images that Move: Analyzing Affect with Aby Warburg." In *Analyzing Affective Societies: Methods and Methodologies*, edited by Antje Kahl, 101–119. London: Routledge.

Schapera, Isaac. 1938. *A Handbook of Tswana Law and Custom: Compiled for the Bechuanal and Protectorate Administration*. Oxford: Oxford University Press.

Scheff, Thomas J. 1977. "The Distancing of Emotion in Ritual." *Current Anthropology* 18 (3): 483–505.

Scheffer, Thomas. 2004. "Materialities of Legal Proceedings." *International Journal for the Semiotics of Law* 17 (4): 356–389.

Scheffer, Thomas. 2007. "Event and Process: An Exercise in Analytical Ethnography." *Human Studies* 30 (3): 167–197.

Scheffer, Thomas. 2010. *Adversarial Case-Making: An Ethnography of English Crown Court Procedures*. Leiden: Brill.

Scheffer, Thomas. 2015. "Diskurspraxis in Recht und Politik: Trans-Sequentialität und die Analyse rechtsförmiger Verfahren." *Zeitschrift für Rechtssoziologie* 35 (2): 223–244.

Scheidecker, Gabriel. 2017. *Kindheit, Kultur und moralische Emotionen: Zur Sozialisation von Furcht und Wut im ländlichen Madagaskar*. Bielefeld: Transcript.

Scheidecker, Gabriel. 2019. "Unfolding Emotions: The Language and Socialization of Anger in Madagascar." In *The Routledge Handbook of Language and Emotion*, edited by Sonya E. Pritzker, Janina Fenigsen, and James M. Wilce, 49–72. London: Routledge.

Scherer, Klaus R., Angela Schnorr, and Tom Johnstone. 2001. *Appraisal Processes in Emotion: Theory, Methods, Research: Theory, Methods, Research*. New York: Oxford University Press.

Scheve, Christian von. 2011. "Die soziale Konstitution und Funktion von Emotion: Akteur, Gruppe, normative Ordnung." *Zeitschrift für Erziehungswissenschaft* 14 (2): 207–222. doi: 10.1007/s11618-011-0206-3.

Scheve, Christian von. 2012. "Collective Emotions in Rituals: Elicitation, Transmission and a 'Matthew Effect'." In *Emotions in Rituals and Performances*, edited by Axel Michaels and Christoph Wulf, 55–77. London: Routledge.

Scheve, Christian von. 2018. "A Social Relational Account of Affect." *European Journal of Social Theory* 21 (1): 39–59. doi: 10.1177/1368431017690007.

Schild, Wolfgang. 1980. *Alte Gerichtsbarkeit: Vom Gottesurteil bis zum Beginn der modernen Rechtsprechung*. München: Calwey.

Schoenbrun, David. 1998. *A Green Place, A Good Place: Agrarian Change, Gender, and Social Identity between the Great Lakes to the Fifteenth Century*. Portsmouth: Heinemann.

Schomerus, Mareike. 2012. "Even Eating You Can Bite Your Tongue: Dynamics and Challenges of the Juba Peace Talks with the Lord's Resistance Army." PhD Thesis, Department of International Development, London School of Economics.

Schroer, Sara Asu, and Susanne B. Schmitt. 2018. "Introduction: Thinking Through Atmospheres." In *Exploring Atmospheres Ethnographically*, edited by Sara Asu Schroer and Susanne B. Schmitt, 1–11. New York: Routledge.

Sedgwick, Eve Kosofsky, and Adam Frank, eds. 1995. *Shame and Its Sisters: A Silvan Tomkins Reader*. Durham: Duke University Press.

Seidel, Katrin. 2015. "State Formation through Constitution Making in Emerging South Sudan: Unveiling the Technicity of the Rule of Law." *Recht in Afrika* 18 (1): 3–16. doi: 10.5771/2363-6270-2015-1-3.

Seidel, Katrin, and Timm Sureau. 2015. "Introduction: Peace and Constitution Making in Emerging South Sudan on and Beyond the Negotiation Tables." *Journal of Eastern African Studies* 9 (4): 612–633.

Seyfert, Robert. 2012. "Beyond Personal Feelings and Collective Emotions: Toward a Theory of Social Affect." *Theory, Culture and Society* 29 (6): 27–46. doi: 10.1177/0263276412438591.

Shaw, Rosalind, Lars Waldorf, and Pierre Hazan, eds. 2010. *Localizing Transitional Justice: Interventions and Priorities after Mass Violence*. Stanford: Stanford University Press.

Shklar, Judith N. 1964. *Legalism: An Essay on Law, Morals and Politics*. Oxford: Oxford University Press.

Sieben, Barbara, Åsa Wettergren, eds. 2010. *Emotionalizing Organizations and Organizing Emotions*. Basingstoke: Palgrave Macmillan.

Silverstein, Michael. 1976. "Shifters, Linguistic Categories, and Cultural Description." In *Meaning in Anthropology*, edited by Keith H. Basso and Henry A. Selby, 11–55. Alberquerque: University of Arizona Press.

Silverstein, Michael. 1993. "Metapragmatic Discourse and Metapragmatic Function." In *Reflexive Language: Reported Speech and Metapragmatics*, edited by John A. Lucy, 33–58. New York: Cambridge University Press.

Skoggard, Ian, and Alisse Waterston. 2015. "Introduction: Toward an Anthropology of Affect and Evocative Ethnography." *Anthropology of Consciousness* 26 (2): 109–120. doi: 10.1111/anoc.12041.

Slaby, Jan, and Rainer Mühlhoff. 2019. "Affect." In *Affective Societies: Key Concepts*, edited by Jan Slaby and Christian von Scheve, 27–41. London: Routledge.

Slaby, Jan, Rainer Mühlhoff, and Philipp Wüschner. 2019. "Affective Arrangements." *Emotion Review* 11 (1): 3–12. doi: 10.1177/1754073917722214.

Smith, Adam. 1759. *The Theory of Moral Sentiments*. London: A. Millar.

Smith, Adam. 1759. "The Glasgow Edition of the Works and Correspondence of Adam Smith". In *The Theory of Moral Sentiments*, edited by A. L. Macfie and D. D. Raphael, 267. Indianapolis: Liberty Fund.

Smith, Anthony D. 1996. *The Ethnic Origins of Nations*. Malden: Blackwell.

Solomon, Robert C. 1984. "Getting Angry: The Jamesian Theory of Emotion in Anthropology." In *Culture Theory: Essays on Mind, Self, and Emotion*, edited by Richard A. Shweder and Robert A. LeVine, 238–254. Cambridge: Cambridge University Press.

Spear, Thomas, and Richard Waller. 1993. *Being Maasai: Ethnicity and Identity in Eastern Africa*. London: James Currey.

Spinoza, Baruch de. 1677. *Ethica, ordine geometrico demonstrata*. Amsterdam.

Star, Susan Leigh. 1999. "The Ethnography of Infrastructure." *American Behavioral Scientiest* 43 (3): 377–391.

Starr, June, and Jane F. Collier. 1989. *History and Power in the Study of Law: New Directions in Legal Anthropology*. Ithaca: Cornell University Press.

Stewart, Kathleen. 2007. *Ordinary Affects*. Durham: Duke University Press.

Stodulka, Thomas. 2015. "Spheres of Passion: Fieldwork, Ethnography and the Researcher's Emotions." *Curare: Journal of Medical Anthropology* 38 (1/2): 103–116.

Stodulka, Thomas. 2016. *Coming of Age on the Streets of Java: Coping with Marginality, Stigma and Illness*. Bielefeld: Transcript.

Stodulka, Thomas, Nasima Selim, and Dominik Mattes. 2018. "Affective Scholarship: Doing Anthropology with Epistemic Affects." *Ethos* 46 (4): 519–536. doi: 10.1111/etho.12219.

Stoler, Ann. 1995. *Race and the Education of Desire: Foucault's History of Sexuality and the Colonial Order of Things*. Durham: Duke University Press.

Stoler, Ann, and Frederick Cooper. 1997. *Tensions of Empire: Colonial Cultures in a Bourgeois World*. Berkeley: University of California Press.

Stoler, Ann Laura. 2002. *Carnal Knowledge and Imperial Power: Race and the Intimate in Colonial Rule*. Berkeley: University of California Press.

Stoller, Paul. 1989. *The Taste of Ethnographic Things: The Senses in Anthropology*. Philadelphia: University of Pennsylvania Press.

Strathern, Marilyn. 1988. *The Gender of the Gift: Problems with Women and Problems with Society in Melanesia*. Berkeley: University of California Press.

Stromseth, Jane E. 2007. "Pursuing Accountability for Atrocities After Conflict: What Impact on Building the Rule of Law." *Georgetown Journal of International Law* 38: 251–322.

Surrallés, Alexandre. 2003. *Au cœur du sens. Perception, affectivité, action chez les Candoshi*. Paris: CNRS Éditions.

Tait, David. 2001. "Popular Sovereignty and the Justice Process: Towards a Comparative Methodology for Observing Courtroom Rituals." *Contemporary Justice Review* 4 (2): 201–218.

Takemura, Hitomi. 2012. "Reconsidering the Meaning and Actuality of the Legitimacy of the International Criminal Court." *Amsterdam Law Forum* 4 (2): 3–15.

Tamanaha, Brian Z. 1993. "The Folly of the 'Social Scientific' Concept of Legal Pluralism." *Journal of Law and Society* 20 (2): 192–217.

Taylor, Katherine Fischer. 1993. *In the Theater of Criminal Justice*. Princeton: Princeton University Press.

Teitel, Ruti G. 2000. *Transitional Justice*. Oxford: Oxford University Press.

Thomas, William I., and Dorothy S. Thomas. 1928. *The Child in America: Behavior Problems and Programs*. New York: Knopf.

Thompson, E. P. 1975. *Whigs and Hunters: The Origins of the Black Act*. New York: Pantheon.

Thomson, Susan. 2011. "The Darker Side of Transitional Justice: The Power Dynamics behind Rwanda's Gacaca Courts." *Africa* 81 (3): 373–390.

Thonhauser, Gerhard. 2019. "Feeling." In *Affective Societies: Key Concepts*, edited by Jan Slaby and Christian von Scheve, 52–60. London: Routledge.

Thrift, Nigel J. 2008. *Non-Representational Theory: Space, Politics, Affect*. London: Routledge.

Throop, Jason C. 2010. *Suffering and Sentiment: Exploring the Vicissitudes of Experience and Pain in Yap*. Berkeley: University of California Press.

Ticktin, Miriam. 2014. "Transnational Humanitarianism." *Annual Review of Anthropology* 43 (1): 273–289. doi: 10.1146/annurev-anthro-102313-030403.

Titeca, Kristof. 2010. "The Spiritual Order of the LRA." In *The Lord's Resistance Army: Myth and Reality*, edited by Tim Allen and Koen Vlassenroot, 59–63. London: Zed Books.

Tsing, Anna Lowenhaupt. 2005. *Friction: An Ethnography of Global Connection*. Princeton: Princeton University Press.

Turner, Bertram. 2017. "On Retaliation: Conceptual Plurality, Transdisciplinary Research, Blurrings and Translations." In *On Retaliation*, edited by Bertram Turner and Günther Schlee, 1–25. New York: Berghahn.

Turner, Victor. 1969. *The Ritual Process: Structure and Anti-Structure*. Ithaca: Cornell University Press.

Turner, Victor. 1987. *The Anthropology of Performance*. New York: PAJ Publications.

Tyler, Tom R. 1990. *Why People Obey the Law*. New Haven: Yale University Press.

Tyler, Tom R. 1993. "Legitimizing Unpopular Public Policies: Does Procedure Matter?" *Zeitschrift für Rechtssoziologie* 14 (1): 47–54.

Tyler, Tom R. 2006. "Psychological Perspectives on Legitimacy and Legitimation." *Annual Review of Psychology* 57 (1): 375–400. doi: 10.1146/annurev.psych.57.102904.190038.

Urban, Greg. 1988. "Ritual Wailing in Amerindian Brazil." *American Anthropologist* 90 (2): 385–400.

Vail, Leroy, ed. 1989. *The Creation of Tribalism in Southern Africa*. Berkeley: University of California Press.

Veer, Peter van der. 2001. *Imperial Encounters: Religion and Modernity in India and Britain*. Princeton: Princeton University Press.

Vetters, Larissa. 2014. "Contingent Statehood: Clientelism and Civic Engagement as Relational Modalities in Contemporary Bosnia and Herzegovina." *Social Analysis* 58 (3): 20–37.

Vetters, Larissa. 2019. *Prozesse des State Building in Bosnien-Herzegowina: Eine Verwaltungsethnographie*. Baden Baden: Nomos.

Vindevogel, Sofie, Kathleen Coppens, Ilse Derluyn, Maarten De Schryver, Gerrit Loots, and Eric Broekaert. 2011. "Forced Conscription of Children during Armed Conflict: Experiences of Former Child Soldiers in Northern Uganda." *Child Abuse and Neglect* 37 (5): 551–562.

Vinjamuri, Leslie, and Jack Snyder. 2015. "Law and Politics in Transitional Justice." *Annual Review of Political Science* 18: 303–327. doi: 10.1146/annurev-polisci-122013-110512.

Vismann, Cornelia. 2011. *Medien der Rechtsprechung*. Frankfurt am Main: S. Fischer.

Volkan, Vamik D. 1988. *The Need to Have Enemies: From Clinical Practice to International Relationships*. Northvale: Jason Aronson.

Wallerstein, Immanuel. 1983. *Historical Capitalism with Capitalist Civilization*. London: Verso.

Ward, Kevin. 2001. "'The Armies of the Lord': Christianity, Rebels, and the State in Northern Uganda." *Journal of Religion in Africa* 31 (2): 187–221.

Weber, Max. 1905. "Die protestantische Ethik und der Geist des Kapitalismus II: Die Berufsethik des asketischen Protestantismus." *Archiv für Sozialwissenschaften und Sozialpolitik* 21 (1): 1–110.

Weber, Max. 1919. *Politik als Beruf*. München: Duncker & Humblot.

Weber, Max. 1921. *Wirtschaft und Gesellschaft: Grundriss der verstehenden Soziologie*. Tübingen: Mohr Siebeck.

Werle, Gerhard, Lovell Fernandez, and Moritz Vormbaum, eds. 2014. *Africa and the International Criminal Court*. The Hague: T.M.C. Asser Press.

Wettergren, Åsa. 2019. "Emotive-Cognitive Rationality, Background Emotions and Emotion Work," In *Emotions in Late Modernity*, edited by Roger Patulny, Alberto Bellocchi, E. Rebecca Olson, Sukhmani Khorana, Jordan McKenzie, and Michelle Peterie, 27–40. London: Routledge.

White, Geoffrey M. 1999. "Emotional Remembering: The Pragmatics of National Memory." *Ethos* 27 (4): 505–529.

White, Geoffrey. 2004. "National Subjects: September 11 and Pearl Harbor." *American Ethnologist* 31 (3): 293–310.

Whitehouse, Harvey. 1996. "Rites of Terror: Emotion, Metaphor and Memory in Melanesian Initiation Cults." *Journal of the Royal Anthropological Institute* 2 (4): 703–715.

Whorf, Benjamin Lee. 1952. *Collected Papers on Metalinguistics*. Washington, DC: Foreign Service Institute, Department of State.

Wikan, Unni. 1994. "Beyond the Words: The Power of Resonance." *American Ethnologist* 19 (3): 460–482.

Wilce, James M. 2009. *Language and Emotion*. Cambridge: Cambridge University Press.

Wilson, Richard A. 2001. *The Politics of Truth and Reconciliation in South Africa: Legitimizing the Post-Apartheid State*. Cambridge: Cambridge University Press.

Wilson, Richard A. 2011. *Writing History in International Criminal Trials*. Cambridge: Cambridge University Press.

Wilson, Richard A. 2016. "Expert Evidence on Trial: Social Researchers in the International Criminal Courtroom." *American Ethnologist* 43 (4): 730–744. doi: 10.1111/amet.12387.

Wolf, Eric R. 1982. *Europe and the People without History*. Berkeley: University of California Press.

Woodman, Gordon R., and Akintunde O. Obilade. 1995. "Introduction." In *African Law and Legal Theory*, edited by Gordon R. Woodman and Akintunde O. Obilade, xi–xxix. New York: New York University Press.

Zenker, Olaf. 2014. "New Law against an Old State: Land Restitution as a Transition to Justice in Post-Apartheid South Africa." *Development and Change* 45 (3): 502–523. doi: 0.1111/dech.12092.

Zenker, Olaf. 2015. "De-judicialization, Outsourced Review and All-too-flexible Bureaucracies in South African Land Restitution." *Cambridge Anthropology* 33: 81–96. doi: 10.3167/ca.2015.330107.

Zenker, Olaf. 2016. "Anthropology on Trial: Exploring the Laws of Anthropological Expertise." *International Journal of Law in Context* 12 (3): 293–311.

Zenker, Olaf, and Markus V. Hoehne. 2018. "Processing the Paradox: When the State Has to Deal With Customary Law." In *The State and the Paradox of Customary Law in Africa*, edited by Olaf Zenker and Markus V. Hoehne, 1–40. London: Routledge.

INDEX

CAMBRIDGE STUDIES IN LAW AND SOCIETY

Books in the Series

Diseases of the Will: Alcohol and the Dilemmas of Freedom
Mariana Valverde

The Politics of Truth and Reconciliation in South Africa: Legitimizing the Post-Apartheid State
Richard A. Wilson

Modernism and the Grounds of Law
Peter Fitzpatrick

Unemployment and Government: Genealogies of the Social
William Walters

Autonomy and Ethnicity: Negotiating Competing Claims in Multi-Ethnic States
Yash Ghai

Constituting Democracy: Law, Globalism and South Africa's Political Reconstruction
Heinz Klug

The Ritual of Rights in Japan: Law, Society, and Health Policy
Eric A. Feldman

Governing Morals: A Social History of Moral Regulation
Alan Hunt

The Colonies of Law: Colonialism, Zionism and Law in Early Mandate Palestine
Ronen Shamir

Law and Nature
David Delaney

Social Citizenship and Workfare in the United States and Western Europe: The Paradox of Inclusion
Joel F. Handler

Law, Anthropology, and the Constitution of the Social: Making Persons and Things
Edited by Alain Pottage and Martha Mundy

Judicial Review and Bureaucratic Impact: International and Interdisciplinary Perspectives
Edited by Marc Hertogh and Simon Halliday

Immigrants at the Margins: Law, Race, and Exclusion in Southern Europe
Kitty Calavita

Lawyers and Regulation: The Politics of the Administrative Process
Patrick Schmidt

Law and Globalization from Below: Towards a Cosmopolitan Legality
Edited by Boaventura de Sousa Santos and César A. Rodríguez-Garavito

Public Accountability: Designs, Dilemmas and Experiences
Edited by Michael W. Dowdle

Law, Violence and Sovereignty among West Bank Palestinians
Tobias Kelly

Legal Reform and Administrative Detention Powers in China
Sarah Biddulph

The Practice of Human Rights: Tracking Law between the Global and the Local
Edited by Mark Goodale and Sally Engle Merry

Judges beyond Politics in Democracy and Dictatorship: Lessons from Chile
Lisa Hilbink

Paths to International Justice: Social and Legal Perspectives
Edited by Marie-Bénédicte Dembour and Tobias Kelly

Law and Society in Vietnam: The Transition from Socialism in Comparative Perspective
Mark Sidel

Constitutionalizing Economic Globalization: Investment Rules and Democracy's Promise
David Schneiderman

The New World Trade Organization Knowledge Agreements: Second Edition
Christopher Arup

Justice and Reconciliation in Post-Apartheid South Africa
Edited by François du Bois and Antje du Bois-Pedain

Militarization and Violence against Women in Conflict Zones in the Middle East: A Palestinian Case-Study
Nadera Shalhoub-Kevorkian

Child Pornography and Sexual Grooming: Legal and Societal Responses
Suzanne Ost

Darfur and the Crime of Genocide
John Hagan and Wenona Rymond-Richmond

Fictions of Justice: The International Criminal Court and the Challenge of Legal Pluralism in Sub-Saharan Africa
Kamari Maxine Clarke

Conducting Law and Society Research: Reflections on Methods and Practices
Simon Halliday and Patrick Schmidt

Planted Flags: Trees, Land, and Law in Israel/Palestine
Irus Braverman

Culture under Cross-Examination: International Justice and the Special Court for Sierra Leone
Tim Kelsall

Cultures of Legality: Judicialization and Political Activism in Latin America
Javier Couso, Alexandra Huneeus, and Rachel Sieder

Courting Democracy in Bosnia and Herzegovina: The Hague Tribunal's Impact in a Postwar State
Lara J. Nettelfield

The Gacaca Courts, Post-Genocide Justice and Reconciliation in Rwanda: Justice without Lawyers
Phil Clark

Law, Society, and History: Themes in the Legal Sociology and Legal History of Lawrence M. Friedman
Edited by Robert W. Gordon and Morton J. Horwitz

After Abu Ghraib: Exploring Human Rights in America and the Middle East
Shadi Mokhtari

Adjudication in Religious Family Laws: Cultural Accommodation, Legal Pluralism, and Gender Equality in India
Gopika Solanki

Water on Tap: Rights and Regulation in the Transnational Governance of Urban Water Services
Bronwen Morgan

Elements of Moral Cognition: Rawls' Linguistic Analogy and the Cognitive Science of Moral and Legal Judgment
John Mikhail

Mitigation and Aggravation at Sentencing
Edited by Julian V. Roberts

Institutional Inequality and the Mobilization of the Family and Medical Leave Act: Rights on Leave
Catherine R. Albiston

Authoritarian Rule of Law: Legislation, Discourse and Legitimacy in Singapore
Jothie Rajah

Law and Development and the Global Discourses of Legal Transfers
Edited by John Gillespie and Pip Nicholson

Law against the State: Ethnographic Forays into Law's Transformations
Edited by Julia Eckert, Brian Donahoe, Christian Strümpell and Zerrin Özlem Biner

Transnational Legal Ordering and State Change
Edited by Gregory C. Shaffer

Legal Mobilization under Authoritarianism: The Case of Post-Colonial Hong Kong
Waikeung Tam

Complementarity in the Line of Fire: The Catalysing Effect of the International Criminal Court in Uganda and Sudan
Sarah M. H. Nouwen

Political and Legal Transformations of an Indonesian Polity: The Nagari from Colonisation to Decentralisation
Franz von Benda-Beckmann and Keebet von Benda-Beckmann

Pakistan's Experience with Formal Law: An Alien Justice
Osama Siddique

Human Rights under State-Enforced Religious Family Laws in Israel, Egypt, and India
Yüksel Sezgin

Why Prison?
Edited by David Scott

Law's Fragile State: Colonial, Authoritarian, and Humanitarian Legacies in Sudan
Mark Fathi Massoud

Rights for Others: The Slow Home-Coming of Human Rights in the Netherlands
Barbara Oomen

European States and Their Muslim Citizens: The Impact of Institutions on Perceptions and Boundaries
Edited by John R. Bowen, Christophe Bertossi, Jan Willem Duyvendak, and Mona Lena Krook

Environmental Litigation in China: A Study in Political Ambivalence
Rachel E. Stern

Indigeneity and Legal Pluralism in India: Claims, Histories, Meanings
Pooja Parmar

Paper Tiger: Law, Bureaucracy and the Developmental State in Himalayan India
Nayanika Mathur

Religion, Law and Society
Russell Sandberg

The Experiences of Face Veil Wearers in Europe and the Law
Edited by Eva Brems

The Contentious History of the International Bill of Human Rights
Christopher N. J. Roberts

Transnational Legal Orders
Edited by Terence C. Halliday and Gregory Shaffer

Lost in China? Law, Culture and Society in Post-1997 Hong Kong
Carol A. G. Jones

Security Theology, Surveillance and the Politics of Fear
Nadera Shalhoub-Kevorkian

Opposing the Rule of Law: How Myanmar's Courts Make Law and Order
Nick Cheesman

Ironies of Colonial Governance: Law, Custom and Justice in Colonial India
James Jaffe

The Clinic and the Court: Law, Medicine and Anthropology
Edited by Ian Harper, Tobias Kelly, and Akshay Khanna

The World of Indicators: The Making of Government Knowledge through Quantification
Edited by Richard Rottenburg, Sally E. Merry, Sung-Joon Park, and Johanna Mugler

Contesting Immigration Policy in Court: Legal Activism and Its Radiating Effects in the United States and France
Leila Kawar

The Quiet Power of Indicators: Measuring Governance, Corruption, and Rule of Law
Edited by Sally Engle Merry, Kevin E. Davis, and Benedict Kingsbury

Investing in Authoritarian Rule: Punishment and Patronage in Rwanda's Gacaca Courts for Genocide Crimes
Anuradha Chakravarty

Contractual Knowledge: One Hundred Years of Legal Experimentation in Global Markets
Edited by Grégoire Mallard and Jérôme Sgard

Iraq and the Crimes of Aggressive War: The Legal Cynicism of Criminal Militarism
John Hagan, Joshua Kaiser, and Anna Hanson

Culture in the Domains of Law
Edited by René Provost

China and Islam: The Prophet, the Party, and Law
Matthew S. Erie

Diversity in Practice: Race, Gender, and Class in Legal and Professional Careers
Edited by Spencer Headworth, Robert L. Nelson, Ronit Dinovitzer, and David B. Wilkins

A Sociology of Constitutions: Constitutions and State Legitimacy in Historical-Sociological Perspective
Chris Thornhill

A Sociology of Transnational Constitutions: Social Foundations of the Post-National Legal Structure
Chris Thornhill

Genocide Never Sleeps: Living Law at the International Criminal Tribunal for Rwanda
Nigel Eltringham

Shifting Legal Visions: Judicial Change and Human Rights Trials in Latin America
Ezequiel A. González-Ocantos

The Demographic Transformations of Citizenship
Heli Askola

Criminal Defense in China: The Politics of Lawyers at Work
Sida Liu and Terence C. Halliday

Contesting Economic and Social Rights in Ireland: Constitution, State and Society, 1848–2016
Thomas Murray

Buried in the Heart: Women, Complex Victimhood and the War in Northern Uganda
Erin Baines

Palaces of Hope: The Anthropology of Global Organizations
Edited by Ronald Niezen and Maria Sapignoli

The Politics of Bureaucratic Corruption in Post-Transitional Eastern Europe
Marina Zaloznaya

Revisiting the Law and Governance of Trafficking, Forced Labor and Modern Slavery
Edited by Prabha Kotiswaran

Incitement on Trial: Prosecuting International Speech Crimes
Richard Ashby Wilson

Criminalizing Children: Welfare and the State in Australia
David McCallum

Global Lawmakers: International Organizations in the Crafting of World Markets
Susan Block-Lieb and Terence C. Halliday

Duties to Care: Dementia, Relationality and Law
Rosie Harding

Insiders, Outsiders, Injuries, and Law: Revisiting "The Oven Bird's Song"
Edited by Mary Nell Trautner

Hunting Justice: Displacement, Law, and Activism in the Kalahari
Maria Sapignoli

Injury and Injustice: The Cultural Politics of Harm and Redress
Edited by Anne Bloom, David M. Engel, and Michael McCann

Ruling Before the Law: The Politics of Legal Regimes in China and Indonesia
William Hurst

The Powers of Law: A Comparative Analysis of Sociopolitical Legal Studies
Mauricio García-Villegas

A Sociology of Justice in Russia
Edited by Marina Kurkchiyan and Agnieszka Kubal

Constituting Religion: Islam, Liberal Rights, and the Malaysian State
Tamir Moustafa

The Invention of the Passport: Surveillance, Citizenship and the State, Second Edition John C. Torpey

Law's Trials: The Performance of Legal Institutions in the US "War on Terror"
Richard L. Abel

Law's Wars: The Fate of the Rule of Law in the US "War on Terror"
Richard L. Abel

Transforming Gender Citizenship: The Irresistible Rise of Gender Quotas in Europe
Edited by Eléonore Lépinard and Ruth Rubio-Marín

Muslim Women's Quest for Justice: Gender, Law and Activism in India
Mengia Hong Tschalaer

Children as "Risk": Sexual Exploitation and Abuse by Children and Young People
Anne-Marie McAlinden

The Legal Process and the Promise of Justice: Studies Inspired by the Work of Malcolm Feeley
Jonathan Simon, Rosann Greenspan, and Hadar Aviram

Gift Exchanges: The Transnational History of a Political Idea
Grégoire Mallard

Measuring Justice: Quantitative Accountability and the National Prosecuting Authority in South Africa
Johanna Mugler

Negotiating the Power of NGOs: Women's Legal Rights in South Africa
Reem Wael

Indigenous Water Rights in Law and Regulation: Lessons from Comparative Experience
Elizabeth Jane Macpherson

The Edge of Law: Legal Geographies of a War Crimes Court
Alex Jeffrey

Everyday Justice: Law, Ethnography, and Injustice
Sandra Brunnegger

The Uncounted: Politics of Data in Global Health
Sara L. M. Davis

Transnational Legal Ordering of Criminal Justice
Gregory Shaffer and Ely Aaronson

Five Republics and One Tradition
Pablo Ruiz-Tagle

The Law Multiple: Judgment and Knowledge in Practice
Irene van Oorschot

Health as a Human Right: The Politics and Judicialisation of Health in Brazil
Octávio Luiz Motta Ferraz

Shari'a, Inshallah: Finding God in Somali Legal Politics
Mark Fathi Massoud

Policing for Peace: Institutions, Expectations, and Security in Divided Societies
Matthew Nanes

Rule of Law Intermediaries: Brokering Influence in Myanmar
Kristina Simion

Lactation at Work: Expressed Milk, Expressing Beliefs, and the Expressive Value of Law
Elizabeth A. Hoffmann

The Archival Politics of International Courts
Henry Redwood

Global Pro Bono: Causes, Context, and Contestation
Edited by Scott L. Cummings, Fabio de Sa e Silva, and Louise G. Trubek

The Practice and Problems of Transnational Counter-Terrorism
Fiona de Londras

Decoupling: Gender Injustice in China's Divorce Courts
Ethan Michelson

Anti-Constitutional Populism
Martin Krygier, Adam Czarnota, and Wojciech Sadurski

The Ghostwriters: Lawyers and the Politics behind the Judicial Construction of Europe
Tommaso Pavone

For EU product safety concerns, contact us at Calle de José Abascal, 56–1°, 28003 Madrid, Spain or eugpsr@cambridge.org.

www.ingramcontent.com/pod-product-compliance
Ingram Content Group UK Ltd.
Pitfield, Milton Keynes, MK11 3LW, UK
UKHW020110040726
472853UK00010B/465

* 9 7 8 1 0 0 9 0 6 9 3 5 9 *